DATE			

AMY
LOWELL

AMY LOWELL

Portrait of the Poet in Her Time

HORACE GREGORY, 1898-

 BOOKS FOR LIBRARIES PRESS

PS
3523
.O₈₈
Z67
1969

INTERNATIONAL STANDARD BOOK NUMBER:
0-8369-5008-9

LIBRARY OF CONGRESS CATALOG CARD NUMBER:
69-16855

PRINTED IN THE UNITED STATES OF AMERICA

FOR

Mavis McIntosh

Acknowledgments

I am deeply indebted to the many who have given me information concerning the career of Amy Lowell. Among them are Theodore Amussen, Esther Bates, Malcolm Cowley, E. E. Cummings, Mrs. John Gould Fletcher, Amy Loveman, Robert Lowell, Jean Starr Untermeyer, Louis Untermeyer, John Hall Wheelock, and Mrs. August Belmont.

Others who have supplied me with invaluable details concerning the period in which Amy Lowell's reputation grew to fame are Joseph Freeman, Rose Standish Nichols, De Wolfe Howe, Anne Ford, Edward Aswell and Winfield T. Scott. I owe special thanks to Witter Bynner for lending his file of Amy Lowell letters.

In particular, I owe debts of gratitude to Norman Holmes Pearson and Gorham Munson for their criticism of the book in manuscript. My other great debts are to S. Foster Damon's *Amy Lowell* and Richard Aldington's *Life for Life's Sake*.

Not least of all, I wish to thank Mr. William A. Jackson of the Houghton Library, Harvard University, for his courtesy in permitting me to read letters written to Amy Lowell.

H. G.

Contents

BROOKLINE AND THE WORLD   1

THE LONDON ADVENTURES   93

THE YEARS OF FAME   133

CHINESE GARDENS AND JOHN KEATS   173

Brookline
and the World

AMY LOWELL was born on a Monday, February 9, 1874, in an imposing brownstone house at 70 Heath Street, Brookline, Massachusetts. The house had taken the place of a far less pretentious homestead of colonial design set on a large tract of land. The new house was built in the spirit of the decade that followed the Civil War, and its weight and bulk had caught the eye of Augustus Lowell, Amy Lowell's father, in 1866; there were gardens and terraces around it waiting to be improved and walled. In the suburbs of Boston it represented State Street's rise to recovered wealth and power, of which Augustus Lowell, the "hard man" of cotton mills and banks, was himself the image of a New England post-war generation.

With the birth of Amy, who was the youngest of his five children and the last, Augustus Lowell began to think of his suburban estate as a place to be called "Sevenels," because seven "Ls"—seven Lowells —held it, almost like a fortress or a castle, as their home. Its portentousness was screened by a garden which had received the attention of Augustus Lowell himself, for the sake of which he rose at six each morning in spring, summer and fall to direct new plantings for it; and as Amy Lowell was to write many years later, on one occasion he pruned it by cutting a thousand roses in three days with his own hands.

Much of the local fame that Amy Lowell was to acquire beyond the age of forty had for its origins the plain fact that she was a Lowell of the senior branch, which in Boston and throughout New England was more than a sign of personal gifts and the ability to get things done. It carried with it a family legend of hard-headed, skilfully acquired wealth that had begun before the American War of Independence. It was a reigning house whose sons were directors of law offices and banks, iron foundries and cotton mills; its culture was of the counting house and the courtroom. At the time of Amy Lowell's birth, Boston regarded the Lowell family as an institution, more massive in its weight of invested monies than the gold that shone from the State House dome, and considerably less unworldly than the tower of Old North Church. Although the Lowells had done more than their share of public duties in serving on the board of the Harvard Corporation and in helping to found The Athenaeum with its libraries, reading rooms, and lecture halls, although its family vaults held bones of ministers to God, although James Russell Lowell had succeeded Longfellow in the professorship of Belles Lettres at Harvard College and was to be American Ambassador at the Court of St. James's, the family at Sevenels, coming as it did from the money-making branch of the family, had claims to tangible powers that earned immediate respect. Augustus Lowell was in direct descent of Lowells who provided that wealth to which the rest of the family owed its freedom to indulge in travel, philanthropy, education and the literary arts. Though Augustus Lowell spent two of the Civil War years in Europe, and as though to exercise "a robust mind" he chose early hours of the morning to read in higher mathematics and science—enough to conclude with disfavor that Darwin's *Origin of the Species* was "an arsenal in which the advocates of Pantheism will find their surest and deadliest weapons . . ." he clung securely to a tough-minded branch of the Lowell tree. He became an administrator of at least ten cotton mills and ten banks, and was prominent

among those to profit most in the rise of New England's industrial
power after the Civil War.

The household into which Amy Lowell was born was predominantly masculine in authority and temperament; her mother,
Katherine Lawrence, was the daughter of Abbott Lawrence, an
associate of Augustus' father in the founding of several cotton mills.
Augustus Lowell's marriage to Katherine Lawrence was closer to
being morganatic than any recent contract of that kind in the Lowell
family. Though Abbott Lawrence had made a fortune as an importer
of English goods to Boston, he was self-educated; though his interests in politics had resulted in his election to Congress as a "Cotton
Whig" and his friendship with Daniel Webster had its reward in his
being sent as Minister to the Court of St. James, a taste for that kind
of activity was not shared by Augustus' father, John Amory Lowell.
He considered himself too seriously engaged in business for such
lighter diversions as political campaigns and meeting foreigners. Amy
Lowell's mother was therefore in the shadow of Lowell names and
fortunes. At the time of her youngest daughter's birth she was in ill
health, a victim of Bright's disease. Amy's two brothers, Percival and
Lawrence, and of course, her father, were the authorities to which
the two daughters, Katherine, age sixteen, and Elizabeth, twelve, de-
ferred. It was Elizabeth's duty "to mind" the baby, or in the Lowell
family language, which Amy brought so generously into print, "to
mind" Amy who was called "The Postscript" of the Lowell household.

The name, Amy, was a compromise of the family name of Amory,
making it easier to say and more feminine. But if Augustus Lowell's
decisions ruled his family, it was not by physical bulk and an outward show of dominance. His figure was slight, his manner cool,
neat and tight-lipped. He looked the part of being "the hard," active,
efficient businessman he was. His humor was expressed by the dry
wink of an eye as he showed visitors to his gardens at Sevenels the
new flowering of a rare plant. He believed in living "close," in binding his family to him by an orderly management of its affairs. As a
director of his cotton mills he was no less dry and fatherly—remote in
manner, respected and unloved. He would not permit the poems of
Shelley to be read at Sevenels because he objected to atheism in all
its forms; he took pride in his rejection of Darwin and anything that

might be interpreted as issuing from the theories of Thomas Jefferson; and like most of the Lowells, he believed the Lowells had been born to speak for themselves.

The first glimpses that we get of Amy Lowell—the public Amy Lowell—are out of doors. The year was 1876, and the two-year-old baby was seen on Sundays between the knees of the family coachman, Burns, who allowed her to grasp the reins of the smart team they drove together to St. Paul's Church, Brookline. The image was vivid enough: it was of the darling of the family on a fine day going abroad in bonnet and jacket with the open carriage behind her, very like the illustrations in St. Nicholas Magazine, now come to life. Behind the carriage was brownstone Sevenels, set back some distance from the corner where two unpaved country roads had joined, its entrance from both roads marked by stone posts opening a wall of pudding-stones. The house was also shielded by elms and evergreen, and banked by lawns edged with country flowers, the common daisy and the buttercup. A stretch of meadow, then a small grove of horse-chestnuts grew to the sides of and behind the house, and beyond these through a wisteria-trumpet-vine-hung arbour—Augustus Lowell's sunken, formal garden. All this, which to the child was home, was an expanded version of a wealthy man's estate in New England of the 1870's. It was almost manorial, yet it did not have the slightest resemblance to the holdings of the English gentry. Sevenels for its day was both too "modern" and, as a suburban home, too countrified to find its likeness across the Atlantic. To be the darling "Postscript" of Sevenels was to have privileges beyond the reach of many other New England children.

Amy Lowell's mother, described as a soft-voiced, mildly handsome woman with clear eyes and straight features, was a plump motherly version of one of William Wetmore Story's statues and as chaste.* As they rode out together, little Amy seemed to exert more authority

* In his William Wetmore Story and His Friends, Henry James remarked on the chastity of Story's sculptured figures, their mid-Victorian display of half-draped nudity and modesty. He wrote with his usual circumspection: "To borrow from the list of Story's productions alone, we no more see . . . a naked Saul, a stripped Sardanapalus, a Medea without her robe or an Alcestis without her veil . . ." Amy Lowell's mother was not unlike some William Wetmore Story version of Niobe, the opulent, always proud, yet kindly image of maternal love.

than the serene woman leaning backward in the carriage. Amy's
sister, Elizabeth, twelve years her senior, had been delegated to take
care of her, but without the authority that small Amy had already
assumed, and the child took her orders only from men: from Burns,
the coachman whom she said was "born to command," from an elder
brother, or from an almost silently expressed wish of her father. If a
joke was told at the dining table and the company seemed to enjoy it,
Amy, quick to take advantage of any situation, would say, "On the
strength of that, can't I sit up later tonight?" She was then the kind
of child who even in her day was beginning to be called "typically
American." She was, in truth, more innocent than she seemed: yet her
brightness verged on a kind of impudence that had come to be associated with well-to-do children of the American 1870's. The bright
little boy of Henry James's story "The Pupil" is one who, but for the
lack of stability in his relations to his parents, might have been one
of Amy Lowell's cousins. She had learned, even then, the family
trait of speaking up for herself. Yet she was not quite the terrible
"Infanta" of the American household of her day. If her manners were
too pert for favorable comparison with English children of her class,
the delicacy of her small features, the charm of quickening intelligence in her very observant gray-blue eyes, modified the impression
of her forwardness.

Meanwhile Augustus Lowell had acquired a Boston town house
at 97 Beacon Street, so as to supplement during the months of a New
England winter the household's living quarters at Sevenels. The
return to Sevenels gardens on the first of May became a part of his
family ritual. To Amy at five the move to town became an introduction to the larger world in which her parents moved with appropriate
poise and well-established ease. It was a Boston of brick-paved walks,
great naked elms in winter, and houses that retained, in their polished
brass name plates, knockers and handles on front doors, memories of
a colonial heritage. At the brick turning of a corner, the quiet streets
seemed to reflect fragments of Queen Anne's London near the Strand;
and inside the houses with their transatlantic Chippendale and
Adam furniture, darkly polished stairwells delicately tooled, their
China plate and screens brought from the Orient in elder shipping
days, held a bright serenity in contrast to the heavier monuments of
1870 brownstone. Amy Lowell's love of fine bright bric-a-brac, of

bright colors in small objects, in threads of cherry-colored silks, has hints of its beginnings here.

The house on Beacon Street permitted the child to have glimpses of the world that other branches of the Lowell family inhabited, the Literary Lowells, the Lowells who were junior branches of the tree three generations before her, children of the second and third wives of John Lowell, "The Old Judge," who after Sarah Higginson died had married Susan Cabot and soon after her death had married Rebecca Russell Tyng. All these half-cousinly Lowells made up a family of remarkable variety, extending their friendships and professions in a tightly woven net around Boston and Cambridge. The most famous of these was James Russell Lowell who lived in a great square-built frame house at Elmwood, Cambridge, a half mile from Craigie House, already famous as Longfellow's home. The Augustus Lowells took five-year-old Amy to a dinner at which the business, social and literary strains of the Lowells were intertwined, and the elderly poet of the white beard and "The Children's Hour" trundled her around the room in a scrap-basket.

How much this small incident had bearing on Amy Lowell's childhood it is impossible to say, but there is little doubt that the atmosphere surrounding it and the presence of an extremely well-known literary figure in the family itself left its impression. The James Russell Lowell of Amy Lowell's childhood, being sixteen years younger than Emerson and twelve years the junior of Long-fellow and Whittier, had become the heir of "Little Athens" culture, or at least one who was likely to outlive those who had given New England its claims to literary honors, and indeed only Whittier and Oliver Wendell Holmes lived to an old age beyond him. Yet, at this moment of the 1870's, James Russell Lowell had written nearly everything by which his name is remembered—"*Das Ewig-Weibliche*" alone was yet unwritten. In the 1870's he was less a poet than a man of letters, and less a man of letters and editor (for he had been a stimulating advisory editor of both *The Atlantic Monthly* and *The North American Review*, but with little ability to seat himself at a desk, or to put his mind to the task of routine editorial duties) than the stoutly-built, enthusiastic Professor of Belles Lettres at Harvard. At Harvard he was one of those who encouraged the conference or tutorial system and he loved to talk; puns, quotations, gay references to many books he had been reading since a boy, flowed in a stream through his golden Van Dyke beard. The delivery of a lecture primed the rivers of talk that seemed to pour around him; and students caught up in the currents of his brilliantly winding discourses were enchanted. By temperament and training he was certainly the man for President Hayes to send as American Minister to Madrid and a few years later to the Court of St. James.

As an undergraduate at Harvard, he was the brightest, most promising student in his class; he was also (as Amy Lowell was in hers) the youngest child of an extraordinary family, children of Dr. Charles Russell Lowell, minister of the West Church in Boston, and a member of the less wealthy branch of the Lowells. James Russell had to prove his worth in the company of an elder sister who wrote (anonymously) popular fiction and an elder brother who went into the Anglican Church, who had become head master of St. Mark's School and later Professor of Latin at Union College in Schenectady, and who had written of his experiences as a missionary in Newfoundland, as well as popular verse and prose. One can almost say that in self-assertion—and in self-defence—James Russell developed all the skills of an actor. At one moment he was the dreaming poet; at another, the shrewd, energetic Yankee; at still another, the perfect mimic of literary, even political, styles and manners. After graduating from Harvard and marrying Maria White, herself a poet of distinctly original and feminine perceptions and of strong abolitionist convictions, James Russell's energies were quickened into light verse. He had studied at law; he wrote for anti-slavery newspapers and—as if to celebrate the anniversary of being ten years out of college—he published four books in one year, 1848: *Poems, The Vision of Sir Launful, A Fable for Critics*, and *The Biglow Papers*. The energy required for this production was to be equalled only in the literary career of Amy Lowell, and significantly among his plans for future writings was a life of Keats, a plan which became a reality under Amy Lowell's hands. In *A Fable for Critics* and in *The Bigelow Papers*, the loquacious, quick-witted James Russell came into print; even today he has not been surpassed by any writer of light verse in the United States; granting that *A Fable for Critics* almost tripped its break-neck rhymes and metrics into doggerel, its shrewd appraisals of James Russell's contemporaries—however shallow some of their judgments were—are still fresh, impudent, gay. In *The Bigelow Papers* another phase of James Russell's inventive wit skated the surface of the pages, for James Russell had boldly invented a Yankee dialect. No doubt the language of *The Bigelow Papers* carries some resemblance to the nasal intonations of the provincial New Englander, no doubt it was among the inspirations of James Russell's as he acted out on paper the characters he chose to mimic—yet his dialect (imitated by James Whitcomb Riley who called it "Hoosier" dialect forty years later) had a deeper note in the sounds that came to Amy Lowell's ears. That dialect was what the Lowells heard when they tried to hear the speech of "common people"; much of the same language entered Amy Lowell's prose; the actual roots are of the dialect, shrewd, "business-like," and forceful. As James Russell used it, its energy became transformed into wit; as Amy Lowell wrote it (and with no less energy) it veered in the direction of earnest thinking aloud. One can find a clear parallel in James Russell's Ezekiel Bigelow's "An' you've gut to git up airly/ Ef you want to take in God" to Amy Lowell's explosive speech (in the person of an eighteenth-century lady) "Christ! What are patterns for?" The same Lowell energy pervades them; the same atmosphere surrounds them. If they represent the vigor of American speech, they represent it chiefly as the Lowell family acted, thought and felt.

After the death of his first wife, Maria, James Russell's liberal ardors slowly faded; yet they were never more than the consistently variable tempers of his energy. He was a diplomat precisely because he did not, could not, sustain a deeply felt political conviction. His energy and visible enthusiasm and his love of gestures and rapid play of conversation made his opinions seem more vivid than they were. He converted his love of reading into social activity and public appearances which explains the friendships that he made in London as American Minister at St. James and among English men of letters. Those who heard James Russell Lowell speak never forgot the charm of his voice, which even professional orators like Moncure Daniel Conway envied, and of all visiting Americans to England, his manner had the greatest polish: before making his public appearances, he selected and memorized an amusing story to tell—and the rest of his task would be an ingenious device to make the story relevant to the occasion. His stay in London brought him the lasting friendship of

Leslie Stephen; James Russell stood godfather to Stephen's daughter, Virginia, who was to become Virginia Woolf. The two men had much in common: They rejoiced in heartily shouting bookish quotations at each other by the hour, in loudly denouncing indecency in literature, in tossing books at each other across the room—as though the expression of literary opinions was a form of strenuous athletics— and both men had been and still remained bright college boys. Certainly the atmosphere that James Russell created in his own presence provided Amy Lowell, even as a child, with an athletic ideal in literary enthusiasms; and when she grew up there is little wonder that her public appearances seemed to echo the histrionic charms of James Russell's voice, and that her stoutness (which was her private grief) reflected something of his sturdy figure rising behind and over the glittering table service at a public dinner.

Meanwhile the child, who spent her winters in Boston, was being prepared for the years at school to follow. If Boston's joke was that Amy Lowell was being brought up by Burns, the coachman, gossip was true enough whenever it implied that her early teachers were masculine, and in this one finds an example in her eldest brother, Percival. In the 1870's Percival, then entering into his twenties, was employed by his grandfather, John Amory Lowell, in the family business, and succeeded so well in managing its trust funds and acting as treasurer of a cotton mill, that in six years he had earned enough to retire. His earliest schooling was in Paris where, because of his mother's ill-health, Augustus Lowell set up temporary quarters away from the distractions of the Civil War in the United States. At ten, Percival was at M. Sillig's boarding school in Switzerland at Vevey and was writing to his mother in French. At Harvard his career was equally brilliant, both in mathematics and literature. Seven years earlier he had composed a hundred lines of Latin hexameters to celebrate the sinking of a paper boat in a pool at Sevenels. Professor James Russell had called him the brightest young man in Boston, which was high praise from a member of the junior branch of Lowells. At the Lowell dinner table at Sevenels or in their Boston town house, Augustus Lowell's children talked immoderately, none listening to the others, so that young Amy was frequently told "Be quiet! Don't you hear Lawrence talking?" Yet in this household it was clear that Percival was considered the genius: his aptitude for business had already proved itself and he had won his independence. He was a handsome Lowell, fair-haired and with sharply cut curved lips, and his clothes were fitted with more smartness than other members of the house at Sevenels; he was also the most romantic of the Lowells. His experience in business had not dulled his fancies for far-off places: at thirteen, a toy telescope had given him a view of the moon from Sevenels; before his adventures in business, he went on a tour with his cousin, Harcourt Amory, from England to Syria, and he then attempted to enlist as a soldier of fortune in the Turko-Serbian war. If any voice was overheard by his youngest sister, it was Percival's.

Amy Lowell's later interests in French and in Oriental literatures seem to have had their true sources in the adventurous examples set before her by Percival, for Percival in 1883 sailed for the Far East to Japan and to Korea. It had been hinted that, since he was the handsomest of the Lowells, certain unmarried young women of Boston, including Lowell cousins, were determined to welcome him as a husband—and the very Far East was his destination away from them.

At this moment one need not imagine how Percival Lowell looked. There is a photograph of him standing behind solemn-faced and seated Korean officials: his slenderness made him seem taller than he was; his fair hair was curled and wavy, parted in the middle. Signs of a dandy are obvious in a light-colored silk tie and the fashionable, Byronic low-cut collar. His chin tilts upward, and he looks as though it is an effort for him to stand still long enough to have the portrait taken. He was probably the brother who dared Amy (she was then six years old) to eat a double portion of rice at a Boston party—which she did, and then found that she could not button her coat across the front when she put it on to go home. A kind of inward terror possessed her at this bodily transformation which was to haunt her for the rest of her life, as though her stoutness was like a childish nightmare which came true. Twenty-eight-year-old Percival outran the more respectable instincts of the Augustus Lowell household and chose among his friends adventurous young men of Boston. Since Sturgis Bigelow, a brilliant young physician, had given up his practice and had ventured to Japan, Percival was eager to outdo him. He followed him to Japan, rented a house in Tokyo, fitted it with Japanese servants, and in a few months (with his usual facility) had acquired a conversational knowledge of the language. Sturgis Bigelow urged him to accept the post of Foreign Secretary and General Counsellor to the Embassy sent from Korea to the United States, and though he held the lease on his house in Tokyo for the next ten years his stay was punctuated by residence at the Foreign Office in Seoul, Korea, and visits to Washington, Boston and Sevenels.

It was natural enough for his youngest sister, Amy, to adore Percival who never forgot to remember her when he wrote letters home from Japan and Korea. He was an ardent photographer and an enthusiastic buyer of small objects such as a child would love—paper fans and fishes, toys and gay prints—and these arrived for her in floods of mail from the East, while his photographs illustrated his gay letters. Nor was she alone in yielding to the Far Eastern charms of her adventurous brother; his facilities, along with his genial spirits, extended to the writing of three popular books on the Far East: *Choson: The Land of the Morning Calm: A Sketch of Korea, The Soul of the Far East*, and *Noto*, an account of a journey to an unexplored part of Japan. The three books, all written between 1884 and 1891, show, and not without a conscious display of charm, the character of his intelligence, his levity, his mind. In his young manhood Percival Lowell intensified his gifts of rapid observation, the seeing and hearing of multiple things around him, that had made him a brilliant boy. His proficiency in acquiring French and Latin had also been applied in the phenomenal speed with which he picked up Japanese as well as Korean dialects, and which enabled him with photographic accuracy to write down numerous details on the habits and customs of the island peoples of the Far East. The spirit in which he pursued this activity was that of a pioneer, but it also contained a great measure of the enthusiasm that inspires a boy of fourteen to collect, admire and cherish postage stamps from far countries. Of all the Lowells who took to writing, Percival had the most neatly-clipped, brisk, and logical style. As one rereads his books on the Far East, one has the conviction that more of Percival Lowell's soul came to life on paper than any definition of a soul in the island of Japan and the peninsula of Korea. He saw the Far East as possessing a soul which was the direct antithesis of the Lowell soul that had chosen to live in the neighborhood of Boston: both the first and last chapters of his book, *The Soul of the Far East*, make this distinction clear. To introduce his commentary on Japanese art, topography, religion, customs and philosophy he advanced the idea that there was more than a grain of truth in the boyish belief that the world of the Orient was upside down. He explained this by saying that the actions of the Japanese in everyday life were the reverse of what people did in Boston. His picture reminds one of Lewis Carroll's *Through the Looking-Glass*. His examples were that the Japanese struck matches away from themselves instead of toward them, that they rested and drained a wet umbrella on its handle instead of its point. Nor within these limits could one dispute his logic, which denied, and with considerable charm, the literal fact that Orientals walked on their heads.

The logical clarity of his remarks was of the same order which appeared in the "Little Rollo" books which his youngest sister, Amy, had begun collecting; he had much information about the Far East which was certainly new to Boston and to the whole of the North American Continent. Though he viewed Japan (he had made a hazardous trip across broken and snow-swept trails to a far region of the island) as being held in a state of "arrested civilization," he saw a certain kind of ugliness making its way as its people adopted Western dress and customs. In his book on Korea he elaborated this observation in his description of his room at the Foreign Office in Seoul which on one door had a "realistic" imitation Western mural of books and papers in contrast to the more attractive flower designs on the other. His notes on Japanese politeness at inns and overnight hotels show the same appreciation of elder manners held to in the East, but they were observed as seeming quaint, and they were reported as being decidedly unlike the habits of those who walked on Boston's State Street and attended service at Old North Church on Sunday. He looked at Japanese prints as though they represented caricatures of human dress and action; and his deepest appreciation of Japanese taste came forward when he described the Japanese love of natural scenery—for this love was of a kind that the athletic Percival Lowell fully shared. His adventurous journey from Tokyo to Noto was carried out in the high spirits of one who welcomes all things out of doors, who walks through the discomforts of his trip as though on holiday. Mud, rain, snow, and hail seemed to heighten rather than to depress his ardors for further explorations. His only complaints were of the Oriental foods he tried not to eat, and against which he fortified himself by filling his luggage with American canned goods.

In the last chapter of *The Soul of the Far East* one finds his trenchant, reiterated criticism of Far Eastern thinking and its way of life—all that to Percival Lowell were the various aspects of the Oriental soul. His main objection was that they lacked room for the expression of individual tastes and personalities; in other words, a Lowell, particularly a Percival Lowell, would find his habits, his eccentricities, his ideas of right and wrong, his love of travel and need for change of scene, cramped by the traditions, even conventions of the Far East. Percival Lowell was a passionate evolutionist: to see things *move* was his delight, even the progress of his own legs up and down cliffs and mountainsides in his trip to and from Tokyo to Noto gave him an exhilaration that flows between rather than in the words of his little book on travels across Japan. Certainly Oriental habits of meditation and desires for Oriental serenity were not his. They led to what he called "dreamy metaphysics" and "inevitable numbness of monotony" and not to his own intense belief, which was summed up in his statement: "Change of scene is beneficial to others besides invalids . . ." to him the act of sitting still was a sign of being sick.

Percival's interpretation of Oriental art stemmed from the extremely active duties of being a latter-day American pioneer, of putting into order with logical accuracy the many details of information he had gathered in the seven years of his visit to the Far East. It was natural for him to ignore the classical aesthetics of the Far East, the "Six Canons" of art as they had been written down by Hsieh Ho in the sixth century, and to favor his own ability to find exotic contrasts to Western art. He was unaware that Kuo Jo-hsu in the twelfth century wrote "The secret of art lies in the artist himself," which makes his denial of personality to the Oriental seem absurd. It was not that Percival Lowell lacked abilities for research and understanding, but that he had the temperament of an explorer—one who wished to discover whatever may seem strange to Western eyes. This in his later life led him into the science of astronomy. His book, *The Soul of the Far East*, went through many printings before 1916 when it was supplanted by Laurence Binyon's far more authoritative study of Oriental art, *The Flight of the Dragon*. Western readers who had

been amused and attracted by Percival Lowell's remarks on the position of a father in a Japanese home being like that of a king were
beginning to turn to more serious studies in Oriental culture, of
which *The Flight of the Dragon* was one. But in the 1880's Percival
Lowell's books were among the few that provided glimpses of the
world east of Hong Kong.

It was Percival who was a friend of the equally handsome and
romantic John Jay Chapman. Chapman was the son of a New York
stockbroker, and with as lively a career at Harvard behind him as
Percival enjoyed a few years earlier. He had received much the same
praise from James Russell that Percival had earned, and was among
the younger set that worshipped him. Chapman's family fortunes
were in a period of decline, and the young man of talent in social
graces and in writing verse held himself to the severities of a graduate course in law at Harvard. This trial was all the more gloomy
and oppressive because he had just returned from a trip with his
parents to Europe, and contrasts between visiting London, Paris,
Venice and Rome made his return to Cambridge seem a martyrdom.
His relief from his self-imposed routine of studies came in his
partially dazed, yet sudden infatuation for Minna Timmins, a sultry,
passionate, half-Italian Boston blue-stocking who was later to become
his wife. Together they climbed to the top floor of The Athenaeum's
library, a widely lighted room which gave them the illusion of being
lost, the last two survivors on the top of the world and read aloud
to each other cantos from Dante's *Divine Comedy*. In his rapture
Chapman was scarcely conscious of having fallen in love: the broad,
chastely-lighted room was not a place made for an overflow of intimate emotions and he was aware only of his great pleasure in hearing Minna Timmins read aloud and listening to his own voice
answering hers.

Chapman's account of his infatuation is like a story told by a man
speaking within the corridors of a dream from which he had scarcely
wakened: "The Dante readings moved gradually like a cloud between me and the law, between me and the rest of life." A strange,
white, resounding cloud one might say—edged with the light flowing
in through the high windows of The Athenaeum. Some kind of
action was forthcoming, and it came at an evening party on the out-
skirts of Cambridge. The two lovers were there and, in Chapman's

words, "a few pleasant people," among whom was a gentleman he had not seen for years and another someone—or was he the same?— whom he fancied had slighted Minna Timmins, had caused her suffering and yet seemed to interest her. The man was Percival Lowell, returned from Japan, and no doubt an attractive figure at the small party—the kind of young man who would take the center of the room to talk of his remarkable adventures, for Percival Lowell was never shy.

Chapman drew him aside and invited him out for a word or two on the lawn, and in a frenzy—he had picked up a stick somewhere— suddenly struck Percival Lowell over the head and shoulders; Percival was severely beaten, probably Chapman dreamed he had killed him. Chapman drifted back to his small, cheap dark room on a side street in Cambridge, still drunk with repressed emotions, alternately cold and hot with the feeling of guilt; he became aware of a hard coal fire burning in the grate. He stripped off his jacket and vest, made a crude torque of his suspenders around his left forearm above the wrist, and thrust his hand deep in the white-hot coals; he held it firmly with his right hand clasped around the torque. Then slipping on a worn jacket and draping an overcoat over his left shoulder, he stepped out of doors and rode a horse car into Boston. He remembered dreaming or saying to himself "This will never do," and walked through the entrance of the Massachusetts General Hospital to be put under ether and to have his hand cut off.

There is, of course, no account of how Percival Lowell got home, or what he said; that his injuries were too slight for notice seems improbable. It is likely that some romantic story was told as to how he received them and it is unlikely that young Amy knew the truth. Like the majority of nineteenth-century well-to-do households in America, family secrets were well kept, and a household fathered by Augustus Lowell kept family skeletons in the deepest recesses of the cellar at Sevenels. Boston and Brookline had in Percival Lowell their strictly New England counterpart of Richard Burton, the Eastern explorer and translator of *The Thousand and One Nights*; certainly he shared Burton's gift for acquiring exotic languages and their dialects, Burton's adventurous energy, his enjoyment in overriding physical discomfort in travel, his elusiveness when prospects of marriage arrived on near horizons, and his facility in writing books of hastily gathered information. The great difference between them was that Percival never forgot that he was a Lowell, that even his eccen-tricities were part of a family heritage that placed a high premium on holding to personal and, in his case, whimsical opinions. It would have been impossible for Percival Lowell to act out the part of being a Korean or a Japanese diplomat in appropriate costume. As for Burton, he always became the living embodiment of what he pre-tended to be. Unconventional as Percival Lowell seemed in Boston, he needed Bostonian conventions to place him in high relief against them; in the East he was always quickly revealed as a fabulously wealthy American.

To the child Amy, he was nothing less than a hero, comparable only to the heroes of her story books. Although her family packed her up with them when they took holiday excursions to Europe, travelling at a relentless American pace through a dozen countries, Percival Lowell's far eastern travels were literally of greater dimen-sions, and therefore to be classed with the world seen in story books, the farther reaches of fancy, space and time. On his return to the United States as a member of the Korean mission to this country, he brought with him a bright seventeen-year-old secretary, Tsunejiro Miyaoka, a visible proof of his being in far places, whom Amy never forgot; and her memory of Miyaoka was underlined because the boy paid special attention to her.

Amy Lowell's early fancies, spurred by the miniature world of Japanese curiosities sent to her by Percival, turned to images of elves and fairies. And indeed the children's literature of the 1880's in the United States was peopled to overcrowding by these amiable, inno-cent, shrewd creatures, seen as it were through the wrong end of a telescope; they filled the pages of *The St. Nicholas Magazine* as "Brownies"—unaesthetic, frog-like beings who were always up to good-humored, half-innocent tricks. Amy, not unlike many children of her day, found Lewis Carroll's *Alice In Wonderland* too compli-cated to follow and much too frightening; it was easier to accept the athletic lightness of elves and gnomes, a lightness that Amy envied as a child and which in later years became something that she re-garded with a touch of wistfulness—she herself had grown so heavy. But by this time, however, she had begun dictating little stories of her own to her elder sisters and to her mother, and, remembering her father's and Percival's success in business, it was not inappropriate that Amy's elves ran a grocery store. This was her substitute for the traditional habit of the American child from well-to-do homes to emulate its elders by going into the "business" of running neighborhood lemonade stands or imitation circuses. The Lowell fortunes were so notoriously well established that in her childhood Amy never carried the images of a "business-like" game into literal practice, nor would her family permit such an indulgence; the best she could do was to introduce the game within the vision of her fancies. She was, through imitation of her elder brothers, Abbott Lawrence as well as Percival, a very boyish, commanding little girl. Being the youngest child of the family meant that she was "spoiled"; she loved to talk out of turn against the stream of her elder brothers' conversation. She expected privileges and got them. These expectations became clear when she attended "Mrs. Cabot's School" in Boston. Mrs. Cabot, a Lowell cousin, hired a staff of grammar school teachers and placed them in a house at 57 Chestnut Street for the purpose of educating her own small children and making sure that their education would be shared only by children of her choice and approval. Amy had already selected as a friend the pliable Mabel Cabot, a girl near her own age who could appreciate her jokes and her quickness at grasping information. The school into which Amy walked was not likely to dispute her claims to holding the center of attention. When she felt inclined, she very nearly took over the conduct of the classroom, talking down her less well-informed classmates, and even limiting the authority of the classroom teachers. In this small school she not only held a position through the respect shown to the Lowell family, but by her own energetic approach to learning. With the exception of the "Little Rollo" series for which she never lost affection, her reading leaped beyond her years. The books she so fervently admired were reflections of the choices made by her father and her wandering brother Percival. Like many an American father of his day, Augustus Lowell at evening entertained the younger members of his family by reading aloud, and to Amy he read the novels of Sir Walter Scott. This was his way of celebrating "The Children's Hour" which Longfellow had endowed with a particular turn of

lyrical magic, the familiar scene in thousands of late nineteenth-
century American homes—the lamp lit and the circle of light embracing the father surrounded by daughters about to go to bed. Within
his poem Longfellow created an image of enduring peace and security that provided an example to the generations between the Civil
War and the outbreak of World War I. To Amy, her father's reading
of *Rob Roy* provided a touch of wild Highland adventure that made
the evening near the lamp even more secure; later she confessed she
loved the Scots novels of Sir Walter with a devotion far greater than
his more consciously historical romances. The scene of her father
reading aloud—particularly her memory of it—reinforced her nearly
nineteenth-century style of dress in the years that followed, as well
as her nineteenth-century habits of thinking, her nineteenth-century
code of sexual morality.

To her affection for the novels of Sir Walter Scott she added an
enthusiasm for Cooper's sea tales and the candid, slapdash pre-
Victorian romances of Captain Marryat. It is doubtful whether or
not she understood—and the greater probability is that she did not—
the lively rakishness of Marryat's narratives. The tumbling, racy,
though not unclear, movement of Marryat's prose—all written as
though a word had never been erased, or a line blotted, or for that
matter reread at all—became a characteristic of her own prose. From
Marryat she turned to R. H. Dana's far more sedate *Two Years Before
the Mast*, and, after this, to the romances of Jules Verne. She cultivated a boyish taste in fiction; one early friend said Amy often
wished she were a boy. At school she appeared as a stout, yellow-
pigtailed little girl, rather than a plump one, who insisted boldly that
she liked to read Wordsworth's *The Excursion*, which impressed girls
of her age—she was then eleven—and remotely shocked them because
they had always found reading Wordsworth a dreary exercise. Her
declaration was probably half a boast, for though she did like to read
verse, her claim of reading so long a poem through was most likely
an effort to balance her lack of learning how to spell. Someone—a
friend of the Lowells—had sent off to *Life* (when that magazine
closely resembled London's *Punch*) a characteristic Lowell family
dialogue:

Papa—But why do you sign it: 'Your loving son, Amy?'
Amy—Why, of course mamma will know, and I couldn't spell daughter.

Its publication and the joy of seeing her Christian name in print were among her earliest triumphs; she pasted the two line dialogue in her scrap book.

If her father encouraged her tastes for adventurous reading, her mother—who was always described by those who knew her as a consistently kind, "motherly" woman, low-voiced and with an ample bosom—proudly took dictation of Amy's fairy stories. Amy Lowell's habit of speaking aloud her writings and promptly dictating them was formed very early. But it is also more accurate to say that she never relinquished a habit, which, along with the pleasure of exercising her fancy, gave the equal delight of displaying her executive ability. One has an image of the sturdy, pink-cheeked, handsome child, whose features are as delicately formed as her mother's, reciting at authoritative speed whatever passed through her mind—and glancing above the child one sees the serene figure of the mother who with the pride of a Boston Niobe receives the gifts of her small daughter's intelligence.

As for the child, she had become proud of her own mental quickness, her "brains," a pride that was sustained throughout her life, for from childhood onward the mainsprings of her self-respect were identified with the force of her opinions, right or wrong. Naturally enough, she was a difficult child to teach; her mind leaped rather than arrived at its conclusions. In French at school it was not to be impeded by dry facts of syntax or the exact meanings of words; and she became a terror to her French teacher. The little girl always knew what she wanted French words to mean—and insisted upon the right to her opinion. She claimed attention and usually received it; something close to fear haunted her whenever she was denied it.

Her favorite poet was a Lowell, James Russell Lowell, so that the shock of not meeting immediate approval in his eyes was all the greater. On the way to a Harvard-Yale boat race Amy had dropped in to visit her Aunt Mary Putnam and was led into the library to meet elderly "Cousin James." As she spoke to him, the fastidiously dressed, side-whiskered, weary mannered, desperately ill old man turned cold eyes down at her; he was indifferent and seemed bored at having to shake hands with her, to see her in the room. She became fearfully unhappy and the meeting seemed to be a bad omen for the race—which it was, for Harvard lost on that occasion—and Amy

Lowell felt that all the joy, the excitement of being grown up enough
to see a boat race had been extinguished. Her pride was so severely
injured that for the moment she lost her sense of well-being with the
world. As for the elderly James Russell, his indifference expressed,
however politely, the gap between the intellectual branch of the
Lowell family and its wealthy cousins.

An index to the *mores* of Augustus Lowell's household may be
found set down in a list of likes and dislikes in Amy's "Complete
Composition Book." Among the questions Amy asked herself (with
answers hastily set down and with misspellings of reckless charm)
are:

> What is your favorite moral caracterestic? Self controll.
> What do you most dislike? deceat.
> What is your favorite exercise? books. [At first glance this listing may
> seem to have been Amy's highly individual choice with its self-tribute to
> her brains. Actually it reflects Augustus Lowell's athletic, early morning
> exercises in reading; aside from the pleasure he derived in reading aloud
> to Amy, reading was placed among his duties.]
> Who is your favorite heroine in American history? Barbara Friche.
> [Throughout her life few women have been more consciously, even stren-
> uously patriotic than Amy Lowell. Nor was there in her conspicuous
> patriotism the slightest taint of false feeling or sign of lip service. In later
> years she was as valiantly American in Europe as Percival had been in
> Japan. Whittier's legend of Barbara Frietchie gave her an image of active
> patriotism to which she never failed to respond. It also embodied a con-
> ception of physical courage shared by all male members of her immediate
> family and shown by Percival's hazardous Japanese travels as well as in
> the incident described by De Wolfe Howe of Abbott Lawrence Lowell in
> middle age, and after he had become President of Harvard, climbing a
> roof of his summer home with hose and buckets to put out a threatening
> fire.]
> Who in the history of other countrys? Josephine. [Childish as this
> choice may seem, it precisely echoes late nineteenth century American
> prejudice in favor of Napoleon's wife. Her face was known on hundreds
> of candy boxes, tinted and oval; the romantic and pathetic story of how
> she was deserted by her ruthless, heartless Emperor, the heroic ignominy
> of her divorce were household tales. Like most legends of its kind it con-
> tained ambiguities and paradoxes: Josephine's legend—drifting into mid-
> dle-class homes—spurred a demand for Empire bedroom furniture. One
> might think that housewives would sleep uneasily on beds which even
> faintly resembled Josephine's; probably the romance of the legend over-
> came such fears and was a stimulus to pleasant and sometimes waking

dreams. Up to the time of World War I many girls were christened Josephine—and by that time the legend had less of pathos in it than the reflected glory of being an Empress.]

What caracter (female) in all history do you most dislike? Joan of Arc.

What are your reasons for your likes and dislikes. Joseph's husband ill treated her Joan of Arc was too masculin. [The shock of seeing Joan in armour, dressed as a soldier, would have been quite enough to discourage too active an admiration for this heroine; it is consistent with the following two entries:]

What quality do you like most in women? Modesty.

What do you most dislike? imodesty. [Certainly this masculine prejudice in favor of ideal and correct womanhood was one that would have been echoed by Amy's mother; it was also an ideal probably set up in the household whenever Amy's habit of talking out of turn ran out of bounds.]

In her choice of books, particularly in her affection for George MacDonald's *At the Back of the North Wind* and *Marco Paul's Adventures on the Erie Canal* can be found further proof of the impression left on Amy by having Percival Lowell as an elder brother. The other-worldliness of MacDonald and Percival's "other world" of Japan—and later of astronomy—complemented one another; even *Marco Paul's Adventures on the Erie Canal*, a notably less memorable choice, had its associations with Percival's adventurousness. Amy Lowell was distinctly the child of Augustus Lowell's domestic environment. Her school, though championed and "made to order" by the cousinly Mrs. Cabot, was of considerably less influence. Indeed, the school was far less exciting to a child of Amy Lowell's vigorous, robust temperament than her father's household. No Boston family radiated the variety of interests that the Lowells in all their branches held out for display. In Amy's branch, wealth was the most prominent of its superiorities—and this in the world that Amy Lowell came to know was not despised. Nor is it extraordinary that in after years, she stayed on until her death at Sevenels, even sleeping in the same bedroom she slept in as a child. Sevenels became her castle, and however far she journeyed from it, her trips were holidays and excursions, not farewells.

2

S HER DIARY entries and her subsequent remarks on her school days show, the late 1880's and the early 90's were to Amy Lowell an extremely painful interlude of "growing up." A few years before her pride, her vanity, and her ego had been sustained by being the acknowledged darling of her family. Whether or not she made friends easily or held them had been matters of small importance, but with the coming of adolescence, a disturbing self-consciousness possessed her. Instead of growing slender as most girls of her age seemed to grow, she felt herself becoming maturely stout, "a great rough masculine, strong thing," she wrote, and in writing these words down she exaggerated the awkward figure she saw in her looking-glass. She was not as ugly as she supposed; she had small hands with tapering delicate fingers, small feet, intelligent grey-blue eyes, a rounded chin, and sharp, finely molded lips. It was true that at school she had made no intimate friends. To classmates who in a few years would be debutantes, Amy talked too much, was too opin-

ionated and bookish, too aggressive. When they would have liked to
have spoken up in class, Amy outtalked them, forestalled them with
highly opinionated information. They were tired of being forced to
sit back silent while Amy, who had a brother in Japan and who
herself had visited more than half of the great cities of Europe, talked
with an air of authority. Their revenge was to make themselves more
attractive, more clinging to boys at parties and to each other than
Amy could bring herself to be. She won respect but was decidedly
unloved; if she went to a dance—and she attended dancing school—
she was left alone; if she played a set of tennis with a boy, after the
game the boy walked home with another girl. "But I am ugly, fat,
conspicuous, and dull; to say nothing of a very bad temper," she
wrote. "Oh Lord please let it be all right, & let Paul love me, & don't
let me be a fool."

If she respected nothing else that nature gave her, she valued her
brains: "don't let me be a fool" was the refrain of all her prayers. It
had become easy for her to become a hoyden, a "roaring girl," * in
self-defense to make herself more noisy, more unpopular than ever.
In school she had never learned to listen to her teachers or to take
advice from them. If she learned anything at all, it had to be acquired
through her own habits of reading, her own ability to see and hear
things for herself. Her school had invited a Harvard lecturer to deliver a series of talks on Shakespeare; and though Amy Lowell did
not record his name it was probably Barrett Wendell. She remembered the lectures which she attended for two years: "We learnt
everything about the plays . . . except the things that mattered.
. . . Not once in those two years were we bidden to notice the
poetry. . . . The plays might have been written in the baldest prose
for all the eminent professor seemed to care." Had she been able to
see all the plays the lecturer tried to make her study, her love of
action and color would have been stirred, for Amy Lowell had a
deeply romantic affection for the stage. Because she felt the slights

---

* Unknowingly, of course, and unconsciously the early Amy Lowell had the
temperament, spirit, and courage of Thomas Middleton's Mary Frith, the
Elizabethan heroine, "Moll Cutpurse," of *The Roaring Girl*. This analogy is
not as far fetched as it may seem; the greater differences in their characters
are those of time, custom, place and social mores. Amy Lowell was as chaste
as Mary Frith, had the same outward show of cheerfulness, the same practical
skill in handling money, and the same kind of public popularity.

she received at Boston parties, the only social engagements that gave her superlative pleasure were the occasions when she joined a group of girls on theatre parties and, later, when the girls performed in amateur theatricals. She had been offered the part of Tony Lumpkin in *She Stoops to Conquer*—but this, because her mother refused to let her play the part of a man, she was forced to reject. Her mother probably knew that if Amy did well in the part (which was doubtful) the child would run the risk of making herself, and therefore her family, ridiculous; and there may well have been a touch of hidden malice in giving Amy a rowdy, shrewd, loud-voiced part to play. The role was too nearly in character with what Amy's school friends thought she was. Her mother's prohibition had more than prudishness to recommend it.

In the dark of the theatre, seated in a box or in the orchestra, Amy was permitted to extend her day dreams, to be vicariously the "Leading Lady" behind the footlights, which was a greater pleasure than being both hero and heroine of a novel. Amy craved love, notoriety, fame, action, all the more so because at this time she had begun a long series of missteps, accidents, in which she suffered broken bones and sprained ankles. She had more bodily weight than her small bones could carry. She thought of herself (and in her lonely moments with great dislike) as strong and active, a misconception of her physical strength which was one of the causes of her death at fifty-one. Although like all girls of her environment and wealth she was fated to "come out," as a sub-debutante Amy Lowell knew all too well that she was not made for "society," that she would be forced to be as reserved as her father (without his excuses for being so); yet she loved public activity—as much as she enjoyed throwing herself upon a sled and coasting down a hill in winter. She learned how to talk brightly, cheerfully to friends at parties, and though adept at "small-talk," she was too consciously aware of its emptiness to enjoy it. She hated the thought of becoming an old maid, but the possibility of that future was so clearly hers that she could not ignore it. Her answer to these problems was to read, to read at home and to climb the winding iron stairs of The Athenaeum to the quiet, nearly empty reading room where John Jay Chapman and Minna Timmins as they read aloud Dante's *Divine Comedy* had found themselves in love.

On her darkest days, reading had become Amy Lowell's retreat, her substitute for the creation of wandering day dreams. She admired her father's example of self-control too deeply to allow herself the luxury of staring helplessly into space, or like her now elderly cousin, James Russell Lowell, who when young lay on his back in a field of daisies and grass to gaze up at the sky, to see the afternoon drift by until the clouds reflected the red glow of sunset. She was far closer in temperament to her brother Percival. Her reading also became her substitute for an education at school, where she dismissed German and Italian as unworthy of study and allowed her French to fall so far behind that her mother's earnest, though mild, tutoring in French during summer vacations became imperative. Even in moments of loneliness she demanded activity. Nothing as passive as continual day-dreaming would suffice.

If she could not take lessons from a teacher, she delighted in the experience of arriving at a charity bazaar in fancy dress with writings of her own, privately printed, to be sold. At the Perkins Institution for the Blind, the fairy stories she had dictated to her mother, *Dream Drops,* actually brought fifty-six dollars in the sale of the small volume. This was her way of making gifts to charity, of doing good, of keeping for herself only the glory of public notice. She had to be at the center of an activity to find herself at ease, to learn something of the world in her own way. The more spectacular the occasion, the better.

In the same active spirit she discovered in her father's library at Sevenels Leigh Hunt's *Imagination and Fancy,* a book of selections from the English poets with an essay in answer to the question "What is Poetry?" As she wrote later: "I did not read it, I devoured it. . . . So engulfed in this new pursuit was I, that I used to inveigle my school mates up to my room and read them long stretches of Shelley, and Keats, and Coleridge, and Beaumont and Fletcher. Guided by Hunt I found a new Shakespeare, one of whom I had never dreamed, and so the plays were saved for me, and nothing was left of the professor's lectures except an immense bitterness for the lost time." The book found Keats for her, but at the moment the important event was that she was lecturing on and reading poetry aloud; she was doing the teaching in her nursery at Sevenels with schoolmates for an audience, and she had full authority.

In dancing school where for a time she did so badly, she responded far better to the teachings of a master, Mr. Papanti. The floor of a dancing school yielded more readily to social activity than the desks and aisles of a classroom or the seats of a lecture hall; and dancing had within it an athletic cheerfulness, a bouncing health that chimed with Abbott Lawrence's pleasure in swimming naked and Percival's hardiness on walking tours in Korea and Japan. As Amy learned to dance, and to dance with the felicity and robustness that stout people master and enjoy, she grew to love the waltz; the swaying, swinging movement of the waltz's measures gave her the sensations of physical lightness that she envied in others—here was an exercise that delivered her from the chains of feeling overweight, slow, stupid. And to be cheerfully in earnest, if not always gay, was a part of the design of the façade that she was making to face the world.

Her horsemanship, or rather her skill at driving horses—seated or standing in a trap, or in a smartly turned out cart—was another joy she mastered. It was this that gave rise to the gossip that Amy had been brought up by the Lowell coachman, Burns. She took great pride in caring for animals, dogs or horses, and there was less sentimental attachment in this ability than a display of efficiency, a ringmaster's showmanship, and a concern for the lower orders of the animal kingdom. Her father saw Sevenels almost as an Eden in which he botanized from spring to winter, secure from the world of cotton mills and banks; and Amy had begun to know it as her manor house, a seat of the American gentry. With this came duties to all living creatures within its gates.

With her debut in 1891 came a round of sixty dinner parties and exclusive dances. There were the Assemblies held at Copley Hall where Society displayed itself at gas-lit entertainments. During the 90's it was not surprising that visitors from England accepted Boston and Cambridge as vaguely familiar. It was not quite the Boston known as "Little Athens"; it lacked that elder dignity and air of spaciousness. It had begun to carry its gas-lit innovations with an air of provincial smartness—with brick paved walks, a "High Street" called Commonwealth Avenue, and rows of Queen Anne brick houses near the Common. Society, in the sense that Amy Lowell knew it, consisted of a half-dozen families, most of them distant as well as near relations; their females were the "cousins" from whom Percival had escaped by his journey to Japan

A debutante's ball in Amy Lowell's circle had strong resemblances to a large family party. It was as though the awkward school girl, now grown to seventeen, had been returned to the center of family affection where she felt, if for the moment only, very much at ease. She danced as vigorously and as noisily as she wished; she joined Boston's famous "Sewing Circle," a group of rich young ladies who once sewed garments for the poor but now exchanged gossip in a luncheon club, the "Circle" meeting at a member's home once a week. Now that her elder brothers and sisters were married or, like Percival, away from home, Amy had the top floor of Sevenels for her own uses: there friends could stay overnight with her and have meals served to them—and all the younger Lowells, including Amy, if they were home loved guests to sit in audience. They enjoyed their guests and put on "homemade" arguments and discussions and acted out murder trials, including the Lizzie Borden Case, for the entertainment of all who dined with them. This hilarity was in contrast to the six days of the week when guests did not arrive, when Augustus Lowell's precisely timed routine was in silent order, and when his wife's long illness made its presence felt. Amy's escape from the lower floors of Sevenels was to the theatre and the collecting of full sets of "authors." She loved good, rather lavish leather bindings and first editions, and she became a victim of this expensive, unshrewd vice. Booksellers were not above deceiving her as to the value of her editions, but if even in her innocence she knew that she was fooled, the delight of book collecting had its way with her. Amy Lowell's love of the theatre had rapidly outgrown her earlier school girl passion of playing "heroine" vicariously or as heroine herself stepping on the stage. It took another form: she became a director of amateur theatricals, and was active on committees for charity performances of all kinds. In these civic, if not always social, duties she followed in the wake of earlier Lowells who had made their influence felt in multiple Boston charities and on the board of Harvard's overseers. However cold their individual exteriors may have seemed to the public, the Lowells took a paternal interest in the fortunes of their communities. Their reward for such favors was the unquestioned approval of their ability to command. To Amy such activities had promise of the same reward, and the spirit with which she entered upon them was anything but cool. Her elder sister, Katherine, had married Alfred Roosevelt, who died early, and it could almost be said that Amy, though she knew him very slightly, had been inspired by Rooseveltian energy as well as by the inherited instinct for strenuous activity within her own family. Meanwhile the need for "something to do" had become urgent; her increasing weight had become a burden as difficult to bear as the repression of activity for her energy. She looked beyond Boston for the relief of both: travel spurred exercise and also created the illusion of accomplishment, and in 1896 (her mother had died the year before) Amy took a six-month tour of Europe.

The immediate reason for the trip was to dispel the sense of loss; another reason was that she had been given full charge of Sevenels by her father, and before settling down to additional duties, a holiday was in order. But she did not, of course, travel alone; she was more than well-chaperoned by school friends and relations. During her travels she found time to write long letters to relatives at home, the kind of letters that were a prelude to the books she was to write in later years. Impressionistic, lively, candid letters they were, written in the style which in later years she dictated freely. It is not surprising that her great discovery on this occasion was Venice. To the American tourist the city has the character of a scene behind footlights: the strange reflected sunlight from its waters, the arcs and arches of its bridges, porticos, bell towers. The colors of the sky, stones and sea, are so visibly unlike any other place on earth that the completely man-made city has the illusion of other-worldliness. It was there that Amy Lowell took practice in the most strenuous exercise that she could find; with the instructions of a gondolier she tried to "gondle." As a futile reducing exercise the results were painful; the lessons did little more than convince her, fatigued and hand-blistered as she was, that she was abnormally strong, "*very* strong," as her gondolier Tita told her. The Venetians probably viewed her, as they had casually observed so many generations of well-to-do tourists, English, German, American, with genial impersonality. The secret of Venetian hospitality is its nearly cat-like indifference, its grace, its quiet smiles; the tourist's own responsibilities to the world seem to melt away in the waters of the Grand Canal. With her usual haste, and forgetting that Venice had less of the earth within its peninsula than sea, Amy Lowell boldly wrote,

"Venice is the land for me," and in her enthusiasm it is impossible to read ironic meaning.

In London, on Amy Lowell's way home to Boston from the Continent, the wife of the fashionable, newly prosperous publisher, Heinemann, took her to visit Whistler in his studio. By this time Whistler was in the mildest and most respectable period of his fame: he was less the Butterfly than the carefully and smartly dressed, aging painter who had resigned himself to living in London and was less well off than his patrons and admirers believed possible. It was not known that his wife's recent death, after the futile and heavy expenses of her long illness, had left him nearly as poor as he had been during his earlier career, and with less energy, more pride, and less assurance to face the world. The little man in his neatly appointed studio with its Japanese screens, the farthing earned in the Ruskin trial dangling from his watch chain, had become a kindly figure to visiting American young ladies. As with other young women who came from the United States to see him, negotiations went forward toward the purchase of a small picture. Whistler suggested one of two; Amy Lowell, to show she was of her own mind, took the other. She fancied that he liked her air of independence in making her own choice; but she also felt that she had left him with another picture that he could sell with greater ease than the one she bought. Her intuition may have told her that the celebrated man was in need of American dollars; and it is also probable that in her presence he exerted a rare show of tact; for since she was obviously impressed by him and flattered, he returned the compliment. In those last years of his life Whistler's visitors dwindled in number. Instead of Whistler the younger generation in London sought out the contributors to *The Yellow Book*, and in Paris Degas was "The Master." At Whistler's funeral, a few years later, his crowd of curious followers was absent; only a few of his older friends were present.

After a Boston season at home, Amy Lowell returned to Europe: it had been rumored that she had fallen in love, and that her emotion was not returned. This was Boston gossip that was to be repeated in many similar rumors later. Yet no evidence has ever been discovered that would substantiate a serious affair. The greatest likelihood is that she did meet with an unpleasant experience with a young man who had been attracted by her wealth and that her vanity was wounded. This alone would be enough to dampen the habitual vigor and cheerfulness which so often was her shield against the world. It would cause her to do much serious thinking, and to curse the fate of having a glandular disease which gave her such an unwieldy bulk, to make her angry, to make her close doors to visitors and to reject the affectionate inquiries of her friends. It would lead her to hope that further exertions in travel would reduce her weight and distract her mind from fears of the future—for to be unloved was a nightfall terror of her childhood.

To go abroad again, then, was to effect a break in the provincial routine of Boston society and its duties. Her brother, Percival, now returned from his far eastern travels, had found himself by becoming an astronomer and setting up an observatory in Arizona. Travel had done much toward completing his education; it had made him the author of four books and with finality had turned his attention beyond the Far East to the planet Mars. His example was not to be ignored. Amy Lowell had always felt that her education at school had been, if not disastrously harmful, certainly useless, and that she had to continue to learn in her own way. Travel provided means to that end, and since she had had her glimpses of Europe, Egypt and Africa were farther reaches into the unknown world—and though accompanied by friends, she would be on her own.

For certain Americans, particularly those of Amy Lowell's vigorous temperament, Africa has been a haven; after Naples, Sicily, and Capri, the other, the southern, side of the Mediterranean offers both romantic excursions into antiquity and deep green jungles. Big game has been sought and shot there; it became the haunt of Theodore Roosevelt and Ernest Hemingway—both of whom, by the way, made their African journeys long after Amy Lowell's venture in 1897. Curiously enough, all three of these romantic Americans looked far more robust than they actually were; it was as though that dark continent offered singular challenges to high blood-pressure, hidden frailty and physical courage. Its pyramids, its dark-skinned natives, its visible antiquity, its snakes, lions and tigers, its glimpses of primitive jungles, its swift river courses, its deserts offered inspiration for tests of courage; and because of its exotic and large animals, it also contained childlike associations with the traveling circus—the glamour of "the greatest show on earth" under billowing sheets of canvas. All these attractions held their charms. Its mysterious largeness of hot sky above, wastes of sand below, and the deep greenery of the tangled jungle caught the imagination of restless Americans. Certainly Africa would provide subjects for writing letters. Amy promised her father that she would write him every Sunday of her trip (twenty-three weeks) and she kept her promise; it was the next best thing to writing a book. She felt—it was instinct rather than a logical conclusion —that she needed something to *make* her write. With her two friends, Frances Dabney and Polly Cabot, and her trusted maid, Mary, she had proper chaperones and companions. The day after Christmas, 1897, she was in a *dahabeah*, seventy-five feet long, going up the Nile.

The *dahabeah, Chonsu,* was to become her "boat of the rising moon." And from the accounts of her friends, as well as from her letters, we are given the first of the Amy Lowell legends that furthered her notoriety two decades later. Naturally enough, as her brother Percival had learned in Japan, rich Americans in the wildernesses of strange countries seldom fail to excite the shrewd instincts of native guides and porters. The Americans always look so very rich, and are so often ignorant of local customs, dialects, and means of travel. The *dahabeah* had to mount a three-mile stairway of rapids up which the boat was steered, lifted, and dragged by Arabs, who made much of their exertions and demanded extra fees. As the boat was being guided up the stairway, Amy Lowell sat on deck writing notes with her fountain pen and—as the story runs—the natives seemed impressed by the magic power of ink flowing from a pen that needed no refilling from an ink well. They gathered around her curiously. Slowly she came toward the Arabs with her pen held high as though to open fire, and the frightened natives speeded back to their task. This episode was immediately followed by a further incident when the crew of the *dahabeah* refused to mount the boat to the island of Philae and Amy Lowell hauled the boat to shore herself.

The more colorful details of the story may be dismissed in favor of its greater importance: Amy Lowell could and did command. Without the religious fervor of a General Gordon in the Sudan, Amy Lowell had the same fanatical gift of leadership; Gordon's bamboo walking stick was his sword, even his substitute for fire-arms;

his frail, slender physique equaled the hidden frailties of Amy
Lowell's bulk—yet the spirit of his physical courage was also hers.
A furious disregard of physical, visible handicaps always transcends
what seems the impossible—and if presented in terms of action (beyond mere use of words which are so often misunderstood) the actor
wins the day. So Amy Lowell had her moment of complete victory,
which proved her worth, in a stranger country than any in the entire
continent of Europe. If her journey up the Nile yielded no further
knowledge of her own gifts than this, it was worth the discomfort,
even the trials of journeying up the Nile.

To choose a dramatic moment and to build upon it was a means of
overcoming the visible shock to others of her growing bulk; it gave
Amy Lowell her necessary poise. It also gave her a valuable, an
inventive, "original" substitute for the ambition to act behind the
footlights on the stage. The little adventure on the Nile was a
rehearsal for larger, even more successful scenes in public. To her it
was more rewarding than four years at college; it was the discovery
of an executive gift that she possessed without the aid of teachers or
the advice of others. It made her happy to say "I am glad I am an
American and was brought up like a boy, and I am glad for every
single time that I have been spilt out of a carriage."

An earlier adventure, not so fortunate, had taken place near the
gates of Sevenels, when she lost control of a swiftly pacing horse. A
small nephew was with her in the carriage which was near to being
overthrown—and if her brother Lawrence had not been with her to
right the disaster, all three might have suffered grave injuries. It was
Lawrence Lowell's destiny to see his younger sister, Amy, when
she was not at her best. Or did the presence of the sober, somewhat austere, critical elder brother unnerve her self-confidence?
Abbott Lawrence was of a temperament that rejected flattering indul-
gences to others; he inspired respect but seldom held affection. To
one, like Amy, who needed the assurance of being loved and admired, his critical eye weakened the poise so necessary to her well-
being.

On her way home from Egypt she stopped at Rome to visit the
small apartment at the foot of the Piazza di Spagna where John Keats
died. At that time the room had a barred gateway; this was, one
supposes, to keep souvenir hunters from chipping off flakes of plaster

from the walls or splinters of wood from lintels and window frames, for at the end of the nineteenth century the names of Keats and Shelley had become sacred. Shelley's elegy on Keats, his "Adonais," had linked his name irrevocably with that of Keats; both poets had died young and the sentimental affections of all who read poetry for its biographical interest were stirred. Popular feeling toward both poets had blurred the distinctions between them. At the moment, however, Shelley was in his ascendancy: sixty years had passed since Mary Shelley's four volumes of her husband's collected poems had gone through the press; but she had done her work of editing the poems so well—and all with an air of Victorian widowhood, crowned by laurels—that the revolutionary ardors of the poems she published were forgotten. To Amy Lowell's generation of readers, Shelley was Matthew Arnold's "beautiful and ineffectual angel," and to maternal ladies, inclined to rhapsody, a "fallen angel" to be embraced by womanly arms. Such demonstrations, however, were not permitted in Augustus Lowell's household; to him Shelley was a dangerous atheist, and no more. He refused to allow the real distinctions between Keats and Shelley to be erased, and with the logic of stern common sense, permitted Keats's entry while Shelley's was firmly banned. Amy Lowell's admiration of Keats, though for the moment less fashionable, held no taint of fatherly disapproval; it could run unchecked, unguarded, and in later years it became the greatest of her literary passions.

Looking back to that day in Rome in 1898, Amy Lowell's nineteenth-century heritage seems greater than that of any public literary figure who appeared on lecture platforms in the cause of the "new poetry" which flowered so rapidly between 1912 and 1920. It no longer seems so extraordinary that her ethical and moral principles were so very New England-Victorian, that she dressed in a mode that was at least ten years "behind the times." Nor does it now seem curious that her behavior had the vigor and enthusiasm of the emancipated Boston women in Henry James's novel *The Bostonians,* who flourished—much to his distaste—in the 1870's.

Today, the emancipated woman in America may be regarded as a nineteenth-century phenomenon, for it was then that she received the broadest reaches of her notoriety. The granting of women's rights in the twentieth century and the general acceptance of their legal

and political equality with men destroyed the romantic—and idealistic—elements of their cause.

Keeping Sevenels in order for her father was of short duration,
for in 1900 Augustus Lowell died, and as part of her inheritance,
Amy Lowell became sole mistress of Sevenels. She ran the estate in
the same spirit that the matriarchies in the nineteenth century were
founded. The trip to Egypt, valuable as it had been in self-discovery
of her talent to command, did not improve her health nor decrease
her figure; the glandular disturbance which had resulted in her
abnormal weight and bulk showed no signs of being checked or cured.
She complained of prolonged headaches, and whenever she came
within hearing of strange noises, her body felt shaken, as though, so
she wrote abruptly, "the slightest sound jars you all over." It was in
this period of five years, that she began her habit of staying in bed
until early afternoon. Now that she was mistress of Sevenels, her
childhood desire to put off bed time to the hour she chose (which
was dawn) could be indulged.

Among the outward signs of the Amy Lowell who was to become
famous two decades later was her interest in Brookline public schools.
An elderly official was in control and at a town meeting which had
been called to remove him, speakers gave him so much praise for his
past record that the purpose of the meeting was deflected. Because
she saw the danger to the welfare of the children in her community,
Amy Lowell mounted the platform and restored the purpose of retiring the old man as the principal issue of the meeting. A new official
took his place, and though her relatives, both men and women, were
shocked at the thought of a lady, particularly a Lowell, assuming the
right to speak in public, this victory was one that capped her success
in frightening natives of the Nile.

She was then elected to the executive committee of the Brookline
Education Society and chairman of its library committee; in fact she
had taken over duties that would have fallen into her father's hands
had he been alive. In this office she delivered a paper on the question "Is the Present System of High School Education Prejudicial
to Individual Development?" Nothing more clearly illustrates her
heritage of masculine Lowell thinking than this document. "Character means courage," said Amy Lowell, "and there is a great difference between the collective courage of a mass of people all thinking

the same way, and the courage of one man who cares not at all for
public opinion, but goes on his way unswervingly . . . it is not
. . . easy to find men who are willing to think and act at variance
with the opinions of their neighbors." "Character" and "courage"
were nineteenth century American virtues in the very words and
spirit that Amy Lowell spoke; she herself lacked neither, and she
held to them with a righteousness that was her substitute for religious
feeling. In her paper she quoted a phrase from a Mr. Hughes who
had written a book on education: " 'Evolution, not revolution, is the
order of development,' " and in this quotation one also hears the echo
of her brother Percival's voice. She went on to say, "Nature cannot
be hurried, there is no such thing as cramming. . . . And what can
we think of a primary school taught by one teacher, in which the
children were taught seventeen subjects, with fifteen minutes given
to each subject, as was the case in one school in Brookline!" She had
been thinking of her own education which had meant so little to her.

With the same vigor she applied to the writing of a paper on
suburban education in the primary schools, she took her stand, a conservative one, on the question of moving the quarters of the old
Boston Athenaeum. In the hopes of making a profitable exchange in
real estate, the majority of the Athenaeum's directors welcomed a
plan to move that library from its site on Beacon Hill to a plot across
the Public Garden. Amy Lowell received the few who opposed the
scheme in her bedroom. Shielded from the drafts of two open
windows near her bed by a huge black umbrella set up behind her
shoulders, clad in an old-fashioned wool and cotton nightgown, she
was smoking a pipe. Although the hour was mid-afternoon she had
just finished breakfast. Quickly and like a Civil War general—the
image of General Grant in his tent with his cigar and unbuttoned
jacket comes first to mind—she briefly outlined a successful strategy
for keeping the Athenaeum where it was. She enlisted the help of
her brother Percival, who sent a letter to *The Boston Transcript* in
defense of her cause. It is believed that her poem on the Boston
Athenaeum was written at the same time and she probably read it
aloud to her friends with dramatic effect. With decisive practicality
she bought an extra share of Athenaeum stock so as to raise the
power of her votes, and with the same courage that she displayed on
the Brookline school board, she carried the day. The issue as she

saw it was clear enough: the site of the Anthenaeum had true historic associations, and to lose it was to dilute the cultural heritage of Boston. To change the Anthenaeum's site was to surrender her own associations with the place; it would mean the giving up of a reading room where she had found an escape from the authority of school-room readings and the authority of a teacher's voice. The Athenaeum was a visible symbol of her own independence as well as a symbol of inherited Lowell authority on its board of directors.

Meanwhile as if by and for herself—her salvation from the doom of headaches, of strange prolonged periods of lassitude—Amy Lowell had discovered the impulse to write verse. In 1923 in a letter to Eunice Tietjens, who as a guest editor of *Poetry* (Chicago) was preparing an issue of early verse written by well-known poets, she wrote of her experience in seeing Eleanora Duse act in a cycle of d'Annunzio's plays in the month of October 1902. On two previous occasions she had seen Duse act in Boston, in 1893 and in 1896, but on this particular evening she felt the inspirational force of Duse's acting: it moved her to write in verse, and as she expressed it, "it loosed a bolt in my brain and I knew where my true function lay." The verse that she submitted with the letter and which was published in Eunice Tietjens's issue of *Poetry*, August 1923, has a distinct affinity with Arthur Symons' essay on Duse written in 1900 and a relationship to Sara Teasdale's tributes to Duse which were republished in her first book of poems, *Sonnets to Duse and Other Poems*, in 1907. Whether or not Amy Lowell had read Symons' essay in a periodical it is impossible to say; it is improbable that she at this date had ever heard of Sara Teasdale, who later was to become one of her best friends. The point is that her impressionistic and romantic affinities with Symons' and Teasdale's comments on Duse are clear, and that they moved in the direction of her writing poetry. Arthur Symons in his description of Duse wrote:

Eleonora Duse is a great artist, the type of the artist, and it is only by accident that she is an actress . . . She is the artist of her own soul, and it is her force of will, her mastery of herself, not her abandonment to it, which make her what she is. [Certainly this was consistent with Amy Lowell's desires and character.] . . . if, in the street, some words of one of her parts come to her with a shiver, it is some passage of poetry, some vivid speech in which a soul speaks. Why she acts as she does, and how she succeeds in being so great an artist while hating her art, is her secret,

she tells us; hinting that it is sorrow, discontent, thwarted desires . . .
As one talks with her one begins to realise the artist through the woman
[Amy Lowell always relied, more than anything else, on the force of her
visible personality—on her actual presence] . . . Her stillness is the stillness of one in the act to spring . . . [How much, how often Amy
Lowell saw in action itself an expression of art] . . . When she speaks,
the words leap from her lips . . . always in coloured clothes . . . As
she listens silently to music, she seems to remember, and to drink in
nourishment for her soul, as she drinks in perfume, greedily, from flowers,
as she possesses a book or a picture, almost with violence. [All this might
well describe the qualities Amy Lowell sought for in her own verse, as
well as the joy she had in amassing a large collection of books at Sevenels]
. . . she never touches one . . . remains impersonal, though so close.
Her intent eyes see nothing but the ideas behind one's forehead; she has
no sense of the human nearness of body to body, only of the intellectual
closeness of soul to soul. She is a woman always, but she is a woman
almost in the abstract. [The two last statements have a close affinity with
Amy Lowell's emotional life: during her mother's last illness, Amy
feared that she would lose her own mind, and righted herself by force
of will to hold on to the virtue of having a strong mind; if her body was
awkward, she persisted in keeping her mind keen, sharp enough to feel
that she was all mind, not body. In later years when doctors offered to
modify the bulk of her body through surgical treatment of her glands,
she promptly refused, and said she feared an operation would "slow down
her brains." Both her fears and common sense probably prolonged her
life, for at that time surgical treatment of glandular abnormalities was
highly experimental.]

Symons' quotations from an interview with Duse in which he
wrote what he remembered from her remarks were statements that
now seem to foretell Amy Lowell's efforts and attitudes toward the
making of her "new poetry." In the heat of Amy Lowell's campaign
for *vers libre* and when she wrote that she, a poet, was "putting
cosmic poetry on the blink," there is an affinity to the following statements that Symons remembered:

To save the theatre, the theatre must be destroyed, the actors and
actresses must all die of the plague. They poison the air, they make art
impossible . . . We must bow before the poet, even when it seems to us
that he does wrong. He is a poet, he has seen something, he has seen it in
that way . . .

These convictions are of the same fabric of ideas and feelings that
Amy Lowell expressed almost two decades later, and her image of
Duse was not far distant from the lines that Sara Teasdale wrote "To
a Picture of Eleonora Duse as 'Francesca da Rimini'";

If ever I have pictured in a dream
My guardian angel, she is like to this,
Her eyes know joy, yet sorrow lingers there,
And on her lips the shadow of a kiss.

The Italian actress with her lithe figure, slender hands, soft movements, great brown eyes, and, not least, her attachment to the violently romantic d'Annunzio, was of a time and spirit that preceded
the twentieth century. Whatever romantic attachments Amy Lowell
possessed, their sources were of an earlier inspiration than her audiences of 1916 suspected. Even her "business-like" approach to being
a writer and making herself known came from the New England of
an earlier generation. If her manner was dictatorial, her rudeness was
seldom calculated; if she smoked cigars,* her appearance of being
different was balanced by an old-fashioned decorum in her dress; if
she lost her temper at a New York dinner table and shouted at her
hostess that she was "The Last of the Barons" and that she had no
sympathy with tolerant Liberals, she was Amy Lowell—surrounded
as she was by the nineteenth-century comforts of her own manor,
Sevenels.

* Amy Lowell's smoking habits and preferences are among matters of
dispute. Mrs. August Belmont's memory of them, since she first met Amy
Lowell in 1909 and the friendship was sustained up to the date of Amy Lowell's
death, has an air of authority. Amy Lowell, according to Mrs. Belmont, hated
cigarettes, and on all occasions, refused to smoke them. In private, after
breakfast at her country house, or in bed at Sevenels, she sometimes smoked a
pipe. She did not sustain this habit in company, and her reasons for not doing
so seem clear enough. In Boston pipesmoking was an indulgence of the lowly
"shanty Irish," even among the women; it was a preference of questionable
taste, far more objectionable and "shocking" than the smoking of cigars. In
actuality Amy Lowell was often more conventional than she seemed to newspaper reporters as well as to those who viewed her as being ultra-modern and
sensational. Even in her smoking habits, there were limits as to how far she
would go. At Sevenels her preferences were for a "man-size" mild Havana
cigar that her more intimate friends saw her smoke, and, on rarer occasions,
strangers saw her smoke it. On formal occasions, when traveling or "dining
out," she smoked a smaller cigar of mild Havana. Why did she smoke at all?
A thoroughly reasonable answer can be found that is related to her energy, her
high blood pressure, her irritability, her glandular disease. Tobacco smoking in
its mildest form created the illusion of "soothing her nerves." It became a
"comfort" so indispensable to her ease that she could not drop it, even as she
debated whether or not she should stop smoking in the presence of her sister-
in-law, Lawrence Lowell's wife. She decided that it would be "out of character" for her, and hypocritical, to shield Lawrence's wife from the sight of her
cigars.

3

THE YEAR 1902, in which Amy Lowell felt that the dramatic inspiration of Eleanora Duse had changed her life, came midway in what seemed to be a grey, unhopeful period in American letters. In actuality it was less sterile than it seemed, but the immediate prospect lacked visible color and excitement. Boston as the site of American culture, its "Little Athens," had been "a long time dying," and first sign of its dissolution came as early as in 1881 when William Dean Howells, who as a young and passionate pilgrim had come east from Ohio, resigned the editorship of *The Atlantic Monthly* to Thomas Bailey Aldrich. Since Aldrich had come on to Boston from New York, a subtle shift in atmosphere was felt, and as if to give the sense of change a final note, Howells left the peaceful scenes of Boston's Chestnut Street for the more glittering and less restful streets and avenues of New York. Henry Adams found Boston tolerable only by making extended trips away from it to Europe; he felt that the clink of coins had been heard at least once too often in

41

the temples of Boston, that *his* world was crumbling. It was best to
rediscover Mont-Saint-Michel and Chartres. As for poetry, the most
highly gifted of Boston's younger men was of Spanish, not New
England's, heritage: George Santayana, who in his nearly perfect
sapphics protested:

> My heart rebels against my generation,
> That talks of freedom and is slave to riches,
> And, toiling 'neath each day's ignoble burden,
>   Boasts of the morrow.
> No space for noonday rest or midnight watches,
> No purest joy of breathing under heaven!
> Wretched themselves, they heap, to make them happy,
>   Many possessions.

Edwin Arlington Robinson, because of a change for the worse in
his family fortunes, had left Harvard and Cambridge—and it was
significant that after a return to his native Maine he went on to
New York and bypassed Boston. Whatever fluttering of literary
ambitions stirred the air, Boston had become a city least likely to
overhear them. James Russell Lowell was dead, so was Longfellow;
the meeting between Emerson and Whitman had gone into legend
and both were dead.

The rest of the country, and this was particularly true in New
York, San Francisco, Washington and Chicago—this last city because
of the Columbian Exposition of 1893—felt the dying of an old
century and the arrival of a new. An "End of a Century" emotion
had its hold on the younger generation of London and Paris and it
came into print with the publication in London of *The Yellow Book*,
edited by Henry Harland, a brisk young novelist from New York.
Like most self-conscious demonstrations of its kind, its feelings were
decidedly mixed: world-weariness fell into place beside a realization,
by no means gloomy, that neither Queen Victoria nor her century
could last forever. Harland was an extraordinarily hard-working young
man and had acquired the habit of rising at two in the morning to
get his own writing done before breakfast at nine. On the eve of
leaving New York for London he said to his wife, "This is worse than
murder—for murder merely stops a life, whereas birth begins one,
and out of blessed nothingness." It was in that spirit he left New York
and it was this brisk, cheerful air of knowing the worst that was to

make his magazine the touchstone of all that was fashionable in London a few years later.

At this moment, other voices with the same convictions were heard. With an urban Irishman's alacrity, Bernard Shaw in his preface to *Captain Brassbound's Conversion* foretold the decline of British Naval power as the American fleet made its round-the-world tour shortly after the Spanish American War; he pronounced the nineteenth century certainly dead. No less cheerfully, Theodore Roosevelt, on the sudden death of McKinley, stepped from the Vice-Presidency into the President's Chair. Within a few years *The Atlantic Monthly* had become a far less robust expression of whatever went by the name of "American culture"; its immediate rivals, *Harper's* and *Century*, edited in New York and lavishly illustrated, offered fiction in brighter dress, and from Philadelphia *The Ladies' Home Journal* carried President Roosevelt's warnings against "race-suicide" in a monthly column dictated to its editor, Edwin Bok. A change of temper in national feeling had left Boston in a backwash of elderly convictions and conventions.

It was characteristic of the American temperament, diffused as it was across a large continent, to welcome rather than reject the prospects of a new century. Americans enjoyed, with less experience than their European cousins, an almost superstitious regard for changes of date in the calendar; they welcomed newness in very nearly everything except domestic relationships, "businessmen" ethics, and the two-party political system. It had been forgotten that the "new spirit" which they celebrated had most of its sources in the ideas and premonitions of 1880. In Europe, popular interpretations of evolution and socialism, as well as industrial and commercial application of scientific knowledge, were both vocal and in print. In America, the date 1900 brought with it elaborated hopes and ideas of progress. Protected by two oceans that had been policed by the British navy for a hundred years, Americans saw no reason why material progress could not rise on an inclined plane upward into infinity. The continent was open to huge immigrations from Europe—and all were welcomed both as cheap labor and as shareholders in a Utopia of universal progress. When in 1905 President Roosevelt acted as mediator in a settlement of the Russo-Japanese War, the incident looked as though it were visible proof that the twentieth century would be an American century—an American vision of material progress which was reiterated and enlarged at the close of World War II in 1945.

It is not surprising that a few younger writers of the decade turned against the optimistic temper of the day. Slum areas in the larger cities of the country had grown far too visible to ignore; material progress had not wiped them out; nor were all the results of the Spanish-American War as glorious as Dewey's brief encounter in Manila Bay. Badly tinned beef, sold in trainload lots to the U. S. Army, was the cause of a greater loss of life among American troops than in any incident of that war. The unromantic aspect of war, foreshadowed by early performances of Bernard Shaw's *Arms and the Man,* began to show its face. The decade in America introduced the "social realists" in fiction and "the muckrackers" in journalism, and in poetry came early signs of a distance between serious writing and the kind of fiction and verse that were eagerly read and quickly forgotten. The serious writer, unless blessed by a private income, however small, had grim alternatives to face. There were three: journalism, an editor's chair, or teaching in a university or college. Stephen Crane, the most promising of the younger generation, chose the first; Theodore Dreiser, the second; Trumbull Stickney and William Vaughn Moody, the third. Accepting none of the three, Edwin Arlington Robinson—the most enduring poet of that day and the most vehement in his doubts of material virtues—resigned as it were to poverty and hard-won rewards, took a job as an inspector of tracks on the New York subway, which coincided with his Puritan belief that one must travel through darkness to perceive the light.

The division between the writer who was dedicated to a purpose beyond the entertainment of the reader, and the commercial rewards of doing so, became more clearly marked as the decade approached its end. The Henry James who in the 1870's, '80's and early '90's held an American public through the serial publication of his novels in magazines was scarcely more than a memory, and was regarded as an expatriate, a nearly British writer, resident in London. Rudyard Kipling, who had married an American and lived on a farm in Vermont, occupied a place formerly held by the members of an elder generation, including Hawthorne and Melville, of native birth. In poetry James Whitcomb Riley, as much of an actor as a writer of domestic verses, caught popular attention through recitation of his "child rhymes" in lecture halls. The charm of his performance was as much a part of the welcome he received as Dylan Thomas's recitals in America in the early 1950's. Both Riley and Kipling professed a disregard for art and intellectual seriousness; they admired craftsmanship and deftly practised it. In their writings both exhibited great dramatic éclat and rhythmical ease. Riley's appeal was to an elder generation that had read James Russell Lowell's *The Biglow Papers* and Will Carleton's narratives in verse of provincial America—of which "Over the Hill to the Poor House" provided as many tears as stock company performances of *The Old Homestead*. All these were genre pictures of a rapidly receding American past. Kipling's writings in both prose and verse caught and held the favor of the younger generation—and both Kipling and Riley crossed the gulf between "serious writing" and the demands of popular taste.

Memorable verses appeared in the company of much that was to be forgotten within a few years—all inserted within quarter and half pages of monthly magazines. These were the "space fillers" or "poets' corners" where A. E. Housman's *A Shropshire Lad,* and Louise Imogen Guiney's and Lizette Woodward Reese's poems were published. The first effort in the direction of making a distinction between "magazine verse" and poetry of lasting merit came with Edmund Clarence Stedman's *An American Anthology,* a collection that gave space to the poems of Whitman and Emily Dickinson, as well as to the unknown and early poems of Edwin Arlington Robinson.

It is to be doubted whether or not Amy Lowell was aware of the changes in temper that defined the literary scene in the year she chose to write a tribute in verse to Eleanora Duse. What is certain is that she had already begun her collection of a large library. Going to the theatre and the buying of books had become her dominant passions— along with trips to Europe for a "change of scene," a demand which in the eyes of her brother Percival was a true sign of civilized taste and behavior. Yet much of her later activity had its sources, however well concealed (for she often expressed open contempt for *The Yellow Book's* sensibilities and attitudes) in the apparently dormant, unproductive years of her life.* In her speech she acquired the vigor

---

* Many years later, in 1918, Amy Lowell adversely criticized the writings of Donald Evans, a minor poet, for seeming to reflect the influence of *The Yellow Book.* This was a misreading of Evans' verse, but her prejudices against *Yellow Book* sensibilities were clearly expressed.

of a Theodore Roosevelt, and "bully!" his favorite exclamation and adjective, became her property. Her pince-nez had a resemblance to the pair he wore. His appearance to the world, even his bulk, his semblance of robust action and health, were also similar to the image she presented to friends and enemies alike. She was Rooseveltian in manner as well as—through her sister—Rooseveltian by marriage. She was a staunch evolutionist; and whatever strain of Puritanism she had inherited from earlier Lowells was well overlaid by the commercial Pragmatism of nineteenth century Boston.

In a generation that accepted both Riley and Kipling, enjoyed them and wept and laughed with Riley, and felt a renewal of vigor in Kipling's language, Amy Lowell took from both figures strident examples of their behavior. From Riley came the example of an actor's interpretive skill in reading verse from a platform, the dramatic rise and fall of the voice, the stress of rhythms. Riley in his youth had wished more than all else to be an actor and had run away from a middle-class Indiana home to follow a one-night-stand theatrical troupe; since he was not permitted to mount the stage, he sold patent medicine up and down the aisles during intermissions. His father, a well-to-do small town lawyer, had offered to send him east to college, but Riley, like Amy Lowell after him, had to learn things in his own way, and could not be taught by conventional methods. During the torpid, heat-waved, prairie Indiana summers he read and reread his favorite "modern" poets, Longfellow and Tennyson. To this example, Amy Lowell added her conscious inspiration from the art of Eleanora Duse. Whether or not she was consciously aware of Riley's successes is beside the point; his figure was a part, and a significant one, of the cultural topography of 1902. She did not, of course, imitate his verse; her common sense would not allow her to join him in his all-too-obvious, slightly alcoholic rhyming, nor would it permit her to indulge in fancies which included her in the company of "Little Orphan Annies" and barefoot Hoosier boys.

Kipling's example was of another kind; the boldness, the bluntness of Kipling's *Barrack Room Ballads,* their uses of the vernacular, their dramatic effectiveness when read or sung had general appeal. It is difficult to overestimate the influence that Kipling's writings both in prose and verse had on a generation that came of age between 1900 and 1910, and no less successful were his children's tales, *The Jungle*

Book and *Just-So Stories,* which left their mark on those who were scarcely more than infants. In appearance, if not in actuality, his gifts were an extreme of the extraverted, colorful, masculine; they seemed to be living models of vigorous common sense in anecdote and rhyme. Like Riley's, his example was less literary than generally representative of a day when the expression of ultra conservative emotions and opinions was heard among the voices of the *Zeitgeist.* Riley represented its provincial, domestic American aspect, that was almost feminine and certainly sentimental, and Kipling its realistic, British colonial, Anglo-American, East Indian features. Both figures were examples of trenchant individualism. At a houseparty in Gardiner, Maine, in December 1907, Amy Lowell joined a club which in its enthusiasm over Kipling's "The Brushwood Boy" called itself "The Brushwood Club."

Meanwhile Amy Lowell's admiration of Eleanora Duse had grown so great that she followed the actress from Boston to Philadelphia, and through a friend, Katie Dunham, secured permission to visit Duse at her hotel. As Amy Lowell entered the room there was the large-eyed actress, resting in bed, her voice low and intimate—one of the secrets of her great charm, on stage and off. As Arthur Symons would say, "she talked as if soul to soul," and as another described her, "she looked as though her delicate bones shone through her fair translucent skin, as though a spirit spoke, scarcely a woman, through her lips." Amy Lowell came away from the interview "almost on air."

Since she had become mistress of Sevenels, which she regarded as her permanent home and "town house," she sought out a summer house at Dublin, New Hampshire, and bought a place there called Broomley Lacey—which during the summers she did not spend in Europe became her retreat.

The seven years following 1902 were years of many purchases and gifts: the buying of books and giving them to Radcliffe, of inspecting Wellesley, and of restocking and expanding her own library at Sevenels. Her earlier interest in education in Brookline had increased its range to varieties of education in women's colleges and clubs. To be a director, teacher, patroness of women, were among the ambitions which, to the end of her life, she never wholly lost.

Her virginal energies turned to a remodeling of the ground floor at Sevenels, and she gave it a curiously weighted and mixed Boston-

Victorian-Adam touch—a billiard room converted into a music room, a baronial library, panelled with oak transported from England and embellished with two huge fireplaces, surrounded by heavy wood carvings in the style of Grinling Gibbons. In these costly refurbishings, her taste was in the mode of American millionaire suburban houses of the day. No sight of weighted comfort was withheld; their interiors conveyed the mixed and often dark impressions of the Royal Palace at Bucharest, as well as of British great houses—of Hampton Court and Kensington Palace—with ante-rooms, vaguely resembling the dressing rooms of the Catherine Palace near St. Petersburg, thrown in. No expense was spared. Smaller details, objets d'art, and portable wall fixtures were gathered from the farthest reaches of Europe and Asia; baroque, neo-classic and East Indian designs were all on display within five feet of wall space. To these were added the spoils of six-weeks ardent sight-seeing in Europe: music boxes from Lausanne, cradles from Moscow, enamelled watches and snuff boxes from Paris, Venetian fans and masks, and children's sleighs from Rotterdam. This was a profusion that strove to outdo, and frequently succeeded in its attempt, the overstuffed London apartments of Portland Place and South Audley Street; it was often twenty years behind the London fashion, but the lag in time had the advantage of the buyer's securing more objects of greater diversity. If physical comfort was achieved in these surroundings, mental distraction was also attained—yet the total effect brought about a desire to fall asleep. It had within it the same paradox of violent diversion that attends an evening's entertainment from a television screen. Those who gaze into it beyond fifteen minute intervals are first charmed, then stupefied, and finally, as if in self-defense, sent off to sleep.

Amy Lowell's library did not represent the extremes of American suburban fashion of the moment; it steered between them. Two Constables and her small self-chosen Whistler were on the wall—as well as a series of Japanese woodcarvings and scenes of Egypt by Joseph Lindon Smith. Built-in bookcases lined one wall—and at one end a bookcase was flanked by shelves of dummy books which was actually a door concealing a huge safe, a device that reminds one of the sliding panels and secret rooms described in Sir Walter Scott's *Woodstock*. If Amy Lowell gave this improvement any thought at all, it is more than likely that her childhood reading of *Woodstock* decided her in favor of it. But the most useful feature of the remodelled library was that it could be efficiently converted into a room where private theatricals were given. Amy Lowell's pleasure at seeing and hearing Eleanora Duse both intensified and expanded her earlier enjoyment of the theatre. Professional actresses were invited to perform in melodramas and to sing in the library at Sevenels; young men with a liking for music and skill in playing the piano were encouraged to perform for Amy Lowell and her guests. Amateur theatricals were vigorously promoted on the improvised stage; and Berkeley Updike, a printer and a seller of rare books, from Providence, Rhode Island, who had set up shop in Boston, designed the programs. He later became her favorite typographer, and when her books of verses were published she followed his advice.

It was around Berkeley Updike that Boston club women of that day fabricated legends of another "lost lover" for Amy Lowell. The rumors had certain elements of logic behind them. Updike was a brisk little man, whose spritely manner emulated the taste and the brightness of London's early 1890's. It was probably he who suggested to Amy Lowell that she produce and play the leading feminine role in Oscar Wilde's *The Ideal Husband*. He made frequent visits to Sevenels and there can be small doubt that he entertained its mistress. He was lively, "artistic," unbusinesslike. He was the type of man who promotes rare book clubs, who talks easily to rich women and is stimulated by them, who is mindful of feminine graces and discernments—and women in turn are pleased. To this class successful dress designers belong—and so do the unattached males who are invited by hostesses to be the fourteenth guest at dinner; it is seldom that any thought of marriage or love enters a friendship with them. The logic behind the Updike-Amy Lowell rumors of a frustrated love affair seem most likely to be based on her temporary deference to him in typographical taste and literary enthusiasms. His many visits to Sevenels were cited as evidence, but Amy Lowell's prolonged fits of depression, her headaches, her excessive weight—all made her need to find relief in light discussions of aesthetic matters. The presentable Berkeley Updike supplied it. They could exchange notes on the merits of one typographical style over another, and they could appear to be busily engaged while they indulged themselves in the pleasant relaxation of talking over a theatrical program or planning a book.

Unless she was chairwoman of a committee or hostess at a theatrical evening in the library at Sevenels, Amy Lowell had a lack of ease in social gatherings. She talked as brightly and with more common sense than any member of the clubs to which she belonged, but as she once confessed she felt "like a Fifth Wheel." Her interests were not those that prospered in a round of visits where gossip about neighbors and minor civic duties were topics for discussion at three-hour luncheons and teas. She resigned her offices in the clubs to which she belonged, wrote verses, acquired further collections of Keats's first editions and manuscripts, and increased the number of amateur theatricals at Sevenels. Her summer trips to Europe carried her eastward to Greece and Constantinople.

In the days before World War I, Americans who visited Greece came with preconceived ideas of the "glory" mentioned in Poe's "Lines to Helen," and Byron's "isles of Greece where burning Sappho loved and sung." The search for classical remains among the ruins was overlaid with thick, self-protective layers of romantic emotion, and travelers saw in the rugged landscape much of what they wished to see, rather than the rough terrain. The small cities of Greece, as Amy Lowell wrote to Winifred Bryher, were "a funny jumble of the old and new." The trip was not without the disillusionments reported by many an American pilgrim: the trains were slow, travel by carriage was impeded by overworked and ancient horses, and passage between islands in small, crowded steamers left much to be desired. After a burst of noontide heat, the climate was chilly. Like some few of her fellow-countrymen Amy Lowell triumphed over the usual discomforts by finding Athens was "just like Boston," and she insisted that there was "something very cozy and nice about Greece." She would have felt disloyal to Keats's "Ode to a Grecian Urn" had she thought otherwise.

A year later than her journey—in 1909—two events took place—and the first was of domestic moment—that later were to provide memorable details to the Amy Lowell legend. In the spring of that year the stables at Sevenels burned down and her several horses, including her favorite mare, Aura, perished in the fire. The event was followed by anonymous letters addressed to Amy Lowell which expressed an insane joy at the disaster. The incident probably aroused the feelings of one who inspired by envy of Lowell wealth and influence, as well as by a dislike of Augustus Lowell's cold exterior and his reputation of being a "hard man," could not conceal his pleasure at the thought of destruction falling on Augustus Lowell's heirs. Scarcely a year and a half had passed since the Panic of 1907, which had left in its wake trails of bitterness, grief and terror among those whose earnings and small savings had been wiped out. The Panic of 1907 brought with it the memory of a large body of socio-economic literature that had been in the making since 1879, the date of Henry George's *Progress and Poverty*. At its center were the increasing powers of labor organizations and left wing political parties which had merged into a Populist Movement. In America, it was a belated stirring of the Industrial Revolution, and the distance between the very rich and the very poor was plainly felt and seen. The burning of the Lowell stables at Sevenels was probably the result of carelessness among Amy Lowell's servants and an accident, but to an embittered mind it may well have seemed a portent, a preview of the Lord's wrath that was to fall upon the shoulders of Dives. Generous as the Lowells were in the giving of time and effort to civic enterprises and cultural institutions, including Harvard, they were not known as public benefactors in terms of good, hard cash. If not overtly tight-fisted, they believed in getting a just (and having an ideal of justice has never been a popular virtue) return for their efforts. The family of Augustus Lowell failed in stirring the deeper currents of public affection, and later both Amy and Lawrence received their share of adverse publicity.

After the stables had burned down, Amy Lowell replaced her horses with a litter of huge, highly pedigreed, rough-haired Old English sheepdogs which became the object of her domestic care. Each day they devoured nine pounds of top round beef along with large helpings of fresh mashed vegetables in side dishes—more than enough food to keep a large family of children in robust health. They were trained to roam the grounds of Sevenels, and not to leap over its low walls. After Amy Lowell's guests at dinner had finished their last course, the dogs were fed; guests were given large bath towels to spread across their laps so as to protect themselves, or rather their clothes, from the hearty, rough and galloping caresses of the dogs. At Sevenels the dogs became as much a part of the accoutrement of Amy Lowell's presence as her small, after-dinner cigars.

The other great event of the year was the election of her brother, Lawrence, to the Presidency of Harvard University. In appearance, except for his longer legs and more sure-footed celerity in movement, Lawrence strongly resembled his father, and his mind had the same restraints and withdrawals. During his own undergraduate days at Harvard, his highest grades were in mathematics and in history. Consistent with the somewhat abstract and decidedly pragmatic workings of his intelligence, his graduate studies were in law, and on leaving Harvard Law School he entered the practice of corporation law at 53 State Street. Although at Harvard he had been a favorite student of Henry Adams, he felt no dismay in entering offices in the State Street that Adams had so severely condemned in his *Education*. Lawrence was on the side of "practical education" rather than the caustic, semi-European view of it taken by his great teacher. Upon his father's death in 1900 he assumed full authority in administering the funds of the Lowell Institute and controlling its policy; he added to its funds, and through the Massachusetts Institute of Technology he provided a school for the training of industrial engineers.

Meanwhile he had been writing essays on government for *The Atlantic Monthly*; these were logical abstractions in political science that had the air of being realistic and hardheaded. At Harvard College he gave a course in "modern government," and with the same air of being practical and colorless enough to be regarded as absolutely "safe," he gathered an average enrollment of four hundred students a year. To the world at large, he gave the impression of being a solid man who, unlike his elder brother and younger sister, was to be trusted not to speculate or to indulge his fancies. If he possessed an imagination, that gift was well concealed.

What he actually had were a few soundly formulated ideas and the strength of character to apply them. When in 1902 at Harvard he served on a committee to improve instruction, he insisted that there was too much teaching done and too little studying. "Every serious man," he wrote, "should be encouraged to take honors in some subject." Later, when he became President of Harvard, he carried out his convictions by placing stress on a tutorial system, borrowed from Oxford, which supported a plan, also taken from the Oxford Honors School, of "concentration and distribution"—which meant that six out of sixteen elective courses were in one area of study. For members of his faculty (no matter how strongly his opinion was at variance with theirs) he stood for "personal liberty from constraint," which he believed was of greater importance than mere "academic freedom," because it advanced the rights of a lecturer to speak his mind both on campus and off. These were convictions that held to Anglo-American ideals of the individual's rights to think and act for himself, and Lawrence had the force of executive skill to make them visible at Harvard. Like his sister Amy's, his convictions were less original than strenuously promoted and executed. As President of Harvard he continued the Lowell reputation of gaining more respect than love.

Amy Lowell's own career was still unformed; from 1909 to 1912 her energies were divided between amateur theatricals and the responsibilities of being the mistress of Sevenels. As her official biographer, Foster Damon, suggests, her theatrical interests had been kept alive by a stirring of life in George Pierce Baker's course in playwriting, his famous English 47 at Harvard, and by the successes of William Vaughn Moody's *The Great Divide* on Broadway (1906) and Josephine Preston Peabody's *The Piper* (1909) in Stratford-on-Avon. This last was a Boston-American variation in dramatic form of Browning's "The Pied Piper of Hamelin."

Josephine Preston Peabody, born in the same year as Amy Lowell of an unprospering New England family, was brought up in Dorchester and attended The Girls Latin School in Boston. Her diary confessed her struggles against poverty, her desire to secure an education, her thoroughly romantic ambitions to write poetry, and her feverish hopes of writing for the stage. She felt that the early years of her life had been a progress from one mean, "dark" lower-middle-class suburb to another, through which the distant lights of Shakespearean dramatic verse—as well as the glitter of the Broadway stage—glimmered and shone dimly. Like many parents of the 1870's and '80's in the United States, her mother and father knew whole scenes of Shakespeare's plays by heart and had seen the Shakespearean actors of the period. She read Shelley and discovered Browning, and through the encouragement of her widowed mother, became a special student for two years at Radcliffe. She was more than a conventionally pretty girl; she was an intensely attractive, round-eyed young woman. She had an immense facility for writing verses in high romantic vein, and with her skills she taught the reading and writing

of poetry at Wellesley from 1901 to 1903. This post gave her authority in reading manuscripts of verse for publishers and editors of magazines. Her manner was both bright and decorous. One might say
she was a flower of fading New England's semi-academic literary life;
in that autumnal garden she bloomed like a mid-summer peony,
confident of her charms and fashionable in her taste, for in the
United States, Shelley was at the height of his reputation in the
women's clubs and Browning was their latest discovery. Everything
she wrote and said met with immediate success. In 1906 she married
Lionel Marks, a professor of mechanical engineering at Harvard and
for a year-long honeymoon they toured Europe, renting a house in
Dresden as their headquarters.

While other women of her kind joined clubs to discuss the
mysteries of Robert Browning's poetry, she put her reading of it to
practical use; and like her acquaintances she enjoyed a fashionable
enthusiasm for the Middle Ages. In the circles through which she
moved, the dim lights of the Middle Ages had been relit by
Tennyson's "The Lady of Shalot" and glittered behind the footlights
of his play, *Becket*, but by 1907 their lustres had acquired no less
enchanting shadows in the effort to understand the poetry of Robert
Browning. In preparing Browning's medieval story of "The Pied
Piper of Hamelin" for the stage, Mrs. Marks was less of an "escapist"
than an intelligent rider of a *Zeitgeist*. To take part in her little play,
The Piper, ran parallel to the fun of childish dressing-up in outlandish costumes—and what could be more outlandish than medieval
dress in Boston? With due propriety this fashion was some twenty
years behind a British joy in such performances: the playing at being
lords, ladies, fools and kings at manor-house dinner parties. It was
made respectable by being innocent enough, and in the United
States this innocence was trebled by honest ignorance. The American
generation for which Mrs. Marks wrote her play knew Mark Twain's
A Connecticut Yankee at King Arthur's Court far better than Tennyson's *Idylls of the King* or the poems of the Pre-Raphaelites. Mark
Twain's view of the Middle Ages remained untainted by the rigors
of scholarship and cheerfully unblessed by understanding. If it was
childish, it was instinctively gay, aggressive, boyish—and certainly
to those who read his *A Connecticut Yankee* in their childhood,
memorable. Mrs. Mark's choice of Browning's narrative for children

was in the stream of popular taste as well as in the current of literary fashion. The suburban atmosphere of women's colleges in America, which was then as well sustained as it is today, provided a nearly perfect setting for the success of her play—a neatly tailored "Forest of Arden" where,·for the majority of girls, each stay of four years brings a "happy ending."

In Boston it was inevitable that Amy Lowell and Mrs. Marks should meet, and not unlikely that they should be both friends and rivals. They met at amateur theatricals and at the theatre, on shopping tours and at literary gatherings. If Mrs. Marks lacked Amy Lowell's great wealth and notoriously well-entrenched social position, her literary "connections" were more secure, and the fact that her looks were brilliantly attractive increased them. To editors she looked as a "lady poet" should.

Mrs. Marks was a forerunner of the competition Amy Lowell was to meet from Edna Millay in 1924. Mrs. Marks used ineffable tact whenever she invited publishers to dinner or had lunch with them; she read manuscripts for them and gave them lightly worded, yet positive, advice. As early as 1901, she had been able to place Edwin Arlington Robinson's long narrative poem, *Captain Craig* with a publisher—first by charming him, then bewildering him, and at last carrying the day by warning him that Robinson had an "original mind." She was always more persistent and more formidable than she appeared to be; in her small whimsies, she never failed to charm her admirers, and they were delighted when she pronounced and spelled Bernard Shaw's surname "Pshaw!" She was the kind of woman who could be trusted to patronize Apollo or God himself by tapping him on the shoulder and giving him a nickname.

Meanwhile Amy Lowell began to publish her own verses. The friend of her earliest school days, Mabel Cabot, had married Ellery Sedgwick, who had become the editor of *The Atlantic Monthly*. Sedgwick was a young man of lively impulses and insights, and very nearly the last of Boston's genuine eccentrics, for like Percival Lowell, he had a Bostonian taste for the strange and exotic. He was an excellent editor who never feared his own or the public's opinion; and within the framework of Boston and *The Atlantic's* conservative policy, he was always happy to risk adverse criticism. It is consistent with his career as well as with hers that the first publication of Amy

Lowell's verse, and also the best of her last, appeared in the pages of his magazine. The first publication was in 1910, a year before "The Lyric Year," 1911, brought the decade of a conscious "poetic renaissance" into American literature.

At the distance of nearly half a century, the forerunners of that phenomenal decade seem to have been four men and one woman. The first of these was scarcely a poet and his name was Edmund Clarence Stedman. Stedman was a Connecticut Yankee who had gone to Yale, had been a newspaper editor and an assistant in the office of the Attorney General of the United States, and had made a fortune as a broker in Wall Street. He had written verses in the style of James Russell Lowell's *The Biglow Papers*, and had proved himself to be a hospitable man of affairs by throwing wide the doors of his large house in suburban Bronxville, New York. His neatly trimmed beard, his fashionable dress, his finely cut features, his quickly ignited enthusiasm made him seem to be a *beau ideal* among men of letters; he was as genial and as vigorous as the quick-stepping rhymes and meters of his verse—and so obviously wealthy that his opinions were listened to with respect and praise. He compiled a Victorian anthology of British verse and capped it with *An American Anthology* which included (a startling innovation for the year 1900!) large selections from the poetry of Walt Whitman and Emily Dickinson—and even a poem by Edwin Arlington Robinson, who gladly accepted invitations to his house for weekend dinners. His warmth, his excitement at discovering new poets was communicated to Harriet Monroe who on her trips to New York from her native Chicago visited his house in Bronxville. He, probably more than any one of her early friends, turned her mind in the direction of founding and editing *Poetry* in 1912.

Stedman's hearty approval of Whitman and Dickinson and early praise of Robinson did much to remove official doubts of the genius of all three poets. Stedman was a discriminating editor and was untouched by the taint of Bohemianism; his anthologies were commercially profitable and, in an academic sense, respectable and well-informed. Through his inclusion of Whitman and Dickinson, "free verse" and irregularly metered, epigrammatic verse became accepted as a "new" kind of poetry, poetry that was American in its locality, its language, and its emotions. Stedman's choices of Whitman and

Dickinson were first steps toward their broader recognition and influence.

With Whitman and Dickinson presented as major figures in nineteenth century American verse, their examples as "originals" became a precedent for the writing of experimental verse, for "self-expression" at the cost of breaking older conventions in the writing of poetry. Henry Adams in 1911 described the situation clearly:

> Poetry was a suppressed instinct: and except where as in Longfellow it kept the old character of ornament, it became a reaction against society, as in Emerson and the Concord school, or, further away and more roughly, in Walt Whitman. Less and less it appeared, as in earlier ages, the natural, favorite expression of society itself. In the last half of the nineteenth century, the poet became everywhere a rebel against his surroundings.

The general feeling of revolt had been extended to the conventions and language of poetry. The language of Tennyson and of Longfellow had lost its magic. Something of the direct, forceful, unrhymed, unpolished character of prose was demanded. Although Edwin Arlington Robinson retained the formal graces of verse (and he insisted that he belonged to the "old tradition") the language of his poetry had a conversational tone, and this same character marked the poetry (then still unpublished) of Robert Frost.

The conscious spirit of change had been in the air since 1900. There is little doubt that Stedman felt the presence of a date-line that had transformed the nineteenth century into the twentieth. Young men leaving colleges were (at the very least) critical of the previous century and hopeful for the reforms, social as well as literary, that were to come. Such cheerful spirits as Richard Hovey and Bliss Carman, authors of the immensely popular *Songs from Vagabondia*, joined Bohemianism with socialism, which gave rise to early formations of radical groups in New York's Greenwich Village. Hovey had written "The Stein Song"—and beer-drinking, art-making, love-making, and readings from Henry George, Marx and Veblen were taken up and practiced with simultaneous enthusiasm for almost twenty years.

Of the younger writers, one who keenly felt and expressed the changing temper of the moment in both prose and verse and who died at twenty-nine, in 1900, was Stephen Crane. It is highly probable that Crane's early inspiration for his famous *Red Badge of Courage* came from a reading of Ambrose Bierce's *Tales of Soldiers and Civilians,* published in 1891, for the same economy of phrasing, clarity of images, and psychological wit applied to men at war are present in both books. It is certain that before Crane wrote his verses (which were unrhymed, "imagistic," epigrams) he had read a book of Emily Dickinson's poems loaned to him by William Dean Howells. Stephen Crane may be considered the fifth and last of the writers—Stedman, Dickinson, Whitman, Robinson are the others—who were true forerunners of America's "poetic renaissance." They did not form a group; their gifts were highly individual and each unlike the others—which explains the great variety of their examples and streams of influence. Taken together, they presented a common cause for "originality," a new way of looking at the world, a new language for the expression of poetic truths. It is significant that in 1925 when Wilson Follett edited *The Work of Stephen Crane* in twelve hand-somely-bound volumes, Amy Lowell had been invited to contribute one of its introductions.

4

IT IS GENERALLY admitted by historians of literature that the five years preceding 1912 produced in England as well as in the United States something that has been called a "poetic renaissance." No one doubts the phenomenon, but few can give coherent reasons for it. In England, a few negative causes for it were clear. In 1909 in Putney, that stolid, most respectable of middle-class London suburbs, where nursemaids wheel their perambulators up and down the hilly High Street, Swinburne died. He had been the last of Victorian poets who could lay claim to greatness. Matthew Arnold, the two Rossettis, Christina and Dante Gabriel, the two Brownings and Tennyson were long since dead. The echoing, ambitious Stephen Phillips, the tinkling Alfred Noyes could not fill the vacuum left by the several deaths behind them—and the Poet Laureate, Alfred Austin, least of all. When Albert Edward, Prince of Wales, that gay, robust, hard-smoking-gambling-drinking lover of handsome women fell ill, Austin had written with serious concern:

Across the wires the electric message came:
He is no better, he is much the same.

It was clear that Kipling, who did not pretend to write poetry at
all but wrote memorable, trenchant verse, was both below and above
the fastidious banalities of Austin. Housman and Bridges stood apart
from all large claims: Housman was fixed in the orbit of his *Shropshire Lad;* Bridges was respected, but known only by the very few.
In England it had become a period of "magazine verse" that was self-
consciously minor. The great unknown was, of course, Thomas
Hardy, famous only for his novels; the potentialities of W. B. Yeats
were recognized only by Arthur Symons; de la Mare was still in the
green shadows of his first *Songs of Childhood.* Between the intonations of minor verses, silences were echoing this refrain: "the empty
singer of an empty day." If poems were to be written again at all, it
seemed as if an earthquake had to happen.

The situation in the United States was no less uncertain and
vaguely expectant. E. A. Robinson had just begun to fill a vacuum;
the great poet manqué was Edwin Markham. The public literary
figure who held the largest hopes for his admirers was William
Vaughn Moody, who died in 1910. "Magazine verse" was ascendant,
and the finest examples of it in terms of genuine poetry were found
in the lines written by Louise Imogen Guiney who had left Boston
for England to become a brilliantly mad "Bodleian mole" at Oxford.

Yet all these are negative reasons for what was to come, negative
preparations for an anthology *The Lyric Year* of 1911. A general and
positive cause may be found in the fact that a great and increasing
number of people both in Britain and the United States had formed
the habit of reading; and these were of a generation who felt that
the prospects of a peaceful Western culture were limitless. Victorian
prosperity carried over into the reign of Edward VII; and as his reign
faded into that of George V, the merest tremor of change was felt in
the air. Victorian standard of thinking and conduct had begun to
shift; Fabian ardors had become full grown; "the Emancipated
Woman" had almost come of age; the "Yellow Sins" of the 1890's
took on a sun-tanned look, for the younger generation had discovered
speed in motor cars and it became easy enough to escape the cities. It
was remembered that nudist camps were fashionable in Germany;
and in an English orchard, with books and lunch baskets near,

clothes were easily unbuttoned and dropped to the ground. Something was needed to express the feelings that had made these experiences memorable and behind them was the broader spread of education to the middle classes, of scientific education as well as a new look—an H. G. Wellsian-Fabian look—at the human body and the beginning of a Freudian look at the human psyche. Among the liberated few, the artists and the poets, there was a brief, delightful shock of post-Pantheism; they felt that they had traveled far beyond Victorian taboos. They had probably not read the short preface written by J. M. Synge for his modest book of poems in 1908, but they felt something of the same urgency in the air. Synge wrote:

. . . modern verse contains a great deal of poetic material . . . The poetry of exaltation will be always the highest; but when men lose their poetic feeling for ordinary life, and cannot write of ordinary things, their exalted poetry is likely to lose its strength of exaltation . . . In these days poetry is usually a flower of evil or good [of course Synge was thinking of the French pre-Symbolists and Symbolists]; but it is the timber of poetry that wears most surely . . . the strong things of life are needed in poetry . . . to show that what is exalted and tender is not made by feeble blood. It may almost be said that before verse can be human again it must learn to be brutal.

A like spirit was shown by some of the contributors, D. H. Lawrence, John Masefield, W. H. Davies, Rupert Brooke, in the poems Edward Marsh selected for a *Georgian Poetry* anthology of 1911–1912. It is significant that when in September of 1912, Robert Frost went to England, he found friends among the Georgian poets; there was true affinity in the youthful post-Pantheism of Frost to the younger Georgians. His advantage was that his speech had sloughed the softer, looser, nearly Wordsworthian decadence of simplicity that his English friends had clung to; his speech was tougher, sharper.

In the United States the larger forces at work behind the new movements in poetry had a different aspect. At the turn of the century, grade and high schools of the public school system, crude as many of its rural teachings were, were in a stage of progressive advancement and reform. In Cambridge, Massachusetts, Greek was taught to boys; so was Latin. While never surpassing the standards of established prep schools in this country or in England, the public school system in American towns, which were growing into cities, had merits that are not practiced in public schools today. The ears and brains of school mistresses and masters were still ringing with the sentiments and periods of Emerson's "The American Scholar." There was a general conviction that the public school system was proof of the goodness inherent in democracy and that it *had* to succeed. It was an all-embracing faith that united Emersonian idealism with Puritanical disciplines, that combined an eagerness to teach with the hope of seeing bright students enter the best universities. The teaching of elocution, of oratory, was not neglected and through this channel languages and literature were taught. This was a distinctly middlebrow culture which encouraged recitations of verse: these were quotations from *The Lays of Ancient Rome* as well as from *The Concord Hymn* and *Evangeline,* quotations from *Thanatopsis* as well as from *Marco Bozzaris.* Often enough these passages were memorized with appropriate gestures and took on a closer kinship to calisthenics than to a reading of verse, yet it was impossible for the grade school student, however dimly he understood the lines, to leave school without some memory of Poe's "The Raven," Byron's "Isles of Greece" and Mark Anthony's speech over Caesar's dead body.

No doubt many of the results of these teachings prejudiced many brighter students against the reading of poetry at all, but more than a few, even those who did not enjoy the strenuous exercise that accompanied the recital of it, as well as those who were moved to laugh at it, looked forward to the reading of a "new poetry" that was to be quite different from the verse which they had been taught or heard. Like their contemporaries in Britain, they felt the presence of a vacuum in poetic literature. The verse published in magazines seemed (and was more often than not) childish, trivial or thinly feminine. Even the ranting lines of "old favorites," remembered from grade school platforms, were less anaemic than the "poets' corners" in newspapers and periodicals. The need for something "new," something more nearly contemporaneous was felt, something that had a twentieth-century air about it—that reflected the growth of American towns into cities, the transformation of young women into "emancipated" girls who had "love affairs" and went to college, of events and things seen *now,* as if for the first time. In America the adjective "new" has a touch of magic in it; a demand for something new, if generally felt, is usually supplied; its value may be reserved for later judgment.

The new poetry that was being written in the five years before 1912 was nearly certain to find responsive readers. Amy Lowell's discovery of a source of inspiration in the acting of Eleanora Duse was not an isolated experience. One of the impulses at work behind the poetic renaissance in the United States was histrionic and oracular. Amy Lowell's theatrical evenings at Sevenels had their parallels in the thousands of public school recitals and dramatic societies. After brief moments of glory on school platforms or in public school debating and dramatic societies, only the very few had the boldness to risk the chance of going on the stage. The greater majority became politicians; others, like William Jennings Bryan of an earlier generation, combined journalism with law, politics, and oratory; still others in large numbers became salesmen. In an earlier day, it was no wonder that Whitman had ambitions to be an orator as well as a poet. Amy Lowell's ambitious loneliness in Brookline during the moments she wrote the verses published in her first book was the kind of isolation known to a multitude.

Like others who were inspired to write verse, Amy Lowell had already found, even among her friends in Boston, avenues for publishing her more serious efforts. Twenty American poets of a variety that extended from Ezra Pound in London to Robinson Jeffers in California, from Edna St. Vincent Millay at Vassar to Vachel Lindsay selling "rhymes to be traded for bread" to Chinese laundrymen in the streets of New York, from Edgar Lee Masters to Elinor Wylie—all had begun to write; and more than a few were then writing the very poems that were to make them famous during the following decade.

It would be madness to say that the writers mentioned in the list above had a common cause in being "revolutionary" and "new," yet a kind of unity prevailed among them that was non-political and embraced traditional as well as strenuously experimental attitudes. The common cause was in protest against the dominant materialism of the age. It revived—and in this sense it *was* a "renaissance"—the meanings of Emerson's 1844 essay on "The Poet," which contains the apotheosis of his idealism: he spoke of the poets as "liberating gods," saying further, "Therefore we love the poet, the inventor, who in any form, whether in an ode or in an action or in looks and behavior, has yielded us a new thought. He unlocks our chains and

admits us to a new scene." In his definition of the poet Emerson had
opened barn doors widely, but he stressed inventiveness and the
need for viewing a "new scene." Whether or not the poets who were
growing toward publication in 1912 had read his essay on "The
Poet" is beside the point. The greater likelihood is that their schoolmasters had, or if not their schoolmasters, their elder friends, relatives or editors. His remarks are still part of a cultural atmosphere
that expresses American feeling; it welcomes the inventive and the
new. If it was not conscious thinking, it could at least reawaken
sleeping sensibilities.

The temper of the day embraced "Votes for Women"; the strictly
political aspect of women suffrage held scant appeal for Amy Lowell,
but the general atmosphere was becoming more sympathetic to the
idea of women being active in large affairs. Certainly the writers
who were moving toward a "poetic renaissance" welcomed the writings of young women as well as men. Editors feared to repeat the
mistake of neglecting some new, unknown, unheralded Emily
Dickinson, and the twentieth-century woman writer had been liberated from the earlier convention that had forced her to assume a
masculine pen name. Even the most conservative of women writers
—and this was the class to which Amy Lowell belonged—were happy
to see their own names on the title pages of books. More than that,
they could expect masculine critics to be gallant. If in emulation of her
elder brothers, Amy Lowell in childhood had wished she had the
power to change her sex, to be a boy, that time was past, particularly
as she gave herself over to the writing of verse. Of women poets she
consistently admired Alice Meynell. As early as 1899, after spending
a summer with her friend and companion, Miss Frances Dabney, in
Devonshire, she had read Alice Meynell's *Poems;* Miss Dabney had
made her a gift of the book, and the book provided examples for the
verses she wrote and selected in her first book, *A Dome of Many-
Coloured Glass.* In that first book, she had no desire for an outward
show of unconventionality—quite the contrary; the verses in the book
were to prove the fact that Amy Lowell *could* write poetry.

However unknowing of the general scene Amy Lowell appeared
to be in 1911, she had made a choice that was in the fashion of the
day. The decision to publish a book as soon as she could, was one
that meant more than the usual appeasement of personal vanity. She

had seen the enthusiasm with which Josephine Peabody's verse had been received, and she spoke to her of the possible chances her own book might have if submitted to the Boston publishers, Houghton Mifflin. Josephine Peabody told her that they "did not care much for poetry which had no human interest, but why should they?" which was an evasive answer. Was Josephine Peabody critical of *her* poems? It was enough to make Amy Lowell thoughtful, a trifle hurt, but determined. In later years, she came to regard Mrs. Marks, née Peabody, as a decided enemy to whom she could give no quarter, but in 1911, Josephine Peabody's reputation as a poet could be taken as a sign of the times. Surely the sister of Harvard's president could not fail when lesser creatures were becoming famous.

At the moment Amy Lowell held her discouraging conversation with Josephine Peabody in a Boston florist's shop, Harriet Monroe of Chicago was engaged in getting support for a new monthly magazine, *Poetry,* to be published in Chicago. *Poetry: A Magazine of Verse* was to have great influence upon Amy Lowell's inspirations and accomplishments for the next five years, and the contrasts and parallels between her character and Miss Monroe's are pertinent. Miss Monroe was fourteen years Amy Lowell's senior, and her family, if considerably less wealthy than the Lowells, held a position in Chicago not unlike theirs in Boston. Miss Monroe's father was a prosperous lawyer, her brother-in-law was John Wellborn Root, a famous architect and one of the fathers of the "skyscraper." Whatever cultural or social pretentions Chicago had, the Monroes and the Roots were at their center. They were as steadfastly Chicagoans as the Lowells were Bostonians. When Oscar Wilde visited the city, Miss Monroe was one of a small company of young women who guided him about, and on Robert Louis Stevenson's short stay in New York, Miss Monroe in a new flowered spring hat, with her blond hair tucked under it, and her slender figure tense with the prospect of meeting a great writer, was welcomed into a large darkened room of a hotel where he rose from his sickbed to take her hand. He frightened her: his dark hair was too long and lank; his mustache looked foreign and Japanese; the few words he spoke were in a sibilant, moist whisper. She was to carry this youthful image of romantic disillusionment with her for many years. In situations where Amy Lowell was robust and commanding, Miss Monroe

appeared sharp and, if displeased, tight-lipped and caustic. Her
charms were those of being light and half-casual in conversation;
then with a show of enthusiasm, her eyes would light up behind
the inevitable, brightly-polished pince-nez. Beside her, Amy Lowell's
weight always seemed enormously large; and when later they met,
both were ill at ease in the meeting. Amy Lowell would talk too
loud, and Harriet Monroe's lips would grow tighter; and Amy Lowell
always felt the need of "impressing Harriet."

Yet the two women had more than a few experiences in common:
in Miss Monroe's love of travel (she had seen as much of the world
as Amy Lowell) and her earliest attempts to write were joined to her
great enjoyment of the theatre. Though her reading and knowledge
of poetry were of greater range and had been pursued with more
orderly precision than the younger woman's, by 1911 she, too,
regarded poetry as a "cause." Her friendship with Stedman in Bronxville, New York, her excursions into journalism, her criticisms of
painting and the ballet gave her greater authority in speaking of
poetry as one of the living arts than the Amy Lowell of 1911 could
command. In opening the campaign to raise funds for her magazine,
Miss Monroe granted an interview to a reporter from *The Chicago
Tribune* in November of 1911; her manner was decisive: "a Milton
might be living in Chicago today and be unable to find an outlet for
his verse," she said, ". . . In other words the modern English-
speaking world says 'Shut up!' to its poets, a condition so unnatural,
so destructive to new inspiration, that I believe it can only be temporary and absurd." Miss Monroe's language was not unlike the
Lowellese Amy Lowell spoke in pleading for the same cause.

Miss Monroe too was of an older generation than the majority of
poets who were the heroes and heroines of the poetic "renaissance";
like Amy Lowell she held firm admiration for the conservative,
romantic-classical verse of Alice Meynell, and she was impressed by
the dramatic verse of Josephine Peabody. Yet she had less concern
for the publication of her own verse, and was more directly eager to
read young poets and to find something "new" than Amy Lowell
was. Therefore, when she wrote letters asking for poems to fill the
pages of her new magazine she cast a wide net and guaranteed pay
for the contributions: W. B. Yeats was invited as well as John
Masefield, Harold Munro as well as the unknown poets, Amy

Lowell, Vachel Lindsay and Ezra Pound. Her long sustained hope was that her magazine would attract American poets, whether they remained at home or lived abroad. As for the money with which to print the magazine and to pay its writers—her appeal went to the well-to-do men and women of Chicago. Her friend, the painter Mary Cassatt, had been brilliantly adroit in convincing the patrons and directors of the Chicago Art Institute *not* to buy "old masters" with their money, but the *new* paintings of the French Impressionists. So successful was she that the Chicago Art Institute overlooking Lake Michigan had a distinctly Parisian air. Miss Monroe also had the experience of being an art critic for Chicago newspapers. It was never too difficult for her to brush past secretaries and office boys into the private offices of bank presidents and railroad executives. She entered with the knowledge that her pleas for publishing poetry might seem ridiculous, but she also knew that most of the men she interviewed would not be entirely indifferent to the claims of art. They had supported the Art Institute, which in their language "had helped to put Chicago on the map"; they could scarcely do less for poetry. Slender Miss Monroe was like a wraith of Civic Virtue; no one could doubt her honesty or the firmness of her purpose. Within a few months she had accomplished something similar to the mission with which Mary Cassatt gave distinction to the Art Institute. So far as America was concerned, *Poetry* of Chicago was at the center of the "poetic renaissance."

Two immediate signs of promise—and both were optimistic signs to Miss Monroe, and later to Amy Lowell—were the early careers of two widely different poets: Ezra Pound and Vachel Lindsay. On one of her transatlantic journeys (this time a journey around the world, for which she bought a ticket at Cook's in Chicago for a trip "From Chicago to Chicago") Miss Monroe picked up in London two small books of poems, *Personae* and *Exultations,* by Ezra Pound. She read them on her roundabout way through Siberia from Moscow to Peking. The year was 1910. In London the Pound legend was twelve months old; and it was one of a handsome and bearded young American, with the manner of the late James McNeill Whistler, who strode into a restaurant in Soho shouting "Damn it all! all this our South Stinks peace." This alone would have been more than enough to recommend him to the attention of Miss Monroe. But she had also heard that he had been born in Idaho—where poets seemed least likely to be born. She had heard the romantic story of his having an instructorship at a small Indiana college, where on a winter's night he rescued a stranded actress from the streets and gave her lodging in his rooming house. His sincerely romantic gesture of chivalry was doubted by his landlady, and though next morning the girl had left his room and there was not the slightest sign that he had shared a bed with her, the landlady reported the incident to the college authorities. On being questioned by them, Pound resigned in fury and sailed for Italy. Later, he arrived in London where W. B. Yeats gave him introductions to other poets. The little books Miss Monroe read were "different"; they delighted her. When she began to write letters asking for poems from younger writers she thought of him, and the letter she received in reply from London was both so engaging and so sharply critical of "magazine verse" in the United States—with its postscript, "our American Risorgimento . . . will make the Italian Renaissance look like a tempest in teapot!"—that she promptly appointed him *Poetry's* Foreign Correspondent, an impulse and a decision which she did not regret.

At a polar extreme from her admiration for Ezra Pound she welcomed, and in later years was a faithful friend to, Vachel Lindsay. Lindsay was no less unworldly and chivalrous than the younger poet, but he remained (despite his occasional brief trips to Europe) a provincial, Middle Western American; he was as clearly so as Amy Lowell was a Bostonian. Indeed this was always a barrier between them. There was also a deeper lack of affinity, for Lindsay was illogical and "idealistic" while Amy Lowell was "business-like" and pragmatic. The heroic example he offered to Miss Monroe was one of cheerful disregard of circumstances; he never feared to seem ridiculous. Although he attempted to earn his meals and lodgings by printing his poems in pamphlets and selling them on the streets of New York, his poverty was self-imposed, for his father was a moderately well-off, small-town physician. Lindsay's mother, an ardent Campbellite, was determined to make her son "a Christian cartoonist," a crusader in the causes of the Anti-Saloon-League and the Y.M.C.A., and therefore sent him to the Chicago Art Institute and later to New York art schools to study drawing and poster design. As long as she lived, and he was forty-three when she died in 1922,

Lindsay's attachment to his mother was unbroken; she was always dubious of his poetic gifts, and as a militant, evangelical Protestant, she made valiant attempts to keep him "pure," to drive him and "mold" him into the image of the "Christian cartoonist" to whom she had given birth. His poverty was that of the son of domineering parents who made sporadic efforts to be financially independent. He was a poet in spite of, and not because of, the strong, fanatical wills that guided him. He tramped the length of North America, reading aloud his poems from sheets he had printed. As Ezra Pound in London opened a campaign for the "serious artist" and the recognition of poetry as art, Lindsay in Springfield, Illinois (the town where he was born), issued "War Bulletins" advancing the causes of Single Tax, Buddha, Christ and St. Francis against "business axioms that make this a land of death. If any man has a dollar in his pocket let him throw it away, lest it transform him into spiritual garbage." The passion behind his "War Bulletins" was not unlike the spirit in which Pound fought against usury and for Social Credit. The difference was that Pound, who saw himself in the image of his own "serious artist," had a far more profound understanding of the culture he chose to advance. Lindsay's appearance—which was that of a farm boy dressed in "store-clothes," with a shock of straight yellow hair fallen across his forehead—both charmed and frightened those who met him. His trick of throwing his head back and closing his eyes was in the manner of an evangelical preacher at a revival meeting. Yet he did not frighten Miss Monroe, who was quick to see that he was neither a charlatan nor completely mad—and also to see that his hard-won victory in becoming a poet (against the will of his mother and against the half-amused, half-startled bewilderment of those who heard him read his poems) was an accomplishment of extraordinary power. Surely if a "poetic renaissance" was to come to light in her magazine, it needed the evangelical genius of Lindsay as well as the transatlantic activity of Ezra Pound. Pound had written to her that with the aid of W. B. Yeats he had secured for publication in *Poetry* English versions of the Bengali poet, Rabindranath Tagore's poems, and closed his letter with the slogan: "TO HELL WITH HARPER'S AND THE MAGAZINE TOUCH!" The campaign was to carry the writing, encouragement, appreciation and publishing of poetry beyond the reaches of mediocrity.

Amy Lowell, who had been receiving Miss Monroe's announce-
ments of her new magazine, was quickly stirred by news that seemed
to have all the excitement of pitched battles, counterattacks, reprisals,
and last-minute victories. The exuberance of Ezra Pound was contagious—even at transatlantic distance and in the pages of a magazine that was published in Chicago. Amy Lowell caught fire from it.
Although nearly a year was to elapse before Amy Lowell was to
meet Miss Monroe, their correspondence had already well begun and
Miss Monroe, aware of her Boston lineage, held her in mind, and at
letter-writing-distance, as "a daughter of the Caesars." Even during
the first year of its arrival, various groups of poets who were writing
and publishing poems, quickly staked claims for their participation
in the "new" movement. If not consciously "revolutionary," all felt
equally "new" or at least rejuvenated, and the spirit of something
like a revolution pervaded the air.

In New York a source of inspiration came from John Masefield's
narrative poem, *The Everlasting Mercy,* the story of a rural British
juvenile delinquent who grew up to be sent off to jail nineteen times
for various misdemeanors, and who after a prolonged bout of fighting,
drinking, whoring, suddenly discovered Christ. The poem was a
lively *tour de force,* paced with the speed of a stallion, and written
in octosyllabic rhymed couplets. In England its language, which
skirted only by the narrowest margin the use of forbidden four-letter
words, shocked respectable British reviewers, but it was applauded
by younger readers of "new" poetry in New York. It was written as
though Masefield had accepted with literal conviction J. M. Synge's
warning, "before verse can be human again it must learn to be
brutal." In New York it was remembered that Masefield—sixteen
years before the writing of *The Everlasting Mercy*—had been a bar-
keep's assistant for a few months in Luke O'Connor's saloon at the
corner of Sixth and Greenwich Avenues in Greenwich Village, a
distinction which gave him the aura of being almost a New York
poet, and almost an American. *The Everlasting Mercy* also had its
moments of "spiritual exaltation." To New Yorkers it was Synge's
preface brought to life. It could also be read as a document in a
literature of "Christian Socialism": its characters were sufficiently
proletarian and its message evangelical. Its spirit was "mad, bad" and
—for Americans—not too "dangerous to know." It set the tone of

verse that embraced the feelings of those who were vaguely Leftist in sympathy, all the way from those who believed in "Votes for Women" and "sexual freedom" to those who had heard of Henry George and Veblen and had read Upton Sinclair's *The Jungle* and Jack London's *The Iron Heel*. There is no doubt that the pretty little red-haired girl, Edna St. Vincent Millay, who was to graduate from Vassar in 1917, had read *The Everlasting Mercy* and redramatized it. Her poem was called "Renascence," and in it the same rush and flow of octosyllabic couplets was overheard. If its exalted passages were less humble, they were, if anything, more ecstatic. The results of publishing the poem were as sensational as the reception given to *The Everlasting Mercy*. Early in 1912 it appeared in the anthology, *The Lyric Year*, and did *not* get the prize offered by that publication. To defend "Renascence" became a cause in itself. Its author was nineteen, amazingly pretty, and had all the poise of an accomplished actress; she was the figure, voice and spirit of "flaming youth." If in New York a poetic "renaissance" was to put on wings, certainly Miss Millay was the figure to wear them with dazzling effectiveness, and, as her poem seemed to say, she could also "come down to earth" in a manner that would delight those whose convictions were even dimly Socialistic:

> A man was starving in Capri;
> He moved his eyes and looked at me;
> I felt his gaze, I heard his moan,
> And knew his hunger as my own.

If it had not been for "Renascence" and the controversy it aroused through *not* receiving a prize for being the best poem in the collection, *The Lyric Year* would have been quickly forgotten; as it was, the very title was associated with Miss Millay and the "new" poetry of which Miss Millay became New York's image of all that was young, appealing and feminine. Upon leaving Vassar five years later, she took parts in the plays on the stage of the Provincetown Theatre in Greenwich Village, and her conquest of the city was complete. She wrote plays and verse, and though her voice was too thin and shrill for the memorable recital of poetry, her presence on the stage insured applause. Undergraduates on weekend visits from Harvard, Yale and Princeton decided (as they saw her cross the stage) that the "new" poetry was something to be seen as well as heard. It was believed that the girls who wrote the "new" poetry *had* to be beautiful (a few of them were), and that their love affairs were gratuitous, well-advertised, and brief. Refugees from middle-class homes found in Greenwich Village a retreat from the moralities too often quoted by parents and watchful aunts and uncles. Without the need for further travel, the Village had become a substitute for the more dignified Bohemianism of London's Chelsea, as well as for the less decorous practice of the arts in Montparnasse and Montmartre in Paris. Whatever was meant by art and love in Greenwich Village was expressed in the image of Miss Millay: she filled a vacuum that had been left after the earlier residence there of Washington Irving, Edgar Allan Poe, Henry James and Mark Twain.

At the moment when the arrival of the new poetry was being felt at Oxford—largely through the handsome presence of Rupert Brooke ("I first heard of him as a Greek god under a Japanese sunshade, reading poetry in his pyjamas," wrote D. H. Lawrence), at the Poetry Bookshop near the British Museum in London, at the Art Institute in Chicago where Miss Monroe approached its directors to talk of her new magazine, at Vassar where Miss Millay took part in theatrical performances, in New York where *The Lyric Year* was being sent to the printers, Boston alone seemed unstirred by portents of poetic glory. Amy Lowell, however, had found a new friend and companion and, best of all, a sympathetic reader of the poems she had been collecting for her book.

She was Ada Dwyer (Mrs. Harold Russell), daughter of James Dwyer, a bookseller, who had travelled west from Philadelphia to Salt Lake City, Utah, where he was better known for his love of books and reading than for making money. His daughter acquired his tastes, and also through her girlhood friend, Eleanor Robson, one of the most beautiful and gifted actresses of the late *Yellow Book* period in London, she acquired a passion for the stage. James Dwyer sent his daughter to school in Boston and from a girls' school she stepped into Boston dramatic club performances, and then entered a Boston theatrical training school. She and her friend, Eleanor Robson, were actresses in the tradition of Minnie Maddern Fiske and Maude Adams. Ada Dwyer, off stage, lost none of her charm by an interest in reading poetry aloud and a modest, seemingly self-effacing personality. She and Eleanor Robson first met Amy Lowell in 1909;

they were playing in Frances Hodgson Burnett's *Dawn of a Tomorrow* which was a successful play by the now almost forgotten but then famous author of *Little Lord Fauntleroy*—a minor classic among children's stories of the late 1890's. In Boston, as *Dawn of a Tomorrow* made its New England tour, the three women—Amy Lowell, Ada Russell and Eleanor Robson—became friends.

For eight years Ada Russell had been a member of Eleanor Robson's company; if the original script of a play had no part for her, a part would be written in. Her very lack of off-stage histrionics on the stage itself exerted a particular spell, a quality that Amy Lowell sensed and Eleanor Robson valued. Ada Russell was as much at home in a library or at a literary cocktail party as on the stage, and as securely at ease. She had an air of sparkling gently as she talked, as she inclined her head to listen to someone speaking to her, or as she raised a glass of water to her lips. Her easy alertness had the art of putting others, particularly the restless and unnerved, at perfect ease.

In 1910 Eleanor Robson married August Belmont, and with her marriage her career on stage neared its close. Ada Russell also prepared to leave the stage; and within the next four years she, who had always seemed immune from illnesses, fell ill. Meanwhile, before her illness the spring of 1912, Mrs. Russell was on tour again in Boston. She was a friend of Mrs. Charles Bruen Perkins, who in turn was a member of a luncheon club to which Amy Lowell belonged, and because Mrs. Russell was then playing in *The Deep Purple* in Boston, she agreed to be introduced to the group at a luncheon, for the club was then named "The Purple Club."

Amy Lowell felt the need of one who could understand, in a sense that others of her friends could not—not even her friend Berkeley Updike—what she wrote and what she had to say. Mrs. Russell, listening to her read, not only gave her warm appreciation, but could and often did express intelligent, forceful adverse criticism of how poetry should be read. She could also offer helpful teaching of how to read in public, and this, as well as the charm of her personality, made her the companion that Amy Lowell sought. The new friendship brightened the prospect of meeting editors, of gaining support for the publication of the first book of poems. It was a friendship that was sustained to the end of Amy Lowell's life.

To all outward appearances, Boston in 1912 was the least likely of all places to contribute its share to the "poetic renaissance." In 1912 the general air of vacancy that had been felt ever since William Dean Howells had left for New York had become omnipresent; and it was as if all the forces of New England's destiny had appointed Amy Lowell to break the spell.

5

IN THE SPRING of 1912, Ferris Greenslet, a young editor of Houghton Mifflin, kept his appointment with Amy Lowell in his offices that fronted Boston Common. Mr. Greenslet was not the usual Bostonian, and was in fact scarcely a Bostonian at all, for he had come to Boston by way of New York State, and more recently from the editorial offices of the weekly liberal paper, *The Nation*. His manner was brisk and candid, and it combined the alertness of the young businessman with the more professional approach of a well-schooled lawyer. He made it clear that he was unlikely to be won over by any show of nonsense, yet he barely concealed a weakness for reading poetry. Moreover, his tastes and opinions were not governed by Bostonian conventions; they had been formed *outside* of Boston and were of the larger world. Like his friend, De Wolfe Howe, who had come to Boston from Providence, Rhode Island, he retained a nearly foreign air toward Bostonian privileges and manners.

On that day in 1912, he met a woman who looked older than her years (for she was scarcely thirty-eight), heavier in weight, and several inches shorter than she actually was. Her style of dress was, as usual, ten years out of mode, her hair was brushed back in a high pompadour, her collar of net was held stiffly in place by whalebone stays, and her jacket cut wide to ease her ample figure—this was not the expected image of President Lowell's sister or a poet. Yet she did seem to be the mistress of Sevenels, where her routine of living had become so well established (breakfast at three in the afternoon, dinner at nine, a midnight supper and work at her writing desk until three in the morning). The moment she sat down, her great bulk seemed to disappear; she was as brisk and light tempered as the young man who welcomed her, and as always, whenever she took pains to be charming, it was noticed that her features were small and delicate, that her hands and feet were gracefully turned, that the eyes behind the rimless pince-nez had a certain brilliance that spoke intelligence and rejected platitudes. As a visitor she assumed the authority of being, if not the hostess receiving guests, the mistress of the occasion. In later years, shrewd editors came to fear her visitations; she was all too likely to force larger promises from them than they were willing to keep. Unlike most poets she seemed supernaturally sane, and even businesslike in a way that impressed and charmed businessmen and editors. One young businessman and editor (who also wrote verse) confessed that she was always irresistible, though to him she seemed less a poet than a remarkable saleswoman. Yet whatever his feelings toward her were, he never failed to send her pre-publication copies of his books of poems, and whenever she visited New York, he made certain to call at her hotel—usually the St. Regis—or invite her to his home. On these occasions he was always and half-unwillingly overwhelmed.

It was not surprising that President Lowell's sister quickly overcame the natural resistance of Houghton Mifflin to the risks of publishing poetry. In Mr. Greenslet she had found an editor who had a keener appreciation of verse and far more sophistication in the reading of it than her friends of "The Purple Lunch Club." He could understand why she wished her friendly typographer Updike to design the format of her book of verse in imitation of a first edition of John Keats. He knew that since she admired Keats, her choice made sense. Because she did most of her writing at night to avoid interruptions of the telephone bell and daylight routines, he concluded, rather fancifully, that like Keats' *Endymion*, his new author was a "moon-worshipper," and he spoke of the "pale radiance" that "colors all her works." In these later remarks he was probably thinking of her first book, *A Dome of Many-Coloured Glass*, the title of which she chose from Shelley's famous elegy on Keats, for "pale radiance" is certainly not the phrase that distinguishes the writings of Amy Lowell. Her biographer, Foster Damon, came far closer to a clear description of it when he wrote that it left "the impression of having real things in it, real flowers and real weather."

By the time the book appeared in the fall of 1912, its author felt that she had hoped for too much that had not happened, and her editor remarked dryly that more people seemed interested in it as a book by the sister of Harvard's President than for any other reason. It sold less widely than was expected and was scantily reviewed. Amy Lowell immediately fell ill: neuralgia and the headaches—like those Coleridge so often suffered in his moments of dejection—made their arrival; and from these moments of dejection she was slow to recover. Any disappointment or temporary loss of security was almost certain to bring in its wake Amy Lowell's retreat to the bedroom where she slept as a child; a doctor would be called and he would tell her "not to work too hard." The recurrent cycles of overexertion, of disappointments—either large or small—of the illnesses which followed them, began with her mother's death and ended with her own. Everything that Amy Lowell felt or thought or did was a supreme act of will, as though she had to prove, even to herself, that she was still alive. At one end of the spectrum through which she moved she was always the intelligent "spoiled child" of elderly and indulgent parents; at the other, she was the spiritual sister of her contemporary, Theodore Roosevelt, intent upon living "the strenuous life" even if it killed her. In this respect—that of trying to live beyond herself, beyond her powers to feel or think—she transcended all other members of her family, and went beyond the provincial conventions of Boston and the suburban routines of Brookline. And in this she also resembled certain prominent figures of her day, not the least of whom was Roosevelt himself. Her need for visible success was as great as Andrew Carnegie's, and she shared his sense of

benevolence as well (as it was shown in his gifts to public libraries
and in her regard for education in the schools of Brookline).

She was quick to see that the publication of her book had been
overshadowed by literary gossip about the controversy over Edna St.
Vincent Millay's "Renascence" in *The Lyric Year* and the publicity given to Harriet Monroe's Chicago magazine, *Poetry*. It was
characteristic of her to be less interested in the discussions that came
with the publication of *The Lyric Year* than those which surrounded
Poetry. Beyond the fact that Miss Monroe had accepted some of her
poems for her magazine there was more in *Poetry* that she could not
understand than in the verses printed in *The Lyric Year*. She would
have less to learn of what was "new" from the latter than in some of
the more serious controversies roused by Ezra Pound in early issues
of *Poetry* and, furthermore, the magazine had an "international"
air. Though *Poetry* looked forward to an American "renaissance,"
its pages welcomed poems from Irish writers as well as British, and
its range extended even to Bengal with the introduction of Tagore's
poems to American readers. Such an appeal was far more exotic than
that which *The Lyric Year* had to offer. In the lack of notice that her
own book had received, she had read—and this was between the lines
of scanty praise—that she had not been spectacular enough. One
review appeared in *The Chicago Evening Post* that was to her a
timely warning. It was in a monthly column—"And Other Poems"
written by Louis Untermeyer, whose style in prose, as he so brightly
confessed, had been modeled on the turns and handsprings of G. K.
Chesterton's paradoxes. His complaint was that her book was far too
tame and said "to be brief, in spite of its lifeless classicism, [it] can
never rouse one's anger. But, to be briefer still, it cannot rouse one
at all."

Untermeyer was then a young man of twenty-eight, who as Max
Eastman observed, had a Dantesque profile, an irresistible turn of wit
and a great facility for writing verse and—like Max Eastman—he
was a native of New York State and an ardent Socialist. Both Untermeyer and Eastman were Socialists for the best of impractical reasons
—which were Utopian. Both Eastman's parents had been Congrega-
tional ministers in upper New York State, and Untermeyer's father
was a well-to-do New York City businessman. Both young men were
critical of the respectable status achieved by their families. It had

been hoped that Untermeyer would be a composer and musician and Eastman a professor of philosophy; and both made a dutiful attempt to follow parental instructions, Eastman by becoming a teacher of philosophy at Columbia University, and Untermeyer by vainly emulating a passionate piano teacher who stormed through Chopin and Liszt. In conscious revolt, they both read Heine and wrote verses, dreamed of "absolute liberty" and found a common cause in the editorial offices of *The Masses,* a magazine supported by Piet Vlag, a Dutchman who ran a restaurant in the basement of the Rand School for Social Science. It was an atmosphere in which Dutch cooking and equally indigestible politics prevailed. Young men entered into its activities with the hope of discovering a world they never knew—and found it. This contained the delight of "going slumming" with few of its attendant responsibilities; it had the charm of believing that the world could be reformed by editing magazines, or writing editorials and poems, making posters and drawing pictures. The scene was New York's substitute for *The Lower Depths* of Gorky; it was where the maladjusted intellectuals of New York expressed their discontent with middle-class standards and their hatred of "capitalism" which to them seemed to corrupt the six continents of the world. Untermeyer and Eastman gave their services without any thought of pay, and because of Eastman's attractive personality (he was tall, prematurely white-haired and carried himself with a languid, semi-philosophic air) he was commissioned to raise subsidies for printing the magazine and to be its editor. With Untermeyer and Eastman in the office, the magazine joined forces with New York's poetic "renaissance." It was the self-appointed task of *The Masses* to combine the doctrines of Anarchy, Socialism and Karl Marx with Art—and by these means to overthrow "the oppressive bourgeois majority." However low the depth of its sources were, the hopes of the magazine's editors ran high, and it was from this latter altitude that Untermeyer's comment on Amy Lowell's book was written in *The Chicago Evening Post.*

When Amy Lowell saw the notice she received in Untermeyer's column, she wept aloud. The charge of not arousing interest at a time when so many younger poets were gaining notoriety was a difficult truth to face. She was to make certain from this day onward that she was not to be ignored.

A month and a half before this resolution crossed her mind she accompanied her brother, Abbott Lawrence, and his wife to Chicago. She was recovering from one of her recurrent fits of illness. But her illness did not prevent the writing of her verse; she literally "worked" at it, so recklessly, so devotedly that in her own words (taken from her description of how Keats wrote) she achieved a "fury of delight" —and, therefore, it was little wonder that her efforts were exhausting. She was again in need of the "change of scene" that her brother Percival had always recommended for low spirits or frayed nerves. A trip to Chicago was no great diversion, but it held promise of relief from a routine of Christmas-week duties in Brookline and Boston. It was on this brief visit that she first met Harriet Monroe. Miss Monroe happened to attend a small banquet for the President of Harvard's wife, and as the banquet neared its end, Miss Monroe heard her say, "Oh, there's Amy."

From that moment, Amy Lowell in her slow progress to the table became the most imposing figure in the room. Miss Monroe quickly remembered that she had accepted several of her poems for her magazine, but was scarcely prepared for her abrupt, blunt question, "Well, since you've taken 'em, why don't you print 'em?"

The approach was severe and not without reproof, yet as Amy Lowell "literally sank" into a chair, her good humor asserted itself and, like so many others who met her, Miss Monroe was utterly charmed; her personality was, as Miss Monroe described it, "half-magnificent, half-humorous." The meeting turned Amy Lowell's attention directly to Chicago's *Poetry,* the little magazine that gave so much hope for the publishing of things that were terribly, shockingly "new."

Furthermore the most mysterious of new poems had appeared printed in its January 1913 number, and the mystery was deepened by the strange signature, "H. D. Imagiste." The initials stood for Hilda Doolittle, soon to become the wife of the young English writer, Richard Aldington, and both were living in London, but "Imagiste" stood for something that looked and sounded like a new school of poetry. The poems themselves had an air of distinction: they were unrhymed, clearly cut, and narrow in outline as they ran down the printed page; their references were Greek and their images strictly visual. Only through careful rereading was their music to

be discerned and overheard. Their appeal to Amy Lowell was immediate, for she felt that if this were what "modern" poetry was, she,
too, could be "modern"; she saw "things" clearly, she could describe
them at great speed, and reproduce them on paper in coherent order.
If H. D. could be called an "Imagiste," why not Amy Lowell? At
first reading it seemed that poems of an "Imagiste" kind were childishly easy to write. "Why, I too am an Imagiste," Amy Lowell
thought; to be one would suddenly free her from the usual associations of being the sister of Harvard's President, and joining a new
school of poetry would be immensely more refreshing than joining a
new luncheon club in Boston. The prospect enchanted her with
something of the same spell which led Percival away from Boston
and drew him to Japan. The attraction had much the same kind of
otherworldliness in its removal from the way verse was usually
written and talked about in Boston as would a visit to Japan—and
superficially it had the same sparseness, the same austerity of line
that found expression in the Japanese *tanka* and *haikai*. From Miss
Monroe and the pages of *Poetry*, Amy Lowell was quick to learn
more about *Les Imagistes*, whom Ezra Pound had said "already had
the future in their keeping." She learned that F. S. Flint and Pound
conducted the management of a new group of poets in London and
that it had the air of being a secret society. The French name of the
group also held promise, for she had heard of Verlaine's *vers libre*
and the younger poets who wrote *vers libre*. The unrhymed lines of
Les Imagistes had the appearance of coming from the same source.
When June arrived she decided to go to London; if *Les Imagistes*
had anything to teach, she was going to learn their doctrine from
their masters. Armed with a letter from Miss Monroe to Ezra Pound,
she set sail for Soho restaurants and Bloomsbury; her usual summer
holiday in Europe had been transformed into a journey with a purpose.

A few weeks later Miss Monroe had word (by way of Robert
Frost) that Ezra Pound in speaking of his latest Boston visitor
remarked, "When I get through with that girl she'll think she was
born in free verse."

Amy Lowell, accompanied by her nephew's wife, Mrs. James
Roosevelt, had landed safely at the Berkeley, a luxurious hotel at 77
Piccadilly, whose reputation alone was enough to give an air of

magnificence to Amy Lowell's London visit. It could be assumed
that whoever *Les Imagistes* were they were by no means as wealthy
as their latest convert. Nor would Ezra Pound refuse the invitation
to have tea at the Berkeley.

According to Richard Aldington's memory of early days among
Les Imagistes (he and H. D. were the youngest members of the
group) Pound conducted his campaign for *Imagisme* seated at tables
in the more expensive tea shops in London and restaurants in Paris.
This mild extravagance in drinking tea and eating sweets was part
of the decor that Pound provided for his new school of poets. The
atmosphere (and at the lowest possible cost) was one of elegance—a
meeting with Amy Lowell at the Berkeley was consistent with the
rules of his taste, his chivalry, his discernment and his own youthful
charm. Nothing of the second rate or of middle-class economies was
permitted to compromise them. Pound himself was as out of pocket-
money as the younger W. B. Yeats, but like Yeats, who had introduced him to everyone worth knowing in literary London, he
created settings of luxury on straitened means. This was a gesture
that endeared him to his patrons as well as friends, and was an art
that he learned from the legend that James McNeill Whistler had
left behind him. There is no doubt that on the first occasions Ezra
Pound and Amy Lowell met they charmed each other—and both
were confident of achieving victory should any slight difference of
opinion take place between them.

Without being aware of her intrusion (since she was welcomed)
and without clear knowledge of what being a member of Pound's
circle implied, Amy Lowell entered the list of *Les Imagistes*. She was
a self-appointed member of the group. She cared little enough for
the sacred origins of a closely guarded literary circle that had recently
acquired its intensely private history and short-lived traditions. It
had begun some five years earlier at the Poets' Club which met on
Wednesday evenings in Soho restaurants. The Club itself was a revival of a club formed at "The Cheshire Cheese" by members of W. B.
Yeats's "tragic generation"—which included Yeats, Lionel Johnson,
and Ernest Dowson. The new Poets' Club had as its teacher T. E.
Hulme, a young philosopher who had been "sent down" from St.
John's College, Cambridge, and who had attended the Philosophical
Congress at Bologna and returned with a letter from Henri Bergson

to readmit him to Cambridge and academic society. His temperament, however, was better suited to the revival of a club in Soho
which welcomed a closed group of painters, sculptures, poets, than to
the comparatively dull routine of St. John's lecture halls. His theories
had impressed Jacob Epstein as well as Ezra Pound, and they
embraced his aesthetic for the writing of poetry. He had a tough,
penetrating, inquiring mind that insisted "beauty may be found in
small, dry things"; he protested against "smoothness" in writing verse,
and was vehemently anti-romantic. With youthful exuberance he
wrote, "We shall not get any new efflorescence of verse until we get
a new technique, a new convention to turn ourselves loose in." His
own style in writing manifestos was both dogmatic and unformed;
its virtue was in the radical thinking that he forced on those who
heard him talk. His close-cropped hair and trim mustache were of
a military cut; it was characteristic of him to defend Sorel's
Reflections on Violence, and to foresee the fact that twentieth
century Socialism had many anti-democratic aspects. In controversy
he quickly dominated all who heard him; his Poets' Club became
the forum of a new didacticism which had been common enough in
Paris where each literary generation writes with traditional firmness
of its new laws but was rare in London.

Hulme's wholly serious theories were to create a set of new conventions in twentieth century poetry, but "the 'School of Images' "
came out of a not too serious discussion of the Japanese *tanka* and
Haikai between Hulme, Pound and F. S. Flint. Hulme undertook
the pleasure of illustrating the discussion by writing five short poems,
"The Complete Poetical Works of T. E. Hulme," which Pound published as a coda to his own small volume of poems, *Ripostes,* in 1912.
So far "the 'School of Images' " was a high-spirited piece of showmanship and Hulme's experiments in writing verse were brilliant
enough to catch attention: they were quickly, skillfully performed;
they had no pretentions of being "great poems"; and they demon-
strated the fact that lively verse could be written without too many
adjectives and jingling rhymes. They were far from any taint of
the "magazine touch" that Pound justly abhorred, and they fitted
precisely the doctrine that the more elaborate embellishments of
minor Victorian verse must be swept away.

Without the participation of Ezra Pound, "the 'School of Images' "

and the name *Les Imagistes* would never have been heard beyond
the smoke-filled room of a Soho restaurant. They needed the presence
of genius and the gift for writing poetry, both of which were clearly
shown in the poems of Ezra Pound and H. D. In this respect "the
'School of Images' " had a true excuse for being, and for the moment,
it provided Pound with the means to teach the writing of poetry to
readers of Miss Monroe's magazine in Chicago as well as to his
younger contemporaries in London. The name, *Les Imagistes,* caught
on with more success than Pound himself expected, and since some
readers accepted it with eager gravity, it was used to identify the
poetry of Pound's best friends.

At the very least—and in print—Pound was an excellent cam-
paigner in the cause of the "new" poetry, but to this was added the
spell of his personality. Not since the death of Whistler had London
seen and heard an American who dared to storm the fortresses of
aesthetic opinion with so much ease and wit. Even in his dress, worn
with the air of a "dandy," he was the reincarnation of Whistler, but
a Whistler with a lyrical voice that gave charm to a curiously international accent which was both British and American, stressed with
Italian phrases and Western American slang—the drawl was a graceful parody of American speech. He wore Whistler's mustache and
short imperial. His hair had a glint of red in it, and he walked the
streets and into a room with athletic poise; he lived up to what he
preached—a serious levity in everything he did and said. *The Spirit
of Romance* was the title of his first book of criticism, and the
associations of that title were in the gestures of chivalry, either in
attacking enemies or in defense of friends. His staunchest loyalties
were extended to T. S. Eliot, Ford Madox Ford, William Carlos Wil-
liams, James Joyce and Harriet Monroe. Like Apollinaire in Paris
he thought of the welfare of his friends before he considered his
own, and again like his Italian-Polish contemporary in Montmarte,
he had learned to live on almost nothing, to cook his own meals in
his room at 10 Church Walk, Kensington, with good-humored artfulness and to transform dingy living quarters into scenes of "light-
hearted penury." He was less tactful than irresistible—and as a critic
and teacher, less pedantic than highhanded and spirited. No poet of
his generation, either in London or the United States, was more
brilliantly well-read than he: he made his Spanish, Italian and

French serve as an entry into an understanding of ancient languages and he read Greek and Latin with less scholastic fervor than perceptive gallantry. He knew the essential qualities of whatever poems he revived into English verse; he had no patience with merely literal translation.

Like a knight-errant he pricked and exploded inflated literary reputations and fought the standards of merely "popular taste," as well as the accepted values of middle-class, middle-brow culture. His targets were elder statesmen of British letters, including the shrewd and resourceful Sir Edmund Gosse who rested with ease and intellectual indolence upon his early discoveries in Scandinavian literature and upon his autobiography, *Father and Son,* which rivaled the embittered confessions of Samuel Butler in *The Way of All Flesh.* In his efforts to make literature "popular," he entertained his listeners with fragments of literary gossip. Entrenched in his post of librarian for the House of Lords, he sought out political and social advancement rather that literary distinction. Even as he drifted beyond middle age, he was cautious, urbane, and "on the make." "I have no idea," he wrote, "how the spiritual world would look to me, for I have never glanced at it since I was a child and gorged with it"— a confession which justly damned him in the opinion of a rising literary generation. His affable personality and the ease of his manner illustrated almost beyond the power of words, the kind of "smoothness" that T. E. Hulme resented, and to Ezra Pound he stood for all that defined mediocrity in British literature.

The positive side of Pound's campaign against dullness in current criticism and poetry was in his instruction "to make it new," to recreate literary values rather than to talk about literature and books.

But an unwritten law of the groups of young writers whom Pound encouraged was to accept the dogmas of his "new order," and *Les Imagistes* were no exception to this rule. Pound's leadership was not to be disputed, however briefly it was held, for without him the imagist Pegasus quickly become a horse other than the creature he had described. If Amy Lowell was to be welcomed and tolerated at all, it was as a contributor and friend rather than as a collaborator in a literary movement—and this was a situation she could neither accept nor recognize. She was older than Pound and her family name carried its own authority; her readings in contemporary French poets made her feel that she was an imagist at heart—and she also felt that she could advance the names of Paul Fort and Albert Samain with as much authority as Pound could speak of Jules Laforgue and Tristan Corbiére. Among her sources were essays written on French poets by Sir Edmund Gosse. Even at this time there was ground—practically a battlefield—for misunderstanding between Amy Lowell and Ezra Pound.

Amy Lowell's rooms in the Berkeley, her manner that Miss Monroe described as "nothing less than regal" caused her to be viewed by younger members of Pound's circle as a probable patron (since she was both American and wealthy) of the arts. On the one hand she was far too magnificent to be treated as an equal; on the other, her lack of distinction in writing verse made her less promising than the least gifted members of the group. Her literary tastes had been formed with far less disciplined and serious understanding of what she read than Ezra Pound's; and though Pound's own scholarship was perceptive and intuitive rather that academic, his M.A. thesis, *The Spirit of Romance* was a contribution to comparative literatures that is likely to endure long beyond the first half of the present century. She was charmed by Pound and never denied his gifts as a poet, but it would have been inconsistent with her character to admit that her literary intelligence was less than his. She had come to London to learn all she could—and quickly—of what *Les Imagistes* had to say.

Meanwhile Pound had invited Amy Lowell to meet all the younger members of his circle. Within a few weeks she was on friendly terms with the beautiful and tall H. D. who had the figure of Diana, for unlike many poets, H. D. looked the way she wrote—and her poems seemed to be the direct expression of a neo-Greek, neo-classic personality. Both Ezra Pound and H. D. were as unshrewd as Amy Lowell was maternal and practical, and another attractive member of the group was the youthful Englishman, Richard Aldington, who was handsome and innocent in the ways of a world in which he was later to find a destructive World War and its disillusionments, who laughed easily and was young enough to make light of the prospect of earning a living by free-lance critical journalism and translations from the French. It was a pleasure to introduce the sister of Harvard's President to the latest news of what was happening among poets in London. Amy Lowell had noted the way Aldington's fair hair dropped across his forehead and the charming gesture he had of tossing his head back to keep long strands of hair out of his eyes. His conversation was no less boyish and appealing, and echoes of his conversation can be overheard in his autobiography, *Life for Life's Sake*. In his recollections of that moment, the first meetings with Amy Lowell in London, a tea-shop atmosphere prevails; as far as memory sustained him, the Imagist *mouvement* was a child born in a Kensington tea shop, served as it were, under a tea caddy and surrounded by sweet buns and buttered toast. There can be no doubt that he informed Amy Lowell of Pound's approval of H. D., and that Pound's enthusiasm was so great that on reading her poems in manuscript, he slipped off his pince-nez and told her she was an Imagist. This was the kind of "inside gossip" that always delighted Amy Lowell and made her feel that she was near to learning what young people did and why.

In her rooms at the Berkeley Hotel Amy Lowell scarcely had time and perhaps no inclination to visit the cradle of Imagism at 10 Church Walk in Kensington, to learn that the locality was somehow appropriate to the birth of a new literary movement, that it had been the haunt of the Pre-Raphaelites, that James McNeill Whistler had been married at St. Mary Abbot's, that Henry James had rented a flat in De Vere Gardens, and across the street from it, Robert Browning's house stood, the house from which his body, sent from the Ca' Rezzonico in Venice where he died, was taken to be buried at last in Westminster Abbey. It is doubtful if she would have understood Pound's choice of the neighborhood, the reasons why, since he had to find cheap lodgings, he selected them in an area so rich in particular, and discriminating, literary associations. For the moment, Amy Lowell's energies were directed toward finding out what was "new," what was the very "latest thing," and how she could excel in the writing of the very "latest thing" herself.

There is no doubt that Aldington was impressed by Amy Lowell —not by her verse, but by her verve, her "vivacious intelligence" as he defined it, the sharp eyes behind glittering pince-nez, her cordiality which had the ring of being sincere. The only doubts that he remembered were in respect to her verse, which H. D. and he agreed was "fluid, fruity, facile stuff." There the distrust was clear enough, but that was all too easily forgotten in the genial gossip of the tea parties at which Amy Lowell presided and assumed the rôle—since the younger people were notoriously short of cash—of Lady Bountiful. On these occasions she could and did command, and she convinced Aldington that she had learned more French under her mother's instruction than he possessed. Aldington was extremely impressionable and unsure of his abilities, for this was long before he had written his novel *Death of a Hero*. World War I was still an event that could not happen, for during the summer of 1913, World Wars were unthinkable phenomena, known only in the prophetic novels of H. G. Wells and in the premonitions of the Fabians who saw "class struggles" looming in the future. Among poets the atmosphere was, if anything, too calm. Amy Lowell's half-genial, half-belligerent curiosity, her "vivacious intelligence" had in them germs of excitement and of combat. Indeed, when she discovered that Constable, her British publisher had not distributed her book, *A Dome of Many-Coloured Glass*, to London booksellers, she started a small war in Constable's offices. She refused to leave until the staff told her where her books were—and she left only when it was explained to her that her books, shipped from America, were still unpacked, forgotten in Constable's storerooms.

Her London visit also saw the beginning of her friendship with a young American poet from Arkansas who had strayed to London by way of Cambridge, Massachusetts, and Harvard, by way of extended trips through the American Southwest and northern Italy followed by a few months' breathing spell in Venice. His name was John Gould Fletcher, whose father had been a captain in the Confederate Army during the Civil War, and after the war had become a prosperous dealer in cotton in Little Rock, Arkansas. The death of his father in 1906 insured Fletcher, then at Harvard, of a comfortable income, and he left the University without taking his degree. He was a strange young man of middle height, with broad shoulders, a broad, high rounded forehead, and a formidable, out-jutting jaw. Despite the powerfully built, aggressive body and jaw, an air of helplessness surrounded him and a naive light shone from his pale blue eyes. From time to time a kind of mental blackness possessed him, a madness that seemed to be related to epilepsy. Since late adolescence and throughout his life he was subject to fits of week-long illnesses which were brought about by any test, large or small, of his abilities. At Harvard the thought of an approaching examination immediately unmanned him; and in his private journals he set down the curious warnings of his malady: as he walked the streets of Cambridge (and later any town or city) he seemed to see windows of houses lift and a face, very like a mysterious self-image, stare down at him. In terror, he would hasten home, to his rooms or flat, collapse into a chair, and for the following week would be only semi-conscious of whatever he said or did. He would know he was ill, and would have the symptoms and sensations of having a slight cold, carrying with it a fever—and would discover, after the week had passed, that he had been subject to violent rages, that he had written insulting letters to friends as well as to those he feared were his enemies. Or, like someone violently drunk, he would walk into restaurants, and fuming at his table, shout in an angry voice at any face he knew.

The explosive fits of madness that he suffered left him exhausted, yet after his struggles he turned to his reading and writing at demonic speed, and even experimented briefly—this to increase his speed—by taking a drink or two of whisky as he sat down to write. Drinking did not become his habit of solitude; he soon discovered that it sent him off to sleep which defeated the purpose he had in mind. With much of the same compulsive energy that drove his hand in writing, he read voluminously in nineteenth-century French poetry. He sought out Baudelaire, Verlaine, Rimbaud—but found no true affinity with the Symbolists until he read the latter-day French poets who had begun to read and translate Whitman, poets who were closer to Impressionism and Naturalism than their predecessors, and who celebrated "external things." These were Verhaeren, Paul Fort, Francis Jammes and André Spire who was an open champion of *vers libre*. Fletcher enjoyed the pleasure of writing loosely and at length, and Spire, the Impressionist, pointed that direction to him; the four French poets he enjoyed freed his hand and led him toward the writing of his almost endlessly diffused "color symphonies." During 1913, Fletcher published five separate books of verse, a tour de force which no one in London cared or hoped to equal. However hastily written or inept some of the poems were, Fletcher at twenty-seven created the impression that he could move mountains. He was so prolific that some future good in his verses seemed imminent.

Moreover, Fletcher's independent income—and he had rented a flat in Adelphi Terrace, an address made famous because Sir James Barrie and George Bernard Shaw lived nearby—gave him the distinction of wealth among poets who drank tea in Kensington but lived in furnished rooms near the British Museum or in Bohemian Chelsea. In that year, 1913, Ezra Pound had decided to "discover" Fletcher, and since he was foreign editor of *Poetry*, to insist that Harriet Monroe publish Fletcher *en masse*. He wrote to Miss Monroe:

> Of course one of Fletcher's strongest claims to attention is his ability to make a *book*, as opposed to the common or garden faculty of making a "Poem," and if you don't print a fairish big gob of him you don't do him justice or stir up the reader's ire and attention.

Almost instantly Amy Lowell chose Fletcher as her guide through Impressionist French poetry as well as through Anglo-American imagism; with Fletcher she shared the need of writing and reading hastily and with fluid ease. In her eyes Fletcher made a better impression than others in the group. After leaving Harvard he had lived a year in Boston. It is true that his manner was often abrupt and aggressive, but it was gentlemanly, correct in a way that good Bostonians could always understand. His clothes were conservatively tailored and his white collars were starched; at will his voice took on the modulations of childish humors, or could be raised to a masculine shout of rage or derision, or at a lighter moment turn into a parody of itself. Together, Fletcher and Amy Lowell viewed the more aesthetic, more discriminating, more Bohemian Pound with a touch of middle-class patronage. At the same time the genuine air of helplessness which would suddenly cloud Fletcher's talk and behavior aroused Amy Lowell's maternal instincts; she felt centuries older than Fletcher, more deeply self-taught than he, and even in her worst hours of self-distrust, more self-assured. She staunchly admired a young man of twenty-seven who would dare to publish five books of verse within a single year; to her this in itself was an accomplishment not to be ignored.

Amy Lowell's summer holiday in London was far more invigorating—and refreshing to her spirits—than the more healthful retreat she had come to enjoy in New Hampshire. To an American, the heat of London, despite its seasonal stretches of gray, heavy days, is more temperate than most sections of the New England countryside. In 1913 even "out of season" London, and largely because of Ezra Pound being there with his young friends, had more literary activity than any city in the United States. Only Harold Munro's Poetry Bookshop, which was in sight of the British Museum, showed signs of summer. From her hotel in Piccadilly, Amy Lowell chartered a taxi to its door; she alighted and for a quarter of an hour gazed into its windows. As she stared, the ragged children of the neighborhood (for at that time—and for at least twenty years later—the tree-haunted region of Russell Square concealed run-down rooming houses and slums) crowded around her. They were dazzled by the presence of the large, obviously rich woman standing where shabbily dressed members of the professional classes usually strolled on their way to the British Museum. On entering the shop she discovered that Harold Munro himself was on holiday and there was nothing for her to do than to return to her hotel.

Her holiday included a brief visit to Henry James at Rye. Though he could not be otherwise than courteous to a Lowell, the aging novelist and the portly, vigorous woman nearing middle age had little enough in common. James had his own reservations concerning Bostonians, but on learning that Amy Lowell was about to launch out on a literary career, he drew her aside from his other tea table guests and strolled with her in his garden. He himself had grown bald and portly, and one has an image of those two large figures, pacing slowly, talking earnestly, the elder giving advice with great deliberation and solicitude. In Foster Damon's biography of Amy Lowell a curiously bitter conversation is reported; it is of James warning his Boston visitor against England and expatriation: "I have cut myself off from America, where I belonged, and in England I am not really accepted. Don't make my mistake." This may have carried some of his feeling at the moment, for in 1913 his own literary fortunes, despite his prestige, were at low ebb; his lack of success in the writing of plays still haunted him. Though Sargent had painted his portrait that very year, for several years past he had been signing his letters to Hugh Walpole "your dismal friend" with a half-affectionate, half-ironic intonation. When Sargent's portrait was placed on view at the Royal Academy (which was a short walk from Amy Lowell's hotel) a suffragette slashed it in protest against the smoothly shaven masculine figure with his right thumb hooked into the armhole of his fashionably cut, horizontally striped waist-coat. The act was an index of James's lack of general popularity of which he never failed to be painfully aware.

Yet the tone of his warning is distinctly un-Jamesian; and it is far more like Amy Lowell's reporting of a slightly different kind of warning with the pronoun "I" left out. His sensibility—perhaps a gift of prophecy—would have been alert to the possibility that Amy Lowell herself could not sustain a respected literary reputation in London—which later, her British critics proved. James was probably acting as a not-unfriendly American in her behalf. But, of course, she did not accept James as her "master," nor for that matter, did Harriet Monroe; James was decidedly "out of step" with the enthusiasms that Amy Lowell wish to acquire and which swept through the offices of "little magazines."

September brought her home again to Boston and ship reporters made the discovery that the President of Harvard's sister smoked cigars.

The London
Adventures

6

LTHOUGH *A Dome of Many-Coloured Glass*
had not sold as well as Houghton Mifflin had hoped it would, on her
return from England its author had fully recovered from her feeling
that she had failed. Meeting the younger generation of poets in
London, seeing how unsure of themselves (with the exception of
Ezra Pound) they seemed to be, gave Amy Lowell renewed self-
confidence. If she did not understand everything they had to say,
she had actually *seen* them, which for her had dispelled the mystery
surrounding the name, "Imagiste"; she had learned that verses need
not always rhyme and that a kind of rapid visual notation of things
seen, or no more than glanced at, could be accepted as poetry. There
was no reason for her to suppose that she was less able to write
vividly than the young people she had met on her London tour.

Nor had she stopped writing verses of her own. She had also
learned of Ezra Pound's admiration for the poems of Robert Browning and nothing was easier for her to remember than the story of

"Porphyria's Lover," to redramatize its theme and shift it to a story of
frenetic jealousy and then to rewrite it as "After Hearing a Waltz by
Bartok." Certainly the verses held an echo of Browning's vigor:
there was murder in them—one jealous lover strangling another—
and a sufficient number of exclamations:

> One! Two! Three! And his corpse, like a cold
>   Beats me into a jelly! The Chime,
>   One! Two! Three! And his dead legs keep time.
> Air! Give me air! Air! My God!

On the boat she tested the effectiveness of these lines by reciting
them to a delicate young man who had been persuaded to listen to
her readings; the young man was terrified, and Amy Lowell felt that
she had scored a complete success. This with the attention she
aroused from ship reporters by smoking one of her small Havana
cigars, was enough to reassure her that her personality at least had
valid character.

In 1913 that personality was clothed in the immense bulk that
distinguished her for the rest of her life: when she rose to her feet
she was nearly as broad as she was tall. The cigars she smoked
(falsely described as "big black" cigars) were of a size appropriate to
be held between her small, tapering fingers, and only because in
1913 few women of fashion smoked in public at all (Queen Alex-
andra and Queen Mary were among the few, and Alice Roosevelt
was another, and they smoked cigarettes) did the habit seem extraordinary. Newspaper reporters made the cigar her trade mark. Her
tailored dresses and suits were of dark cloths to make her bulk seem
less conspicuous, relieved by white lace collars held neatly to her
short neck by whalebone stays; the costume made her seem to be a
"grande dame" of over fifty. Yet her bulk gave her—as in the case
of several literary figures, including Samuel Johnson, who had been
afflicted by overweight—an air of authority. She had only to take
advantage of the necessary burden of flesh she carried—and so she
did. There could be no mistaking Amy Lowell for anyone else; once
seen in public she would be remembered.

If a few years before she had had to acknowledge her failure as
an amateur actress, she had begun to discover that she need not give
up the stage. She would act the part of "Amy Lowell, poet," to newspaper reporters, editors, younger poets—anyone who would listen: in

her library at Sevenels, or on ship docks, train platforms, in hotel suites in New York and London, or wherever an engagement could be procured, behind the lectern in a classroom, concert or lecture hall. The attention she had received from newspaper reporters had shown the way.

No sooner had Amy Lowell settled herself again at Sevenels, than she received a note from Ezra Pound asking permission to print one of the poems she had shown him in a small anthology, *Des Imagistes*. The unrhymed lines were called "In a Garden"; they were unspectacular, but their descriptive passages were clear and graceful, and had something of an impressionistic charm that might well have gone into an unwritten nocturne by Debussy. Certainly the choice was dictated by Pound's highly discriminating taste and was far less forced and noisy than "After Hearing a Waltz by Bartok." Meanwhile she had also received a letter from John Gould Fletcher. Though Pound had introduced him to Amy Lowell, though Pound had bullied Harriet Monroe into accepting a large group of Fletcher's poems for *Poetry*, a chill of loneliness surrounded the unhappy young man from Arkansas. His mind was darkened by its illnesses, and was shot through with fits of envy of Pound's brilliance, Pound's levity, his quickness in making *Des Imagistes* seem important and exclusive. He told Amy Lowell how Pound had helped him, but also hinted that Pound was a literary politician. Because he admired her, he was letting her know that *Des Imagistes* were nothing more or less than a group of Pound's friends; he hinted that Pound and Aldington were determined to make themselves famous, and that other Imagistes were to be mere followers; as for himself, he would not let *his* name be used. Fletcher's moments of mental illness provided a background of nightmare to whatever he knew about his friends; he saw them spinning plots against him and each other; and their air of cheerfulness—(a few weeks later Aldington and H. D. were married)—increased his feeling of discontent.

Through October to mid-December Amy Lowell translated for the Boston Music Company Rostand's trifle, *Pierrot Qui Pleure et Pierrot Qui Rit*. Her London interviews with Aldington, Fletcher and Pound had reinforced her interest in French poetry; at Sevenels she formed a group to hear piano concerts given in the library once a month and to the group she invited Magdelaine Carret, teacher of

French at Wellesley, who became a useful addition to her friends, one who would be willing to assist her toward a more authoritative knowledge of French, to guide her beyond the vocabulary and grammar she had learned by her mother's promptings.

Early in the new year of 1914 Amy Lowell decided to shift her publishing activities from Boston to New York, from Houghton Mifflin to the Macmillan Company. Both of her brothers were published by the New York firm: Lawrence Lowell as Harvard's president held his position securely by prestige, and Percival by the continued sale of his books on the Far East. She made the most of their connections with the firm, as well as of the newly acquired confidence she had gained in being a "personality," and with a sharply executive air she played off Houghton Mifflin against the Macmillan Company. In making investments or securing a contract from a publisher, she was her father's daughter; no shading of poetic romance centered her dealings with publishers. As businessmen they understood her language; as a Lowell, not unfamiliar with business tactics and the management of banks, Amy Lowell saw publishers as businessmen and know how to manage them.

With the same determination and understanding of editors, she sold new poems to magazines. The contract for her new book, *Sword Blades and Poppy Seed*, was signed with the Macmillan Company— and this was proof enough that Boston had grown too small for her. From New York she went to Chicago to renew her acquaintance with Miss Monroe and *Poetry,* to announce her new book and to make sure that some of her new poems would appear in an early issue of Miss Monroe's magazine. To the end of her life Amy Lowell always felt that Miss Monroe had to be "managed," forced into publishing her verse, and her instincts concerning Miss Monroe were not entirely wrong. Miss Monroe's manner, habitually cool and not given to loud-voiced enthusiasms, grew a shade cooler in Amy Lowell's presence. Miss Monroe's preferences ran in the separate directions of Ezra Pound, Carl Sandburg, Vachel Lindsay and Wallace Stevens (then quite unknown)—and like many Middle Westerners she sustained a mild distrust of New England's, particularly Boston's, representatives.

Meanwhile it was in Chicago that Amy Lowell again met the charming actress, Mrs. Ada Russell; they had met several times before in Boston, and on each meeting their friendship and respect for each other increased. Mrs. Russell in Chicago moved in the same company that supported and financed Miss Monroe's magazine, *Poetry,* and one of her best friends there was Mrs. Chatfield Taylor, wife of one of *Poetry's* earliest patrons. It was at this time that Mrs. Belmont urged Mrs. Russell to leave the stage; Mrs. Russell had been ill, and her prolonged illness made theatrical connections difficult to sustain. Moreover, she was growing older, and the Broadway-Shaftsbury Avenue prospects of a middle-aged actress, however bright they may have seemed at eighteen, tend to grow dim. Mrs. Russell had a daughter to support; she feared her own loss of energy, her lack of aggressiveness in meeting theatrical managers and producers. Her friend, Mrs. Belmont, happily married, had left the stage, and could no longer insist that Mrs. Russell be given parts to play. Mrs. Russell needed means of earning a living, and when Amy Lowell offered her the post of being "companion" to herself at Sevenels there was a tentative acceptance of certain terms; Mrs. Russell, still convalescent, was to take the post on trial to learn whether or not she and Amy Lowell could remain friends in the new relationship. Amy Lowell was to pay her a salary equal to what she had earned on the stage. Fortunately for both women the trial period was a highly optimistic experience; the experiment "worked"; the friendship survived Amy Lowell's bursts of ill-temper and wilfullness, her domineering manner of being mistress of Sevenels—for if Amy Lowell saw a piece of unwashed silver or china in the Butler's Pantry at two in the morning, her household staff would suffer one of her blind rages. She was, as she claimed herself to be, "the Last of the Barons," absolute ruler of her domain. In public Mrs. Russell (whose temperament was anything but histrionic in voice and manner) soothed Amy Lowell's insulted guests and servants. In private— and against Amy Lowell's insults even to her—she held her ground and taught (for a brief moment) her friend the merits of tact and humanity. She often forced (and again in private) Amy Lowell to keep her promises to others, to be scrupulous in keeping social as well as public lecturing appointments.

For these reasons it was rumored among Amy Lowell's New York acquaintances that Mrs. Russell "had given Amy Lowell a heart," which was a claim that Mrs. Russell, whatever she may have felt about their relationship, would not have put into words. She was too restrained, too modest, too well-poised in her position as Amy Lowell's companion to claim an "influence" on Amy Lowell's behavior. Mrs. Russell's poise also gave rise to an anecdote, a New York legend, concerning Mrs. Russell which was said to have taken place that winter in Chicago. One evening on driving to dinner in a taxicab to meet her director at a restaurant, she dropped her fur wrap from her shoulders; she stepped out at her destination, paid the fare, but as the taxi disappeared she found her wrap gone. Her director met her at the door, and as he met her, she warned him that she would not go on the stage that night—or any night thereafter until her wrap was returned. The director was called on to perform the nearly impossible, but by nine o'clock the wrap was restored to Mrs. Russell's shoulders; the curtain rose and the play went on. The friend whom Amy Lowell chose to share Sevenels was not to be her servant; in matters of authority within her province, Mrs. Russell's will was quite her own. She made no agreement to share Amy Lowell's travels and fortunes until she had earned the respect of her future hostess.

The story was merely a half-truth. Mr. Theodore Ammussen, Mrs. Russell's grandson, corrected it. One night in London during the 1890's when Mrs. Russell was a member of Eleanor Robson's (Mrs. August Belmont's) company, on her way to the theatre, she stepped into a hansom cab. The night was cool; she wore a fur wrap, a luxury on which she had spent her savings; her wrap was treasured, yet her mind was full of the need to arrive at the stage door of the theatre "on time." She dismounted hastily, paid the cabman and it was not until after the cab had vanished, that she discovered her wrap was gone. Though the loss nearly made her ill, she went on stage and told no one of it. After the last curtain, upon leaving the theatre, she hailed a cab to take her home. Settling into it, her hands slipped between its cushions; there was her fur wrap, securely hidden, left for her to find again. She told the story to her grandson as one that proved miracles *could* happen on earth. The rumor of the incident taking place in Chicago was false; more than that, it was "out of character" for Mrs. Russell to put on a show of histrionics off stage. As Amy Lowell's companion, her position was one that stood in contrast to Amy Lowell's rages and commands; Mrs. Russell's weapon (and sometimes in self-defense) was one composed of unhistrionic poise and tact. In public she complemented Amy Lowell's spectacular entrances and exits; like Henry James's famous "Brooksmith" she was the hidden spirit of conversations in the drawing-room-library at Sevenels. When Amy Lowell came down late for dinner, sharing with her guests only the last moments of dessert, Mrs. Russell steered conversation into light and orderly progress; and when guests left, it was she who soothed those whose tempers were ruffled while guiding them to the door.

As the spring of 1914 arrived, Amy Lowell's correspondence with London had increased. Ezra Pound offered her the opportunity of being owner of *The Egoist*, a "little magazine" that had taken the place of *The New Freewoman* which John Gould Fletcher had partly subsidized. She hedged on this question, for however promising certain young poets seemed to her, she was slow to risk large sums of money for their support. Her business instinct told her that "little magazines" consumed more money than they seemed to need, that they died almost at birth—and she for one, since she was always a Lowell, had no wish to participate in a business venture that was almost sure to fail. This particular kind of distrust was part of her character: to certain individuals she would offer and give small sums of money outright, but in dealing with poets, not as rich as she, a protective wariness possessed her. She became conscious of the fact that she was *very* rich, and was therefore subject to large demands from those who had less than she. In this respect she was uniformly "tough-minded"; in matters of handling money she had no soft illusions, and in her commerce with the world, no desire to be made a fool.

Fletcher's warnings against Pound had put her on guard; for herself she saw with one eye closed that Pound in money matters was impractical. She underrated his generosity to others; she feared his brilliance almost as deeply as Fletcher did. When one of the younger members of Pound's group in London wrote to her that Pound was crazy, she believed it. All these elements of distrust entered into her relationship with Pound, and her counter-suggestion was to bring the main office of *The Egoist* to the United States where she could watch and manage it. She was also wary of Pound's selection of European contributors; she had heard of D. H. Lawrence, but not

James Joyce—what did *he* write? "Who is he?" she asked, withdrawing from most of Pound's suggestions as though she were being led into a grass-covered pit—and then sent him as a gift a check to celebrate his coming marriage to Dorothy Shakespear.

Her taste in reading had none of the finer discriminations Pound fought for, nor at this early date in 1914 had Boston or New York heard of James Joyce.

According to Patricia Hutchins ("Ezra Pound in Kensington," *New World Writing* Number 11, 1957) it was Yeats who recommended a reading of Joyce's writings to Pound. During that very summer of 1913, Pound spent part of August sharing Stone Cottage in Sussex with Yeats. The two poets exchanged literary opinions and confidences, and because Yeats's eyes were weak the younger poet read aloud to the elder. Amy Lowell knew nothing of the means by which Pound had discovered Joyce. *The Egoist* was yet to carry Pound's essay on *Dubliners* published that year, for although Joyce's small book of lyrical verses, *Chamber Music*, had been published in London in 1907, knowledge of its existence had not crossed the Atlantic—and it would have taken a delicately tuned ear for Elizabethan lyricism to discern the merits of *Chamber Music*. This was what Pound possessed and Amy Lowell did not. Knowledge of Joyce would merely distract her from her recent discoveries in "free verse."

In her eagerness to know what Imagism was, Amy Lowell always underrated the traditional aspects of Pound's position. She was unaware that through his friendship with Yeats he was one of the heirs of the Dante Gabriel Rossetti circle. She did not know that in matters of forming literary groups the Pre-Raphaelites were masters of that art, that Pound learned the art, not from Yeats alone, but was reenforced in tactical detail through his friendship with Ford Madox Heuffer (Ford), a descendent of one branch of the Pre-Raphaelite tree. No Bostonian of her generation, however adroit, could compete with the civilized forces Amy Lowell had ranged against her. In knowledge and in learning she was hopelessly outstripped; she lacked "background" and though impractical enough, Ezra Pound could easily outpace her efforts.

Meanwhile a first publication of *Des Imagistes*, an Anthology, appeared as a fifth issue of *The Glebe*, a periodical edited by Alfred Kreymborg in New Jersey in 1913, but now shifted (through the

Bachrach

Amy Lowell in her Garden at Sevenels

Michel Faran

SEVENELS

Harriet Monroe

Thomas Hardy

CARL SANDBURG

WILLIAM STANLEY BRAITHWAITE

ROBERT FROST

E. E. CUMMINGS

ELINOR WYLIE

Sir Osbert, Dame Edith and Sacheveral Sitwell

Center figure EDNA ST. VINCENT MILLAY in Benavente's *Bonds of Interest*

strange mutations suffered by so many "little magazines") to New York and published by Albert and Charles Boni. The pamphlet contained about forty poems with Aldington and H. D. prominently represented and Ezra Pound given a modest place (which should have been proof enough to Amy Lowell that Pound remained untainted by vanity and personal advancement). Her lines on "In a Garden" were included and so were Joyce's unrhymed lines (reprinted from *Chamber Music*) which began "I hear an army charging upon the land." "I hear an army" was also one of the poems read by Yeats, who recommended its publication to Pound. In Yeats's eyes the poem was indicative of a new movement in verse. Yeats had been kind to the very young Joyce, offering him letters of introduction to his friends in Paris, and he continued to speak well of Joyce's poems to Pound in London. In New York the little collection meant that nine unknown new poets were being introduced; the pamphlet was in fact a supplement to Pound's earlier "A Few Don'ts by an Imagist" in Harriet Monroe's *Poetry*. Pound had elected himself teacher extraordinary to the youngest generation of poets, and not a few of Amy Lowell's later difficulties with him came from her refusal to recognize his selfless devotion to that task.

On an American visit Rupert Brooke, armed with a letter of introduction from Harriet Monroe to Amy Lowell, made a four-day stay at the Hotel Bellevue in Boston. Not since Byron descended upon London had a young graduate of Cambridge University so completely charmed readers of poetry, for like Byron's, Brooke's gifts were of a dual nature: he could write poems of undoubted talent—and his handsome face was of the same unquestionable quality. Harriet Monroe had called him one of the most beautiful young men of the hour; and so he was: fair golden hair with red glints in it—and he was blue-eyed and clear-skinned. Unlike most poets, his movements were athletic, and at twenty-seven, as his poems so clearly showed, he could be heroic, gay, easy, grave, ironic. In appearance he was all a young poet should be—a startling presentation of an ideal, and in sitting for photographs he affected an open collar or naked shoulders. The aging Henry James in England quickly responded to Brooke's charms. Brooke's poem "The Great Lover" was immediately identified with him; and to members of his generation he personified youth and poetry in everything he wrote and did. In many American colleges where girls wrote verses, photographs of him were clipped from newspapers and magazines to hang on bedroom walls. It was not likely that Amy Lowell would refuse him audience; she had him out to lunch and then to dinner.

There is no direct report of what happened at these meetings, for both were silent so far as written documents reveal. Later in London her conduct toward him showed lack of respect and he ignored her, yet it is not difficult to read from that silence a mutual disregard. The self-assured young Englishman made no appeal to Amy Lowell's maternal instincts which young John Gould Fletcher so unerringly aroused, nor was he concerned (since his own reputation had been so quickly established) with new movements in poetry. He could steer his own course without the aid of others, and like many British poets he was both ignorant of and indifferent to American poets and what they wrote. Neither he nor Amy Lowell had anything to learn from the other.

But lack of rapport with Rupert Brooke did not diminish Amy Lowell's interest in the group of poets she had discovered in London, for the group seemed to open a way toward what she felt was "new." Undeniably American as she was, she was also a Lowell which in this situation meant that like her brother Lawrence (who had already remodeled Harvard on lines resembling Oxford and Cambridge) she looked to England for renewed inspiration and ideas. Her interest in French poetry and poets was one that always took for granted a view of French literature through Anglo-American eyes, and in this respect her vision of it was not unlike her brother Percival's interpretations of the Far East. Her sustained interest in Keats was still another reason why she felt the need for further visits to London and the English countryside. She had made up her mind to repeat the English summer of 1913 in 1914, and in order to increase the range of her travels, she decided upon transporting her maroon-colored car and with it a chauffeur in maroon livery. By late May she had also persuaded Mrs. Russell to be her companion on the journey.

In July she returned to the Berkeley Hotel in Piccadilly, and when an afternoon London newspaper carried word of her arrival, she had reason to believe that her conquest of the great city had begun. As in the summer of 1913, London seemed to glow within a twilit dream. Amy Lowell's apartment at the Berkeley was on the top floor, and looking down from its bow-window one saw the traffic of Piccadilly and beyond it the thick clustered tree tops of the Green Park. The summer was unusually fair: a great blue sky with slow-moving clouds hung over the golden-tinted scene—or at least that was how the summer was afterwards remembered. To ward off reflections of her own portliness, Amy Lowell draped the mirrors of her apartment in red or black which concentrated the view outward across the Green Park to St. James's, and as clear evenings fell, the traveling lights of Piccadilly had behind them the street lamps of the two parks, glimpsed through waving boughs. Never before nor since had the grey and timesooted, yellowed facades of London seemed to gleam so prosperously. Though Edward VII had been interred since 1910, his genial, luxury-loving spirit continued its reign into the Georgian era; as Sir Osbert Sitwell noted, the theme song of that moment was an echo from the music halls:

> "There'll be no wo'ar
> As long as there's a king like good King Edward."

The effect of the lingering, continued peace and the calm summer with its threatening news that Franz Ferdinand, Archduke of Austria, had been assassinated, made the atmosphere seem as though something had to happen. Young Englishmen had grown increasingly restless; some planned hardy trips in mountain climbing—anything to break the unnamed tension in the air. Amy Lowell's maroon-colored car that could be driven with the top let down was in keeping with the high fashion of the moment, for the younger generation suddenly demanded all the sensations of speed, more speed on wheels; and through this desire a dividing line between the reigns of Edward VII and George V began to be felt. Still it would have been rash for anyone to predict the immediate arrival of a world war.

From his second floor flat in 10 Church Walk, Kensington, in a little close behind St. Mary Abbot's, Ezra Pound veered from the cause of *Des Imagistes* to Vorticism. On Kensington High Street, a few steps from his door, Pound walked like a reanimated vision of Whistler. His living quarters were far less well appointed than that of any of the rooms where Whistler lived beyond his means, for Pound was modest in his poverty, which forced the presence of an ugly white-enameled iron bedstead into a hallway which preceded a

loftlike chamber and his writing table. But on the High Street the
Whistlerian image prevailed. Hatless, with bristling red hair, mustache and imperial, a dark cloak thrown across a brown velvet jacket
and pearl-grey flannel trousers, and carrying a silver-headed cane,
Pound met his friends—the most recent of whom was the young
painter and writer, Wyndham Lewis, who had chosen Paris, "the
city of light," as his university. To Pound he brought the excitement
of "The Vortex," which was, so Lewis explained—and he was a
broad shouldered, clear-eyed young man whose intellectual integrity
and enthusiasm had a flash of fire in them—"the point of maximum
energy." *Blast* was the name of the magazine he edited to promote
the claims of Vorticism, and its subtitle read: "Review of the Great
English Vortex." Lewis's effort was to bring all the arts, sculptural,
linear, literary, into an unvarnished, vigorous parallel with machine-
made action and strength. Lewis's temper was "tough-minded" and
of a radical conservatism; and its expression was an "inside" Bohemian revolt against Bohemianism, against mere "artists," the middle
class, the rich, the poor, the people who patronized art and who
promptly sentimentalized whatever they bought or praised. *Blast*
(between pink covers like a sporting sheet) shouted its manifestos in
bold-face Gothic type, the type of the headlines on the fronts of
tabloid newspapers. It announced its war—and because the British
twilight summer of 1914 was so glittering and serene—against:
"ROUSSEAUISMS (wild nature cranks), DIABOLICS—raptures and roses
of the erotic bookshelves culminating in PURGATORY OF PUTNEY"—
this last a reference to Victorian concern over Swinburne. *Blast*
insisted "LONDON IS *not* A PROVINCIAL TOWN"; it was to be aware of
twentieth century arts as they were practiced on the Continent
across the Channel.

 Blast was also a counterblast against the very neighborhood where
Amy Lowell had set up her headquarters on the top floor of the
Berkeley Hotel: "we do not want the GLOOMY VICTORIAN CIRCUS in
Piccadilly Circus. IT IS PICCADILLY'S CIRCUS." Ford Madox Hueffer
(Ford) remembered Pound's new friend Wyndham Lewis as a
black-steeple-hatted figure in a loose cape who mounted the stairs
toward him saying nothing, yet at the same time seemed to extract
endless rolls of manuscripts from countless pockets, thrusting all of
them in the direction of Ford. Freed of its burden, and still without a

word, the figure turned its back and slowly walked down stairs and out the door. Ford's memory was anything but literal, nor was he ever guilty of devotion to factual truth, but he was sensitive to the demands of legendary art. His impressionistic memory of Lewis explains the magnetic force Lewis had for Ezra Pound—an attraction strong enough to reduce Pound's image of *Des Imagistes* to puppets playing at a parlor game—and Lewis's assault on London also attracted the precocious, boyish, gifted Frenchman, Gaudier-Brzeska. Vorticism had the advantage of embracing all the arts, and condemning in the same breath all branches of fashionable diversions in British society. *Des Imagistes* of whom Pound had warned the world that they "held the future in their keeping" were far less threatening than the coming Vorticists, who had greater mobility because their number was so small. Lewis, Pound, and Gaudier-Brzeska were their leaders.

Amy Lowell never clearly understood the reasons why Pound within the short time between two summers grew less concerned with *Des Imagistes* than with other matters. She probably did not realize that Pound like Yeats, his first patron in London, sustained an impulse to walk through "movements" rather than to stay within or to follow them. Without loss of his own convictions, he invented or promoted several of his "movements" simultaneously; and the "movements" were almost as many as the separate interests and talents of his friends. Though he seemed diffident (even to Fletcher) about the progress of his own poems, there is evidence enough that he maintained his high standard in everything he wrote. The one small segment of common ground he still shared with Amy Lowell was an apparently ceaseless love of activity. On this ground, and with frequent misunderstandings, they met and enjoyed each other. He kept his rule of almost never speaking of his own poems, but was dogmatic (according to John Gould Fletcher) in having his say about other poets and poetry in general.

To safeguard a better treatment of her poems in London than her first book had received Amy Lowell interviewed George Macmillan (since the New York branch of his firm had become her publisher) and with him signed a contract for *Sword Blades and Poppy Seed.* The agreement was that he distribute a hundred copies of the book in England, reserving ten per cent of the retail price for himself and giving the rest to her. The contract reversed the usual author-publisher agreement in her favor, and even in England there was little doubt that she knew how to impress and how to take advantage of publishers. The result was that Macmillan invited her to dinner at the Ranelagh Club situated near Richmond on the suburban site of Barn Elms, once the house and estate of Queen Elizabeth's secretary. She was more at ease with George Macmillan than with Ezra Pound.

Through introductions given to her by Pound, she visited the Vorticists, including Gaudier-Brzeska, who received startling recognition for his sculpture from critics and fellow-sculptors in London, but earned so little money that his poverty and hardships comprise a tragic legend in H. S. Ede's brief story of his life in *Savage Messiah*. In July 1914, Henri Gaudier (the latter and hyphenated part of his name came from Sophie Brzeska, his Polish mistress) was as young as Amy Lowell's John Keats. Gaudier was scarcely twenty-two, and in London literary circles his Bohemianism, his unwashed clothes, his jealous devotion to his art, his violent speeches in defense of it, represented the archetypal Bohemian artist of the day. His appearance—long hair, thinly bearded cheeks, narrow chin, slanted eyes, and quickly accelerating nervous gestures—contributed to his rapidly growing legend. The brilliance of his gift, however precocious and immature, was well established. The concern of his friends, many of whom were barely able to support themselves, sustained professional interest in his work; he had no need of encouragement—his needs were for small sums of money and a guardian to dole it out to him at reasonable intervals. His relationship with his Polish mistress was almost feverishly sexless; they quarreled with vehemence, never over lack of money, but rather over aesthetic matters—the way she dressed, and his impracticality in finding the places where they lived in wildest squalor. Sophie Brzeska was like a half-mad maiden aunt, plain-featured, sturdy and with work-stained, chapped wrists and hands, hiring herself out as an inefficient governess (positions which she held for short stays only) for board and lodging. Gaudier depended on her esteem and love, and she on her intuitive knowledge of his genius.

Gaudier's personality, the obviously unwashed condition of his face, hands and clothes, his Bohemian tactlessness (for, not without justice, he had scolded John Middleton Murry and Katherine Mansfield because they saw no beauty in the statue of King Charles at Charing Cross) were signs of conduct that would not attract Amy Lowell. Her common sense would tell her that he was an unwashed, egotistical bright boy whose manners were deplorable—if they could be called manners at all—and more suited to all-night conversations over a table in an out-of-door café than to the interior of the drawing room at Sevenels. It is probable that she judged the other Vorticists in the same light, yet she accepted an invitation from Pound to join them at a Vorticist dinner in a French restaurant, a dinner at which she found herself at odds with Madox Ford. The rotund Ford, who wore a walrus-like mustache, was an editor of lively tastes, shrewd wit, imaginative charm—and his family background was of far greater literary sophistication than Amy Lowell's. His kinship to the Rossettis —Christina Rossetti was among his aunts—and memories of his boyhood contained within them a round of gossip which flowed through Pre-Raphaelite circles. He had been a friend of Joseph Conrad, and at a time when Conrad felt the need of an English editor, Ford assisted Conrad in the writing of two novels, *The Inheritors* (1901) and *Romance* (1903). He had no pretentions to being either an *Imagiste* or Vorticist. He called himself an Impressionist and a friend of Ezra Pound. In a Vorticist group of far younger people, he emerged as military advisor and sage. (The Pre-Raphaelites before him had been masters in the arts of successful literary warfare). When he chose, the genial Ford could display a lack of courtesy to visiting Americans; and he took pleasure in showing a lack of respect for American Lowells, nor would he permit Amy Lowell to preside at a Vorticist dinner.

Beyond these dissensions and in the company of the Vorticists, Amy Lowell was not always "having her own way." Although she could never define the quality of the invisible wall between them and herself, she could feel the presence of the wall and know that there was something wrong. She loved to be hostess and to preside at dinners; therefore at the same restaurant where the Vorticists met and talked—the "Dieudonne"—she had planned a half-ironic, belated celebration for *Des Imagistes*. She invited to it all the contributors to Ezra Pound's little anthology that had been published by Albert and Charles Boni in New York—and all accepted her invitation. After they had settled around the table, she made an attempt to learn more precisely what Imagism was from the very lips of those who were said to practice it; but by this time, whatever the "movement" as a slogan stood for, it was "old hat" to its inventors. Ezra Pound disappeared from the table to return a few minutes later with an old-fashioned tin bathtub worn on his head like a helmet—that was his answer. It was clear that Amy Lowell had failed to preside at the dinner for which she had issued the invitations and had paid the bill. There was considerable talk and much laughter; the dinner was one at which all seemed cheerful, yet the memorable event of the dinner belonged to the inventive high spirits of Ezra Pound. The wearing of a bathtub as headgear could be interpreted as having several meanings: impertinent Vorticism, too much drink, Bohemianism, disrespect for the hostess—but all signs pointed toward a further coolness between Amy Lowell and Ezra Pound. In Ezra Pound's presence Amy Lowell was never allowed to be the center of attraction.

Among Ezra Pound's younger friends Amy Lowell made her choice of four: John Gould Fletcher, Hilda Doolittle (H. D.), Richard Aldington and D. H. Lawrence; and as if in consolation for the slights if not overt insults she received at the *Imagiste* dinner, she invited the newly married Aldingtons and Lawrence to spend an evening at her apartment on the top flight of the Berkeley. That dinner was memorable for several reasons: the date was July 30th, 1914; it had been a warm, fair summer day, filled with the same air of calmness that had preceded it for at least two months, yet the date was only five days before the First World War. Newspaper posters had begun their warnings: "British Army Mobilized," "Germany and Russia Are at War." Glancing down from the bow window of Amy Lowell's apartment, Aldington saw the posters being set up in Piccadilly. The true end of "good King Edward's" reign had come.

As Aldington looked down at the warm evening in the street below and then turned to see dinner table candles being lit above glittering silverware and a white damask cloth, the room was suddenly given life and motion by the swift entrance of D. H. Lawrence —not the red-bearded prophet of ten years later, but a slender young man with a quick, lithe, nervous step and very blue eyes. He did not wait for introductions but burst out with the news that Edward Marsh, well-to-do editor of the "Georgian Poetry" anthologies and private secretary to Prime Minister Asquith, had just told him that the British would be in the war. Lawrence had made his dramatic entrance in a way that thoroughly delighted Amy Lowell.

During the dinner, at which the thin, volatile young man as guest of honor was placed at the right hand of his portly hostess, Lawrence declared his independence from the Georgian poets as well as *Les Imagistes*. He was neither, he said; he was not their kind of poet, but a writer well apart from groups and movements, a position that brought respect from Amy Lowell's reservoir of common sense. His appearance, despite his red hair, was in great contrast to Ezra Pound's; his manner had the brightness, the eagerness in talk of one who had taught (which he did for three years) in a boys' prep school in Croydon. He was distinctly apart from the neo-Bohemianism of the John Middleton Murry-Katherine Mansfield household (where he was welcomed as a friend) and of Pound and Gaudier-Brzeska. There were moments when his poverty neared disaster, but he could never sink to the unwashed physical squalor of Henri Gaudier: if Lawrence had been dressed in the robe and sandals of a Franciscan friar he would have still looked freshly bathed and clean. His appearance, which reflected his personality, held a fascination for Amy Lowell. However lightly or—in another mood—perceptively he talked, he took time out for listening with his vivid, blue eyes fixed on the speaker's face—as though his listening could be taken as an unspoken and direct compliment to his hostess. It is easy to understand why Amy Lowell liked him, and why H. D., Fletcher and Aldington were amused at the thought of a coal miner's son exchanging enthusiasms and literary gossip high above Piccadilly with a Boston Lowell.

Lawrence's recent marriage to Frieda, daughter of Baron von Richtofen, who was beautiful, charming and no less volatile than he, was also appreciated by Amy Lowell; these were the kind of young people who caught her eye and held her regard. She respected Frieda's calm air of being the daughter of a "Baron" and she caught a gleam of Lawrence's intelligence. Though she thought Lawrence's writings were inspired by "some sort of erotic mania," his tactful letters to her smoothed away any doubts she had concerning the propriety of his theories. Meanwhile, she felt that her winning over of Lawrence balanced the scales against her uneasy interviews with

Pound. If Lawrence was on her side, an American Imagist group
could place him along with Aldington and F. S. Flint who had
been unfailingly polite to her. And she was certain that Lawrence
was *somebody,* and that the mention of his name would increase
American interest in Imagism. Read from a platform, Lawrence's
poems could be spectacular enough to offset her loss of Pound's support.

But there were other reasons why Lawrence met Amy Lowell with
deeper insight than his American contemporary, Ezra Pound. In
Nottingham, miner's son though he was, he had known women of
Amy Lowell's kind—her kind, that is, in respect to managing an
estate the size of Sevenels. Women of the smaller gentry in Nottingham did not pretend to knowing or writing poetry, nor were they
anywhere near so wealthy as Amy Lowell of Brookline, but they
shared something of her common sense, her ease and tough-minded-
ness in business matters, and her kindliness to and sense of responsibility toward the animals on her estate. In this perception Lawrence
had an advantage over other younger poets who accepted Amy
Lowell's invitations to dinner; he knew her "type" and so, for that
matter, did Thomas Hardy.

A few weeks earlier and a few days before she had boarded the
Laconia to sail for England, Amy Lowell received a letter from
Josephine Peabody Marks which enclosed a letter of cordial introduction to Thomas Hardy. Between the last rounds of her activities in
London, Amy Lowell and Ada Russell, driven by the liveried
chauffeur in the maroon-colored car, arrived at Hardy's house, Max
Gate, in Dorchester. As Hardy recalled four years later, he saw two
bedraggled ladies emerging from the car. Amy Lowell's car had a
top that could be folded back—but not without an effort—and the
mechanics of folding it back or resetting it forward again could not
compete with the alternating swift bursts of rain and sunshine across
the English countryside. Changes in the weather came more swiftly
than the chauffeur could readjust the top, and by the time his passen-
gers reached Max Gate their hats and dresses were the worse for rain:
a stuffed bird had been washed away from the trimmings of Amy
Lowell's hat—an ironic circumstance that may well have amused
their host and certainly made their visit memorable.

In 1914 the red brick walls, bow windows and trim lawns of Max

Gate had become a shrine in tribute to the expert management of the estate and literary genius of its owner, and they were even more impressive than the landscaped beauties of Sevenels in Brookline. Hardy himself was small, compact and elderly, white mustached and bald, with an inquiring, youthful look in his quick eyes. Like Lawrence he knew at a glance the kind of woman Amy Lowell was; he was taken by her lack of hypocrisy, her forthright manner—and he, as his later letters to her show, was as candid with her as she with him. Though he never regarded her as "the greatest living poet," he admired her intelligence and her visit meant that she had made a friend. He was probably flattered that she knew him as a poet as well as the author of *The Return of the Native* and *Tess*. At this time few Americans knew of his poetry at all; and Lawrence was among the few of a younger generation of English poets who paid him the compliment of emulating his Wessex poems in his own early rhymed verses. Amy Lowell felt honored by Hardy's polite attentions; if he did not pay court to her vanities, he bolstered her ego. In meeting him she felt herself in the presence of a larger figure in English poetry than she did with any one of the younger poets in London. The plain, forthright language of his verse was also something she could understand.

She had far less respect for handsome young Rupert Brooke. At a reading of his own poems in Bloomsbury's Poetry Bookshop, she heckled him from a rear seat of the room by shouting out that he read louder. He pointedly ignored her. She was neither at her best nor at her ease in the company of the Georgian poets who met in Harold Munro's bookshop. Her distrust of Pound was shown by her portrait of him in "Astigmatism," verses which also showed how deeply she resented his critical discriminations. She described his ebony walking stick lopping off the heads of all flowers other than roses because they were not roses—which in turn expressed her feeling that he did not like *her*. Yet she received greater stimulation from the young people around him than from the Georgians who cared nothing for "free verse." The Georgians were not bold enough to hold her attention; she wished to learn something she felt was "new" enough to catch the eye, something that was reflected in her second book of poems, *Sword Blades and Poppy Seed*, which was a title that attracted readers at a time when the world was moving toward its first world war. Chance and instinct rather than a studied knowledge of political events had guided Amy Lowell's choice of a title for her book.

The only Georgian she later learned to admire was the American poet, Robert Frost, who, though he did not contribute to Edward Marsh's Georgian anthologies, had been living in England and had been a friend of several Georgian poets, among whom were Wilfred Gibson and Edward Thomas. She had yet to meet the graceful, formal American whose handsome profile had more "character" than Rupert Brooke's, whose first book had been highly praised by Ezra Pound. She discovered his poems in the Poetry Bookshop and was amazed to find his conventional blank verse contained "our vaunted *mot juste.*" In her apartments above Piccadilly she sat down to emulate his observations of New Hampshire's landscape in verses of her own.

Meanwhile the First World War had transformed London into a war city with American tourists rushing through it to get home. Amy Lowell's brother Percival, then visiting London, had already booked passage home and left, following his earlier traveling habits of quick decisions and disappearances. Her first action, which was eminently practical since automobiles were being commandeered by the British, was to ship her maroon-colored car and her chauffeur home. She had few fears for her personal safety, for her courage always rose to dangerous occasions; in this she was very like her brother Lawrence of Harvard, who would walk calmly into a burning college building to rescue his files. Amy Lowell as well as Lawrence made it a point of family honor to ignore physical risks and handicaps; in this respect they held firmly to the Puritan virtues of their heritage.

In the Lowell tradition, she joined Herbert Hoover who happened to be in London in organizing war relief at the American Consulate and assisted the cause by donating ten thousand dollars of her own money. If for a few days her courage showed a slight lapse in an hysterical effort to book passage on a ship for home, it was characteristic of her to dispel her fears by her devotion to public service at Hoover's direction. She and the future President of the United States were not as far apart in temperament as might have been supposed; however "liberal" certain of their opinions may have seemed, particularly on active occasions and in public view, their convictions were consistently and predominantly conservative. Amy Lowell was never "a votes for women candidate" for fame; she believed that women could take care of themselves, and if one woman who was none other than herself did so in a notorious fashion, that was her privilege because she was a Lowell. She returned to Boston to welcome and advance the sale of her new book, *Sword Blades and Poppy Seed.*

7

IN AUGUST 1914, Amy Lowell's homecoming was something of a triumph: her second book of poems, *Sword Blades and Poppy Seed*, was in press. Its publication date was September 22, and since almost all the poems in it had been recently published in magazines, she was assured of a broader reception than the few notices she received after the appearance of *A Dome of Many-Coloured Glass*. She was writing enough to keep two secretaries busy, and after the verses were rapidly written down or dictated, they were typed. Early in Amy Lowell's day, which was midafternoon, Mrs. Russell listened to her hostess's reading of the typed versions and the work went along so swiftly, so efficiently, so happily that Amy Lowell wished they could hang out a sign over the entrance to Sevenels, announcing "Lowell & Russell, Makers of Fine Poems." The sign, half-joked at, would have given their pleasure more of a "business-like" air and visible accomplishment. Mrs. Russell performed the office of being Amy Lowell's first audience, her prompter, her director at rehearsals. This was the kind of collaboration Amy Lowell delighted in and needed; it trained her voice and gestures, and with training came the effects which make public readings seem spontaneous and easy. The role of playing "Amy Lowell, Poet," to the world could be made professionally successful—and so it was.

The part Mrs. Russell coached her to play was "Amy Lowell, Herself." Outwardly she was—as newspapers wrote of her—the vastly large, cigar-smoking, wealthy poet and sister of Harvard's President. Moreover she talked in familiar terms of the very latest poetry, the poetry that few people knew and few cared to read. Her intention was to make such poetry both dramatic and easy to understand; and her own verses were to represent what it was. To the public of the moment all this was news: this extraordinary woman—so far as appearance could tell and rumor could invent—was in startling contrast to her respectable brother who was President of Harvard. In actuality—and as she grew older, for she had just passed forty—she had become less unlike her brother than the world suspected; her courage was merely one side of her inner resemblance to his character.

The great majority of the verses in her new book were less experimental than conservative and were written in the same verse forms that had been familiar to several generations of New England readers. They were not "modern" in any sense of the word. Familiar forms held fanciful stories of old men who sold sword blades and poppy seeds which were obvious analogies for certain uses of words. Similar verses were of coal pickers who discovered beauties analogous to poetry in rubbish heaps, in the fragments of coal itself. Other verses told of girls seduced or pursued by men—all these were themes that might well have been fancied by a bright child reading in a well-stocked nineteenth-century library. Her boldest experiments in the book were in half-rhyme, half-prose, the stanzas set up as paragraphs and rhyming as Amy Lowell felt inclined; these she called ventures in writing "polyphonic prose." Their merits were in being colorful in action and in using bright, fanciful details as one might stitch gay fragments of cloth together, yet they created a general impression of writing prose that accidentally rhymed at awkward intervals. Heard from a platform their effects were dramatic enough, since they contained stories of illicit love: one of adultery and the other the plight of an unmarried mother. In fact there was little in her new book that would offend the reader of romantic nineteenth-century fiction—the novelty was in having it read as poetry from a platform by a well-trained and confident reader.

The book partly explains what had become an essential point of difference between Amy Lowell and Ezra Pound. Although it was true that some of the shorter verses in the book fell under a general definition of Imagism, they were too long-winded and contained too many words. Only the presence of Amy Lowell reading them aloud justified their lack of economy. Sometimes the verses were good talk, good "Lowellese"; they released her energy, but the writing could not be called an art. Amy Lowell's verses expressed her observations and opinions which were often forthright and clear but revealed little of what she felt. Pound had no patience with her habit of using "poetic license," her inversions of words in a poem to force rhymes, her careless speed in dictating long manuscripts. She was too firmly set in her own prejudices for him to teach—and far too indiscriminate in the love of her own writing to understand his criticism. He saw her verses as being far less "modern" than they seemed to others and to her. Impractical as he was, he knew what Margaret Anderson later saw, "that Amy Lowell would dictate, uniquely and majestically, any adventure in which she had a part." Pound was not prepared to advance the cause of Amy Lowell's Imagism—"Amygism" as it was called—nor could he follow in the wake of her campaign for publicity in the United States.

With the publication of *Sword Blades and Poppy Seed* the legend of her estate at Sevenels, her seven sheep dogs, her habits of cigar-smoking and of rising in midafternoon had a very wide circulation. The heavy, respectable luxury of the rooms at Sevenels began to be noticed by others than women members of her Boston clubs, for she had begun to give dinner parties to friendly editors and poets. Like her brother's position at Harvard, Sevenels was a visible and superficial contrast to what Amy Lowell seemed to be; if her book had "broken away from academic tradition," it also contained ten long poems as well as several shorter lyrics written in a manner that Whittier or Oliver Wendell Holmes would have understood. She made the most of whatever contrasts her personality gave to color an environment and spirit that were respectable and staid. Oliver

Wendell Holmes had chosen carpentry as a diversion from the teaching of anatomy at Harvard, and making chairs and tables was his distraction from the writing of prose and verse for *The Atlantic Monthly*. In much the same fashion Amy Lowell cultivated her care of sheep dogs and the smoking of cigars; these were among the "trade marks" of her personality, and were not at all inappropriate to her size. In contrast to these was her concern in keeping the Lowell gardens at Sevenels in order, and though the garden verses in her new book were more successful than others she included, they were less frequently praised than her dramatic efforts in polyphonic prose.

Aside from building a legend at Sevenels, Amy Lowell sustained a few of the more valuable friendships she had made in England— those with John Gould Fletcher, Richard Aldington and his wife, H. D., and D. H. Lawrence. Since late July, Lawrence and his wife lived in a suburban Chesham cottage called "The Triangle" which Lawrence had rented for six shillings a month in the Chess valley. The place was cheap enough but crudely appointed and very damp; the season, after the nearly perfect summer of 1914, was filled with rain, and the rotted drains of the small cottage steamed with moisture. Lawrence wrote one of his utterly desperate, wistful letters to Amy Lowell, speaking of the rainy cold, of green and rotten water butts, of green apples fallen in the rainy grass, and of the warning of a rainy winter in early autumn. He wrote to ask her to return the poems he had sent her for the *Some Imagist Poets* so he could rework them, to thank her for her promise to see Mitchell Kennerley, the New York publisher, about the manuscript of a novel he had written—"And I kiss your hand, dear Miss Lowell, for being so good to me." He had let her know he was in need of a typewriter and that he was now in need of money. "Nobody will pay me any money," he wrote.

Though Amy Lowell was not given to handing out money to poets even when she knew they were in need, Lawrence's letters opened an unguarded chamber between her "common sense" and her practical desire "to do good." She sent him a typewriter she had discarded and wrote to Harriet Monroe of his illness, his "consumption," and added that he was poor and lived in a cottage that was "horribly cold."

Lawrence confided to her that he was growing a red beard, and then described a scene between his wife Frieda (they had been married less than six months ago) and her ex-husband. The ex-husband said, "*If* you had to go away, why didn't you go away with a *gentleman?*" To which Frieda replied, "He is a *great* man." Lawrence's show of his wife's confidence in *him* was something he knew Amy Lowell would not overlook, and to this he added that the ex-husband would not allow Frieda to see her children. His confidences took the chance of skirting the edges of Amy Lowell's thoroughly Bostonian principles and her dislike of Bohemianism; but by this time he had learned that her sympathies could be balanced against her prejudices and fears. Perhaps he had guessed her love of being "on the inside of things," her hidden loneliness, her feeling of being "left out" among writers of the younger generation as well as the old. In his letters Lawrence never failed to give her something of himself, which was the kind of compliment that Amy Lowell seldom received and which he performed with instinctive artfulness.

Among those of the younger generation who wrote to her, Lawrence was the only one who took the trouble to let her know that he understood her and valued the friendship between them. In his letters he exercised one of his greatest gifts—the gift of making each letter a fragment of autobiography and, in a Lawrencian sense, a work of art. He appealed to her ego rather than her vanity; to her feminine, semi-maternal instincts rather than to the fact that she was a rich woman. Lawrence was living with Frieda, an attractive and *vivid* woman—older than he and daughter of a baron—who regarded him as a "*great* man." He presented himself as an investment in greatness and a guarantee of an immortality for the investor. By these means he placed himself far above Amy Lowell's usual flatterers; he could well afford not to praise her writings indiscriminately.

In a letter thanking her for the typewriter and her new book he wrote:

Why don't you always be yourself. Why go to France or anywhere else for your inspiration. If it doesn't come out of your own heart, real Amy Lowell, it is no good, however many colours it may have. I wish one saw more of your genuine strong, sound self in this book, full of common sense and kindness and the restrained, almost bitter, Puritan passion. Why do you deny the bitterness in your nature, when you write poetry?

Why do you take a pose? It causes you always to shirk your issues, and find a banal resolution at the end. So your romances are spoiled. When you are full of your own strong gusto of things, real old English strong gusto it is, like those tulips, then I like you very much. But you shouldn't compare the sun to the yolk of an egg, except playfully. And you shouldn't spoil your story-poems with a sort of vulgar, artificial 'flourish of ink.' If you had followed the real tragedy of your man, or woman, it had been something.

***   ***   ***

—but how much nicer, finer, bigger you are, intrinsically, than your poetry is.

***   ***   ***

I wish the War were over and gone. I will not give in to it. We who shall live after it are more important than those who fall.

The confident note at the end of the letter renewed his theme of greatness. But the central portions of it were inspired readings of Amy Lowell and her new book. Though Lawrence had been earning his living as a teacher in a boys' school, there was nothing in his criticism of Amy Lowell's verse that recalled the measuring rod, the slide rule or the classroom: he spoke to her with particular direct-ness—almost as though she had come to him for criticism—which she had not. And he took her seriously: her common sense and kind-ness (to him) and her almost bitter, restrained Puritan passion. He gave her a deeper reading of herself than she cared to make public; her restraint was of the same character that made President Lowell's biography of Percival Lowell so barren of personal incident and reminiscence, and it was also consistent with her draping of the mir-rors of her hotel apartments to shut out reflections of her own image. It was rewarding for her to read in his comments deeper resources of her emotions than she was able to show, for him to say "how much nicer, finer, bigger you are, intrinsically, than your poetry is." This balanced the critical truth that he found "banal resolution" at the end of her fanciful long poems. Had she cared to listen to his criti-cism—but Amy Lowell was never to be taught, except by her own impulses which were always immediate and urgent—she might well have adopted him as her best, her most discerning critic. Her "pose," which he had intuitively grasped, was her rôle of acting out the part of Amy Lowell, the poet, on a platform; the "pose" was in the verses she wrote to be read aloud, to shock audiences, to storm their sen-sibilities with vigorous Lowellese and dramatic gestures.

In Boston, Mrs. Marks (Josephine Preston Peabody) had reviewed Amy Lowell's new book with unmodified enthusiasm; and the two women, so frequently wary of each other, had for the moment become great friends. In the cause of Belgian relief funds, Mrs. Marks invited Amy Lowell to join her in a recital at Steinhart Hall on December 17. Amy Lowell opened the performance with a reading of fourteen poems, including newly written verses in prose, particularly "The Bombardment" which throughout its paragraphs carried the reiteration of the word "Boom." Because she could not shout "Boom" loud enough she concealed a friend, Carl Engel, behind the backdrop of the stage who pounded a bass drum whenever "Boom" appeared in the text; the reading as she afterwards described it was a "holocaust of noise and terror." * Neither the piano recital nor Mrs. Marks reading from the same platform could compete with the force of Amy Lowell's demonstration of a cannonade. This was showmanship that anticipated the success of the three Sitwells, Osbert, Sacheverell, and Edith, who eight years later presented Edith Sitwell's *Façade* to an audience in a Carlyle Square drawing room in London. On this occasion, as Sir Osbert wrote in his memoirs, "the sheer volume of sound was overwhelming." And during an air raid of World War II in London, Edith Sitwell read her war poem, "Still Falls the Rain," to the accompaniment of falling bombs. A young American poet in the audience remarked that "Edith always had all the luck: even the horrors of war combined to make her reading go off with plenty of noise." It may be of passing relevance to add that Amy Lowell anticipated Edith Sitwell's imagery of rain in "The Bombardment," and if her poem contained no references to Christ, "the carved head of Saint John" was among its memorable images.

Amy Lowell's performance in reading "The Bombardment" marked the beginning of her more histrionic readings from a public platform. She had become an "entertainer," one who could be trusted not to let those who saw and heard her fall asleep. Behind her public appearances were her rooms at Sevenels where her many verses were hastily written on sheets of paper that drifted to the floor, were swept up by housemaids, typed by a brace of secretaries, reread by the author, corrected by her and retyped, and then read aloud to Mrs. Russell for their final version. Other activities which prospered be-

* From notes written by Amy Lowell on Josephine Peabody Marks.

hind the scenes were her dealings with her editors, Edward C. Marsh, Vice President of the Macmillan Company in New York, and Ferris Greenslet at Houghton Mifflin in Boston who had agreed to publish and distribute annual collections of *Some Imagist Poets.*

Of these dealings, the most important were those that skillfully involved first the interest, and later the awe-tinged admiration, of Mr. Marsh. Nine months earlier Amy Lowell had made a contract with him for the publication of her *Sword Blades and Poppy Seed* which was to bring a flood of letters from him. The first was dated February 18, 1914:

> We are quite prepared to accept the terms of publication which you suggest, i.e., that you shall bear the expense of publication and receive all the returns less our usual commission of 15%.

In this exchange the author demanded and received strict accounting of each book sold, exact costs of paper and binding as well as printing. With the services of her friend Mr. Updike in Boston, she dictated the design and typography of her book and few writers could have sustained the business details of publishing a book as ruggedly as she. In her agreement with the Macmillan Company, Amy Lowell remained in the executive position of an employer; for its fifteen percent commission, the Macmillan Company waited on her orders. The willing services of Mr. Marsh were hers to command. He advised her as to where the kind of paper she wished to buy had the lowest prices and how to secure them; how to keep her books in print slightly ahead of orders for them, which bookstores would be likely to keep them in stock, and how (through means of her platform appearances) to increase the sales. In return for his advice Mr. Marsh had the unusual adventure of dealing with an author who had gifts as a business woman, who could speak his language with more forthright ease than he could understand her verse. In his entire lifetime it was unlikely that he would ever meet another Amy Lowell; he appreciated this peculiar circumstance and valued it—so far as his letters show—sincerely. Whenever she came to New York he was glad to set aside the rush of appointments in his office to receive her; she charmed and refreshed him. He understood the "tough-minded" side of Amy Lowell as clearly as D. H. Lawrence understood and was able to touch the "soft side." It was Mr. Marsh who warned her that the Poetry Society of America in New York was a poor market in which to sell her books, that its members also wrote verse and were ill-disposed toward those who tried to dominate them. In 1922, after both he and she had left the Macmillan Company, he wrote a letter saying that the happiest recollections of his career in publishing were centered around her, that to him the Macmillan Company could never be the same without her.

Meanwhile Amy Lowell's activities in the Houghton Mifflin office with her annuals of *Some Imagist Poets* continued. For these labors she refused to accept the title of editor, yet she collected contributions and handled all the business details for publication; and when royalty checks fell due, she forwarded them with explanatory letters and itemized statements to the poets who were her friends in London. It was also her means of "keeping in touch" with them, and it was done in the same fashion that a toastmaster at a banquet pays compliments and calls upon shy or eager guests to speak, to make themselves known and to receive their prizes. The agreement went forward under the pretext of being "democratic"—with Ezra Pound excluded from the group.

Meanwhile the advertising of Amy Lowell's *Sword Blades and Poppy Seed* had taken a fantastic turn and, in respect to Pound and a few of his friends in London, a tactless one. How far Amy Lowell guided her publishers in making exaggerated claims for herself and her new book it is impossible to say, but it is unlikely that the advertising copy writers at the Macmillan Company—and at this particular moment—had any authoritative knowledge of Pound and *Des Imagistes*. In Margaret Anderson's *The Little Review* (which was the very kind of publication certain to be read by Pound's younger friends) the Macmillan Company published a notice which included the following remarks: that Amy Lowell was the foremost member of the "Imagists"—"a group of poets that includes William Butler Yeats, Ezra Pound, Ford Madox Hueffer"—and then went on to say that she "has broken away from academic traditions and written out of her time with real singing poetry, free, full of new effects and subtleties." The advertisement had all the marks of being inspired by the author of the new book; and it was a shrewd, if somewhat garbled, piece of publicity. Neither Yeats nor Hueffer had made any claims to being Imagists at all, and Hueffer, since he had clearly denied all claims of the kind, would feel that he had just cause for libel.

If Amy Lowell's book sold no more than four copies in London, which was the limit of its sales in that city, the Macmillan Company advertisement was sufficient reason for its lack of popularity—nor did it improve her relationship with Pound. Pound had evidence that his name was being used to advance the sale of her book without his permission or desire.

To Pound, Amy Lowell disclaimed knowledge of and responsibility for Macmillan's advertisement, but her argument (which was scarcely an apology) was unconvincing—all the more so because she had succeeded in getting Houghton Mifflin to publish an anthology called *Some Imagist Poets*—and Pound was not to be its editor: it was to be a "cooperative" venture. Amy Lowell had accepted advice from Aldington and Fletcher, and gossip flowing through "little magazine" and poetry circles converted her half-guilty, half-defensive attitude toward Pound into a "poetic war." She never failed to regard Pound as a rival and, in the light of "business ethics" which guided her, there is no doubt that she saw him as her "competitor." In getting publicity for herself and "new poetry" in the United States, she could easily out-act, out-talk him; her "common sense" had greater appeals to editors and to audiences than his critical intelligence and his "Bohemian" legend.

Amy Lowell's letters from John Gould Fletcher and Richard Aldington throw further light on her relationship with Pound. As early as September 21, 1914, she had received the following report from Richard Aldington:

Ezra is back from the country and looks terribly ill. He lies on a couch and says he has "cursed gout." Poor devil, I wonder if Fat Hueffer was right? Perhaps Ezra is a little cracked. He doesn't seem to be able to talk of anything except himself and his work . . .

Aldington took a dark view of his elders; his earlier observations of Hueffer were as gloomy as this look at Pound and they gave to Amy Lowell a clear contrast with those hours of the day when she felt at her best. These were when newly written manuscripts littered the floor in front of her fireplace at Sevenels and when with refreshed vigor and decisiveness she charmed Mr. Marsh at the Macmillan Company and overwhelmed her friends. To know that Pound had

his moments of infirmity flattered her ability to assume leadership of
his group in the United States. She underrated the activity of Pound
when he felt less despondent than on the day when Aldington saw
him lying on a couch. Amy Lowell understood Pound less than
before, and her lack of understanding opened the way toward one
of the most embarrassing episodes in her career.

Among several of the "free-lance," low-salaried means of earning
his living, Richard Aldington edited contributions to Harriet Shaw
Weaver's little magazine *The Egoist*—the same magazine that Amy
Lowell had refused to buy. But she was not adverse to gaining publicity from it. Therefore, early in May 1914, when she heard that
John Gould Fletcher had contributed an essay about her to *The
Egoist* she was pleasantly gratified. Aldington read the essay and
pruned it and wrote a letter to her telling her what he had excised,
warning her that praise of the kind that Fletcher gave made her seem
ridiculous. He listed a few of the statements that Fletcher made and
of which he, Aldington, disapproved:

   a) that she was the foremost Imagist
   b) that she would take a place among the great masters of poetry
   c) that she was likened to Shakespeare
   d) that she was the only Imagist who practised all forms of dramatic
      and lyric English verse.

As tactfully and as smoothly as his boyish ardor would permit, he
explained that some of the statements were untrue and others—so
far as his critical judgment went—were hilarious. He warned her that
she stood in danger of being damned by excessive praise. He also
observed that no intelligent reader could possibly take Fletcher's
criticism of her verse in the spirit in which it had been written.

When the Macmillan Company had advertised Amy Lowell's
Sword Blades and Poppy Seed as the work of "the foremost Imagist,"
and linked her name with Pound's and Yeats', Amy Lowell guessed
rightly that Pound thought she had dictated the wording of the advertisement and that since Pound and Aldington were living in the
same block of flats, Holland Place Chambers, Kensington, it is probable that Pound knew of Aldington's letter of warning to her. In
public she denied all knowledge of what Macmillan's advertising
man had written, and her friend, Mr. Marsh, Vice-President of the
company, took full responsibility for the phrasing of the advertise-

ment. He was soon shocked to receive an insulting letter from Ezra
Pound, and decided to ignore it. Pound had asked the Macmillan
Company whether or not it would like to be listed with a minor firm
like Mitchell Kennerley; Pound said he felt the same as Mr. Marsh
would, should his work be compared with Amy Lowell's. The episode
was not forgotten by either Pound or Amy Lowell; both felt injured,
and Pound had aesthetic rather than business ethics on his side.
Three years later, in September 1917, Pound wrote to her:

> . . . you tried to stampede me into accepting as my artistic equals
> various people whom it would have been rank hypocrisy for me to accept
> in any such manner. There is no democracy in the arts.

In this exchange neither combatant recognized the need of
humility; the quarrel was decisive, and the breach between them was
as broad and deep as the Atlantic Ocean.

Since her quarrel with Pound had been successfully launched as
a "poetic war," Amy Lowell began the new year of 1915 with a visit
to Chicago. From Harriet Monroe, she secured a letter of introduction
to Margaret Anderson of *The Little Review*. Margaret Anderson
was youthful, blonde, smartly dressed. She was one of few well-to-do
girls who had escaped from the "country club culture" of mid-Indiana
to Chicago. She had come to Chicago to play the piano, but after a
stay of a short time in the city she decided to found and edit the
youngest in spirit, the most dashing, the most instinctively gay of
"little magazines." Although *The Little Review* was as refreshing as
a breeze down the length of Michigan Boulevard, it was anything
but provincial; it had caught the restless spirit of the Chicago "renaissance" which looked wide-eyed at the entire world and adopted Paris
as its second capital. This all-embracing and remotely European view
had already secured transatlantic vistas when the directors of the
Chicago Art Institute went to Paris to buy pictures and sought out
Mary Cassatt. The impressionist torch passed from the hands of
Mary Cassatt and Harriet Monroe to the preternaturally youthful
Margaret Anderson, who thirty-seven years later during the German
occupation of France in World War II, charmed German soldiers
into thinking she was a Hollywood movie star. With herself at wheel
in the driver's seat they let her car pass through the lines into free
France; she was an impressionist in more than one sense of the word.

No less impressionistic was her memory of Amy Lowell. There is no need to dispute her report of the meeting with the poet from Brookline for literal facts were never among Margaret Anderson's recollections. They cluttered storage space within her mind where certain essential and not wholly untruthful impressions boldly took their place. She wrote of Amy Lowell:

She was dressed that morning in the mode of Godey's Lady's Book. Culture and good taste were stamped upon her. She was brunette, her voice was contralto, her nose like a Roman emperor's and her manner somewhat more masterful. But I learned later she wept on the slightest provocation and had more feminine whims and humors than any ten women.
Her first words were congenial to me.
I've had a fight with Ezra Pound. [Pound had yet to exert his charm on Margaret Anderson; so far as she knew, he was still associated with Miss Monroe's *Poetry* and was therefore in a rival "little magazine's" camp.] When I was in London I offered to join this group and put the Imagists on the map. Ezra refused. All right, my dear chap, I said, we'll see who's who in this business. I'll go back to America and advertise myself so extensively that you'll wish you had come in with me.
I gathered that she wanted to subsidize modern poetry and push it ahead faster than it could go by its own impetus. A little review would be a helpful organ for such a purpose.
I love the *Little Review,* she went on, and I have money. You haven't. Take me in with you. I'll pay you one hundred and fifty dollars a month, I'll merely direct your poetry department. You can count on me never to dictate.
No clairvoyance was needed to know that Amy Lowell would dictate, uniquely and majestically, any adventure in which she had a part. I should have preferred being in the clutches of a dozen groups. So I didn't hesitate. I was barely polite.
It's charming of you but I couldn't think of it.
Your reasons?
I have only one. I can't function in "association."
Amy was furious. . . . But she had a redeeming trait—when she was finally convinced that I meant what I said she dropped the subject and never reverted to it.

As in London, Amy Lowell rented a suite in a hotel and had her meals sent up. Her servants ordered taxis for her and however short the drive, even to an office building next to the hotel, she rode. "I always ride," she said. Her rule of "always riding" had its cause in her great bulk; a taxi sheltered her, if only for a moment, from a crowded street. When its door opened for her to alight she could be further sheltered and guided across the walk by a doorman or an attentive taxi driver—the way was cleared with no time left for a crowd to stand gazing at her figure. If she was to make herself a "celebrity," she was also to be the mistress of occasions in which she arranged the decor and was in control of the scene. Her contralto voice took command. To "show herself" was often painful; it took the arts of "personality," the variable tones of voice, an intelligent glance from her blue eyes, and a decisive gesture to prevent the occasions of her arrivals and exits from becoming ridiculous.

On her return to Brookline and Boston in the middle of January the ghost of her differences with Pound still haunted her. *Some Imagist Poems* was on the press at Houghton Mifflin; assurances came to her from Aldington and F. S. Flint that she had the right (in the United States at least) to speak for her Imagism in whatever terms she chose; and with a conscience less clear than bruised, she removed Pound's name from the short historical preface to the anthology.

Her public activities now claimed all her attention. She had translated two operettas from the French, and for the benefit of the Women's Municipal League of Boston, of which her sister Katherine was President, she rehearsed the performances that were to be presented during three days of the first week of February. Although she had secured Maggie Teyte for one of the star roles in the production, like all her theatrical ventures in which "Amy Lowell as Poet" was not on stage, her entertainment failed. On this occasion a four-day snow storm kept her expected audiences at home and, since Amy Lowell had forwarded money to pay the orchestra and opera stars, a loss of several thousand dollars was the unhappy result of all her efforts. Amy Lowell almost never made a bad investment. In her experience this loss of money was unique. Whether she felt so or not she had reason to believe that the forces of nature had combined to frustrate her desires.

At the age of forty, one of her cures for disappointment was increased labor. She accepted an invitation from a Boston friend, Mrs. George Putnam, to deliver a series of lectures on French poets on six Thursday afternoons during Lent, from mid-February through the month of March. These lectures were in the well accepted tradition of club women meetings in America: members bought tickets by invitation; the intentions were cultural and the meetings were held in a large parlor of a hostess' home—in this case the home of Mrs. Putnam on Commonwealth Avenue. The flattered, and now busy, lecturer became involved in the mysteries of ardent and furious research as well as the writing of papers to be read aloud, which was no small task for one who had not made a profession of teaching. In accepting Mrs. Putnam's invitation Amy Lowell was no less deeply stirred than her predecessors, no less conscious of her task, and no less inspired by the hopes of doing supremely well. She soon discovered that an hour's talk demanded the writing of forty typewritten pages—and these to be filled with informative facts and dates, small anecdotes and quotations. She who had once refused to be taught—except by her own inclinations—was to be a teacher herself, and the charm of this experiment had attraction enough to guide her through many nights of what she called "awful" labor.

Another attraction that her invitation held was the opportunity to speak of things of which she had heard so much in England, of names that floated through the conversations of Ezra Pound, Richard Aldington and John Gould Fletcher; talk of Symbolist poetry, pro or con, had been in the air and with it "impressionism" and "vers libre." Now in Boston she was given a chance to voice her own convictions about what she had heard, and she entered the subject of recent French poetry with unbridled innocence and ironclad opinions. The French that she had learned at her mother's knee was revived and forced to revolve around six names: Emile Verhaeren, Albert Samain, Remy de Gourmont, Henri de Regnier, Francis Jammes and Paul Fort. No doubt some of these choices were made with the thought behind them that she could transcend the taste, the knowledge of Ezra Pound. She remembered that he had talked of Rimbaud, Laforgue, Corbiére, and now she would insist with greater vehemance than his upon the superiority of Verhaeren, Samain and de Regnier—whom she called the best of her Symbolist poets. She was determined to make her lectures lively—and of course understood by those who heard her. Of Verhaeren and his first book she wrote:

Then the storm broke, and howled about Verhaeren. The book was strong, vivid, brutal. It was as violent, as coarse, as full of animal spirits, as the pictures of Breugel the Elder, Teniers, or Jan Steen. As one of the critics said, "M. Verhaeren pierced like an abscess." The critics were horrified. . . . The battle rages furiously . . . it is a startling book, written with a sort of fury of colour. The red, fat flesh tints of Rubens have got into it, and the pages seem hot and smoky with perspiration.

Certainly these descriptions of the French poets whom Amy Lowell chose as texts for her lectures were consistent with the more colorful passages in her own polyphonic prose; she convinced herself that the company of French poets she had assembled wrote verse like hers, and that their poems were in a language closer to Boston Lowellese than French. In writing her lectures she had all the excitement of creating a battlefield for the defense of "free verse"; and if she never quite understood the nature of Symbolist poetry, she enjoyed telling her audience how unrestrained French poets such as Paul Fort could be, how he, with his long hair, looked like a poet, and how de Regnier was "the poet of the nude." At the last of her lectures, the lecture on Paul Fort in which she read his *Le Chant des Anglais* with its refrain of "It's a long way to Tipperary" ringing through paragraphs of machine-gun French in prose, her audience broke into tears. It was as if World War I (as imagined by Boston) had entered a Commonwealth Avenue front parlor, and its recording angel was Amy Lowell. From this day onward she was more than well-prepared to face larger audiences in New York, Chicago, or wherever an invitation to read aloud might send her.

The Years
of Fame

8

LTHOUGH AMY LOWELL had prepared her-
self to conquer larger scenes than Boston and though literary circles
in New York and Chicago knew her name, she had not entirely dismissed New England from the topography of her campaign. She
reenforced her earlier knowledge of Edwin Arlington Robinson's
poetry by inviting him out to dinner at Sevenels and in London
made her discovery of Robert Frost's poems. Among the new American poets Pound had talked about in London, Frost was one whom
she could read without pretense of knowing European culture or
Imagism; both Robinson and Frost represented kinds of intelligence
she knew well. She had attempted to find an American publisher
for Frost's *North of Boston*, which as recently as December 1914
had been reviewed and praised by Pound in Harriet Monroe's *Poetry*.
Meanwhile Henry Holt of New York had accepted the book and it
was in press. The most she could do in voicing her appreciation of
it was to write an article on the book and its author for a newly

135

founded weekly, *The New Republic,* edited with trenchant idealism by her friend Herbert Croly. Frost had just completed two years of living in the English countryside. In 1912 he had sold his farm at Derry, New Hampshire, and with the money from the sale the unknown thirty-nine-year-old poet took his wife and children for a change of scene to rural England. Amy Lowell was aware of Frost before he had heard of her, and though he was living in England at the time of her London visit in 1914, the twr Americans did not meet until after Frost returned to New Hampshire in March of 1915 and some time after he had read her review of *North of Boston* in the pages of *The New Republic.* According to legend, he had just stepped off the boat from England in New York and, walking up-town, bought *The New Republic* at a newsstand, opened it and read her article welcoming him to native shores. On this occasion, and later in 1917, she was among the most trenchant of his American admirers.

In writing of Frost Amy Lowell had an opportunity to display the most enduring of her reflections on New England and its people, on her kinship to and her opinions of them. She had no need for re-search, or to prove her self-appointed right to be called a "foremost Imagist." Though she herself was no more than a year older than Frost, both in her appearance and manner of writing she felt old enough to speak of him in the maternal voice of an elder New England generation.

On his return in the first flush of becoming famous, Frost had a discreetly mannered yet boyish personality. Unlike his more spectacu-lar contemporaries, Vachel Lindsay, Carl Sandburg, as well as Amy Lowell herself, his appearance on lecture platforms held all the graces of formal ease and unaffected understatement. He seemed younger than he was, and as he read aloud his dramatic narratives from *North of Boston* his voice, often dropping to a whisper, had lyrical qualities that modulated rather than stressed whatever his-trionics his lines required. His six years of teaching at Pinkerton Academy in New Hampshire, followed by a year of teaching psy-chology in that state's Normal School, and then his two years' resi-dence abroad probably gave him authoritative yet cheerful poise in facing an audience. If a number of the characters in his pastoral narratives were distinctly rural, the poet himself was far above the expression of ungainly rural mannerisms. In the years when many poets mounted the platform to read their writings aloud, Frost was a welcome exception to the rule of strained and overtly dramatic performances. Photographs of an earlier Frost than the white-haired figure of today present a handsome, slender young man in formal dress. At public readings a neatly tailored dinner jacket, worn with ease, accented a manner that was both engaging and precise. He was at the furthest removed from the image of a wild-eyed young poet or of a young provincial, fresh from the farm, wearing a "store-bought" suit of clothes to meet the club women who had come to hear him read his poems. His voice allowed his poems to speak for themselves.

In reading and hearing about him, Amy Lowell was seriously impressed. She saw him as an "intuitive" poet, one who though born in San Francisco—and who had lived there for the first ten years of his life—had adopted New England, where after his father's death in the west he went with his mother to stay with his paternal grandfather. In reading his poems she was surprised to learn that no references to the earliest years of his childhood in the west were visible, that his affinity to rural New England was complete—and that all the observations in his verse were unmistakably gathered at first hand from New England acres, small towns, and a homogeneous people. In writing of Frost she found occasion to say bluntly, critically that his *North of Boston*

. . . reveals a disease which is eating into the vitals of our New England life, at least in its rural communities.

What is there [she wrote, and in the spirit of her Lowell ancestry] in the hard, vigorous climate of these states which plants the seeds of degeneration? Is the violence and ugliness of their religious belief the cause of these twisted and tortured lives? Have the sane, full-blooded men all been drafted away to the cities, or the West, leaving behind only feeble remainders of a once fine stock?

In commenting on Frost's poem "Home Burial" she continued:

Catholic countries, with their insistence upon consecrated ground in which to lay the dead, give no chance for a horror like this. [The burial of a child in a field on its parents' property.] In England, a state church makes such a situation practically impossible. Happily it is unusual, even in New England, but what a travesty of happiness our vaunted freedom has led us into! The old pioneers came here to be free, God-fearing, and upright; and, behold, they are decayed and demoralized.

A poet might well object to having a moral and religious editorial written into quotations from his text, but in her commentaries on Frost and Robinson, Amy Lowell was at her best. She saw the literal environment, the landscape and its people, out of which Frost's poetry came; she saw how steadily he had rejected the influences he might well have acquired during his stay in England. She insisted— and justly enough—that

. . . his imagination is bounded by his life, he is confined within the limits of his experience (or at least what might have been his experience) and bent all one way like the wind-blown trees of New England hill-sides.

With less sureness of taste and understanding of Frost's poetry, she argued that it lacked the resources of dialect in its writing and she quoted James Russell Lowell's *The Biglow Papers* to prove her point. Her grandfather's cousin was, of course, very different from the kind of poet Frost became; their only likeness was that both knew certain aspects of the rural New England temperament and gave it life. But throughout the latter years of her literary career, James Russell Lowell haunted her. From the same source of Lowell civic consciousness, she felt an identity with the entire region of New England. When she wrote of New England's "decadence," she wrote with the same air of authority that Theodore Roosevelt breathed when he warned the people of the United States to have more children and not to indulge in the dangers of "race suicide."

Her comments on Robinson were no less authorative. She knew how clearly the town of Gardiner in Maine had remained a central point of reference in the poet's psyche. She wrote,

I know of no place in America so English in atmosphere as Gardiner. Standing on the broad, blue Kennebec, the little town nestles proudly beside that strange anomaly in an American city—the Manor House. For Gardiner has, so far as custom is concerned, possessed a squire for over two hundred years. And this gentleman's house is as truly the "Great House," as that in any hamlet in England. A fine Tudor mansion of grey stone with rounded bow windows, it stands on a little hill above the river, and even the railroad tracks which modern commercialism has incon-siderately laid along the nearer bank, cannot take away from it its air of dominating dignity.

It is not only in appearance that Gardiner house harks back to English tradition. It is a house not only in material fact, but in genealogical, for there have been Gardiners of Gardiner ever since the first fox-hunting squire transferred himself and his dogs to the New World . . .

At the time the Robinson family went to live in Gardiner, a momentary cloud hung over the fortunes of the "Great House." The openhanded hospitality of a hundred years was showing its effect, and the Gardiner family possessed their house, some of their land, and but little else. The owner was doing all that thrift and skill could do to repair the mistakes of his ancestors, but in order to accomplish this he was engaged in business in Boston. The house was vacant for months at a time, much of it was out of repair, outlying acres had been sold. Still the owner clung to his ancestral hall, to raise it, as he has done, like a phoenix from the ashes. . . . In Mr. Robinson's childhood, it stood as a pathetic monument of the folly of attempting to graft the old order of things upon the new.

Amy Lowell then explained that her image of the "Great House" was not to be given a literal interpretation, that in Robinson's psyche it had more meaning than any description of its appearance could convey. It was associated with the melancholy aspect of Robinson's poetry; its air of a precarious gentility, its reticence, its belonging to the "old order"—all were written in the speech of ironic commentary. She found Robinson "noble," and in meeting the middle-aged poet, who if he spoke at all, spoke slowly and with painful deliberation, she respected his silences. He responded to her with the same seriousness and courtesy. Her "Great House" was Sevenels which Robinson understood and respected; his tenderness in writing to her—and he was always careful to avoid hurting her feelings— was that of one who for many years had lived alone and was writing to a woman who was essentially alone, carrying the burden of an unwieldy body. She was not aware of his wit, yet she understood his shyness; she was never to see a side of Robinson that showed itself to Thornton Wilder, who when walking with Robinson through the grounds of the MacDowell Colony where both were spending the summer months noticed Elinor Wylie, Jean Starr Untermeyer, and Leonora Speyer in the distance bearing down toward them. The three women were famous literary beauties of the hour; they worshipped Robinson and sought whatever opportunities they could to speak with him in the effort to break through his invisible wall of shyness. Robinson drew Wilder out of their view behind a tree and murmured "O implacable Aphrodite!" and with these words retreated to his studio.

Amy Lowell would have called Robinson's remark "ironic" but, with the same silent understanding which he extended to her, she guessed at the motives for his retreats and evasions in meeting people. In stressing the Gardiner "Great House" she had also described the aristocratic aspect of Robinson's poetry—that side of his character hidden behind his shabbily genteel appearance, his tall figure— slightly stooped—and his near-sighted eyes, sharply lit behind pol- ished, rimless eyeglasses. She knew his sense of family pride as well as she knew the results of his New England heritage, his tendency to take an austere view of life and to withhold his sentiments. Mean- while, his relationship with her was not much unlike the rapport he had established with President Theodore Roosevelt, who some years earlier had appointed himself one of Robinson's patrons, had given him a sinecure for four years (1905 to 1909) in New York's Federal Custom House. Amy Lowell reminded Robinson of Roosevelt: her explosive, vigorous manner, her executive poise, her determined cheerfulness in public, her ability to act while others stepped aside, her peculiar slang in speech and in writing were clear to Robinson. His letters are proof that he was at ease with her; they could at least exchange courtesies and small kindnesses without constraint. In a sense, they spoke a common language—and both were innately con- servative.

It is not surprising that Amy Lowell found in Robinson a poet of heroic stature, one of "the most important poets of his nation." Later, when she came to rewrite her papers and reviews to be included in her *Tendencies in Modern American Poetry,* her essay on Robinson was among the best of her ventures into prose. Though she had once said it was her intention "to put cosmic poetry on the blink," none of that determination marred her remarks on Robinson; on the con- trary, she was happy to admit that "the spirituality of Mr. Robinson's work is tonic and uplifting."

Her first public appearance outside of Boston was at the March 31, 1915 meeting of the Poetry Society of America in New York. She had been invited to give advance publicity to *Some Imagist Poets* which Houghton Mifflin were publishing in 'April and was allowed five minutes for her recital. Members of the Poetry Society had already made up their minds that she was an invader upon what they regarded sacred ground in poetry. Hers was a Bostonian invasion of New York; her conquest of the field—if she were to make the attempt at all—would be over their dead bodies. And whatever the members of the Society lacked in poetic reputation, they made up for in forensic skill. They saw Amy Lowell as a formidable champion of all that was foreign to their own taste, a representative of all that was terrifying, horrible and "new." Few discerned that Amy Lowell was more conservative than themselves; they preferred to view her as a dangerous innovator and intruder, a "radical" and a near relation of "Revolutionary Ideas."

On that evening Amy Lowell took the initiative by reading aloud her latest experiment in what she called "polyphonic prose," her "Spring Day." The name she gave her experiment was new enough, but the form she used had been known in French literature since Baudelaire wrote his poems in prose. Still, in the heat of the moment, the Poetry Society rose up against the unexpectedly large figure of the President of Harvard's sister and literary history was totally forgotten. The clamour began as she read the first section of her paragraphs from "Bath":

Little spots of sunshine lie on the surface of the water and dance, dance, and their reflections wobble deliciously over the ceiling; a stir of my finger sets them whirring, reeling. I move a foot, and the planes of light in the water jar. I lie back and laugh, and let the green-white water, the sun-flawed beryl water, flow over me. The day is almost too bright to bear, the green water covers me from the too bright day. I will lie here awhile and play with the water and the sun spots.

To Amy Lowell's audience it was impossible to resist a literal reading of these lines; it saw Lawrence Lowell's sister in a bathtub, and what seems harmless and childish today was at that moment heard as dangerous exhibitionism. In the Lowell family there was great delight in bathing naked in the open air at lake resorts and on broad ocean beaches; the President of Harvard himself enjoyed that liberty and won a case in court against a spying neighbor who watched his bathing near his summer home. Seeing the large woman stand before them, wicked and ridiculous associations floated through the minds of her audience; she had successfully shocked them by her experiment in impressionism. In half a day she could write down hundreds of "experimental verses" of that kind—fragmentary notes of what she liked to touch, to see, to hear. She was a writer of *virtu*. Like her

brother Percival, who during his stay in Japan, delighted in buying
coloured paper fishes, kites, flags, and bright boxes, she loved to
recall to mind many small, familiar or curious objects—and then
describe them. A spring day gave her many objects, some as large as
the blue sky itself, all of which she jotted down in breathless, note-
taking order; that was her pleasure. On this occasion the recital of
her pleasures brought with it arguments. Was "Spring Day" poetry
or not? It is probable—since so many of her inspirations came
from books she had recently and hastily read—that her "Spring
Day" had its source in a quick reading of Rupert Brooke's popular poem, "The Great Lover." Brooke wrote, and these lines delighted many:

> These I have loved:
>   White plates and cups, clean-gleaming,
> Ringed with blue lines; and feathery, faery dust;
> Wet roofs, beneath the lamp-light; the strong crust
> Of friendly bread; and many-tasting food;
> Rainbows; and the blue bitter smoke of wood;
> And radiant raindrops couching in cool flowers;
> And flowers, themselves, that sway through sunny hours.

And the list ran onward for twenty-five more lines, each "lovely"
thing different in kind and texture, which showed a brilliant lack of
discrimination as well as a high-spirited lack of feeling. Most of all,
the list displayed an extraverted, youthful glow of enthusiasm for all
things on earth, and an unprofound, quick-glancing eye. "Spring
Day" lacked the youthful impetus and felicity of the things Brooke
choose to "love" and list, but the kind of writing that it represented
was in high fashion in 1915. Amy Lowell preferred to shock her
audience with "Bath" and to call her listing an experiment in
"polyphonic prose." She was rewarded by spontaneous antagonism.
The controversy over the propriety of writing "Bath" at all gave her
quickly earned notoriety—something for newspapers to quote as "the
new poetry."

The little storm she aroused at the Poetry Society was one of her
most easily accomplished public victories. Her paragraphs on taking
a bath gave her reputation an air of pagan recklessness that amused
some readers, charmed others, shocked a few, and added to her
legend the image of a large bath tub with a large woman enjoying

her bath within it. This was even more amusing to newspaper reporters than the image of the woman smoking a cigar.

Her poem, "Bath," and her recital of it gave further discussions of "free verse" and the "new poetry" a rakish air. It proved that a reading by Amy Lowell on the "new poetry" would receive immediate publicity. From then onward she had no difficulty in convincing her publishers that her books would sell. Meanwhile her readers and audiences had caught something of the exuberance that radiated from her personality. Her poems flashed and sounded their lines, wheeling colors and loud exclamations:

> Hey! My daffodil-crowned,
> Slim and without sandals!
> As the sudden spurt of flame upon darkness
> So my eyeballs are startled with you,
> Supple-limbed youth among the fruit-trees,
> Light runner through tasselled orchards.
> You are an almond flower unsheathed
> Leaping and flickering between the budded branches.

Seen as an after image of a large nude in a bath tub, these lines take on a curious air of naughtiness; their actual meaning was slight enough. Although one hears echoes of Ezra Pound's early poems through them, Amy Lowell's experiments in free verse began to be accepted as a way to write the "new" poetry. One could scarcely read them without a smile, and they reflected, more than all else, the unguarded ease with which they were so heartily written.

Amy Lowell's air of spontaneity in her lectures made free verse and "new poetry" seem more "radical" and "revolutionary" than they were. It was true that for the moment and in her own writing she broke down the usual distinctions between poetry and highly tinted fragments of impressionistic prose. Had she been a painter there is little doubt that she would have been able to dash off fifty water colors between lunch time and a friendly cup of tea at four in the afternoon. (During these very months between lecture engagements outside of Boston, she frequently had tea with her friendly critic, Josephine Preston Peabody Marks. They celebrated a truce in their relationship over hot, invigorating cups of tea which had been deeply spiked with rum.) In addition to and perhaps because of Amy Lowell's rising celebrity on lecture platforms, the kind of free verse she read aloud had results beyond the applause she received from audiences. Her spontaneously written verses encouraged school girls to write millions of impressionistic fragments for the delight of their school teachers and startled yet happy parents. If these fragments could be called "poetry," then almost every child between the ages of six and eight could write it. During the following ten years in America, the "freedom" of Amy Lowell's verse led to the discovery of many girl prodigies. In grade schools throughout the United States something like a children's crusade for "free verse" took fire. Inhibitions which had withheld the writing of verse were quickly overcome, and if a few children still persisted in writing their verse in rhyme, these prejudices may be traced to parents who held to conventional ideas concerning poetry. In New York, teachers and magazine editors—even publishers—inflamed their fancies with verses written or dictated by children who could scarcely read. It is probable that Amy Lowell, even to the end of her life, remained unaware of her influence on the education of children in the United States.

Meanwhile the Macmillan Company was willing to publish Amy Lowell's lectures on *Six French Poets*, but they suggested that she translate in full the poems she quoted in the text, which meant the addition of 139 pages, a formidable task in itself, which she approached with characteristic energy and speed. The translations were the triumph of her personality over art, and in spirit they resembled her own experiments in "polyphonic prose": fanciful, hurried in movement and balanced only by her own vigorous common sense. For a book of its kind, it sold extremely well; and the reasons for its popularity may be found in the American curiosity and good will toward learning—provided it was "new" and could be quickly read and absorbed.

It is also probable that the book attracted readers because it was known to have been written by the President of Harvard's sister. And still another reason for its semi-popularity was because World War I had awakened patriotic curiosity toward all things French. The book was written in a language that could be understood in women's clubs. It assumed that its readers had scarcely heard of (which was true enough in the United States) the more recent descendants of the French Symbolists. Naturally Amy Lowell's choice was made up of poets whose poems were less intense, less "morbid" than others and could be read aloud in her own clear-voiced, yet impressionistic style. It was also true that she herded her six French poets together as though they had been bright school boys who were now about to receive prizes and medals from her hands. As Lytton Strachey wrote in his review entitled "French Poets through Boston Eyes," "Nothing could well surpass the patient sympathy with which Miss Lowell scrutinises her poets, her refined enthusiasm for their achievements, her enlightened tolerance of their faults." Although Strachey's remarks seemed at the moment unnecessarily cruel—and though Amy Lowell never forgot the injury to her ego that his irony inflicted upon her ventures into scholarship—the truth was that she patronized the poets whom she claimed as her "discoveries," whether she found them in her rapid readings of French poetry or at home among young poets of her day.

In her lectures, delivered in Boston and New York, she enjoyed the excitement of being greeted as a center of controversy, and when members of the Poetry Society in New York refuted her statements on "Modern Metres and the Poets Who Write Them," she exercised her wits against them. On one occasion (November 1915) her friendship with Louis Untermeyer, who had favorably reviewed *Sword Blades and Poppy Seed*, took root. He alone of that company came to her defense. The heat of her lectures made way for an attack on the Puritan tradition, which since the arrival of a "new poetry" movement in 1914 had been the target of the younger generation. She saw, and in the spirit of 1915, the figure of Emily Dickinson as "A true pagan poet shut up in a cage of a narrow provincial Puritanism." While Amy Lowell shocked conservative readers of American poetry, she won over to her side many of those who felt themselves to be "radical" and in revolt against conservative opinions.

Today, in the light of Thomas H. Johnson's three-volume definitive edition of her poems, Emily Dickinson is clearly seen as one who wrote within the New England tradition of dissent, rather than existing as a "pagan poet" confined within the toils of Puritanism. Actually, her position was not too far removed from that of Thoreau; her spirit was as youthful, as fresh, as independent as his, and she was as distinctly regional as he. She was a mystic in nearly the same sense that Emerson was a mystic. Her inspirations were "transcendental." Her motives, as far as we can reconstruct them from her poems, were pure. She was an unchurched New Englander whose "transcendentalism" sought out and found an affinity with the poetry of the divine George Herbert which she quietly transcribed and admired. But in 1915 these aspects of Emily Dickinson were shrouded by the vague idea that she was a "rebel" and ten years later there were many fervent biographical speculations as to whether or not she had a "lover," and if so, who he was. The complete discovery of her poetry awaited the patient researches of Professor Johnson.

As she read Joyce Kilmer's interview with Josephine Peabody Marks written for *The New York Times* during January of 1916, Amy Lowell saw danger to her position in Boston, all the more so since Mrs. Marks was represented as an enemy of "free verse." The truce which had been established between the two women was beginning to cloud over. Amy Lowell took all adverse comments on unrhymed poetry as a personal affront and a threat to the supremacy that newspaper publicity had given *her*. She was not content until two months later she talked Joyce Kilmer into writing an interview with *her* on the subject of the "New Poetry." * This was one of her active invasions of New York; she visited her editor at the Macmillan Company with a new manuscript of verse, *Men, Women and Ghosts*, and that evening she spoke at a dinner at which she asked for hisses, "just to make me feel comfortable and at home." During the years of her rising reputation, she never underrated the attraction of always seeming to be at the center of controversy. She knew its value in making friends among lesser known writers than she. Unrecognized young writers are often willing to attribute a lack of immediate success to seeming "radical," or to being "too new" for popular opinion. In their eyes Amy Lowell became their champion, and if not their patroness (which they half hoped she would become), their means of becoming better known to a large and indifferent world. The air of cheerfulness that she sustained in public gave her the authority of a successful actress on the Broadway stage. Her little victory over Josephine Peabody (since the older woman assured her that Kilmer had misquoted her unpleasant remarks about "free verse") had restored Amy Lowell's position in Boston's women's clubs.

* This was the same Joyce Kilmer who had become famous through a poem called "Trees," and a popular book of verse under the same title. He then became a reporter and special feature writer for *The New York Times*.

With this victory behind her, Amy Lowell and Mrs. Russell left
New York for public engagements in Chicago; Mrs. Russell to play
monologue parts in three short plays written and directed by Mary
Aldis, and Amy Lowell to deliver another lecture on the "New
Poetry." It was then that she began her long, enthusiastic friendship
with Carl Sandburg and was introduced to Edgar Lee Masters whose
Spoon River Anthology had begun its memorable career. Amy
Lowell's lack of affectation and her frankness of manner had their
direct appeal to both men. If she was often patronizing she was never
snobbish, for because she was a Lowell, she did not need to be a
snob. These were reasons enough to promote friendliness between
all three. But there were other reasons why Masters and Sandburg
felt at ease with her. Both men earned their livings in the busy,
vigorous world of Chicago—Masters as a lawyer, Sandburg as a
newspaperman; whatever recognition they received had come "the
hard way," and their writings showed the results of everyday, practical experiences. Their realistic view of the world was not far
removed from Amy Lowell's belief that one prospered by the use of
"business" sense, and like them she detested signs of Bohemian
extremes and artiness. She could talk their language with sustained
energy and force. Sandburg had written "the past is a bucket of
ashes" a statement that was to become the theme of what Amy
Lowell seemed to say about poetry. It would have been strange if
they had not been friends.

When Amy Lowell came to write her *Tendencies in American
Poetry*—published in 1917, a year and a half after her enthusiastic
meeting with Masters and Sandburg—all the virtues of her "common
sense" were predominant. Of Masters she wrote:

Mr. Masters is the author of a number of books, but one has made his
fame; and it seems probable that only one will outlive the destructive
work of time. But this one is so remarkable that it may very well come to
be considered among the great books of American literature. I refer, of
course, to "The Spoon River Anthology."

She was correct then, and the same judgment is appropriate today.
Fashions have changed. Masters' sentiments and teachings now seem
outmoded, but the essential value of his *Spoon River* is not. He was
born in 1869 in Kansas and brought up in Illinois. He had inherited
a Middle Westerner's post-Civil War disillusionment, which formed

the background during his own youth for the spread of Populism.
The cyclic recurrence of "panics" in Wall Street, the rapid, uneven
progress of an American industrial revolution made obvious the fact
that the rich got richer as the poor neared the level of starvation.
The frontier civilization of the Middle West was not merely raw in
its external signs of rugged living, but was raw and crude in its
efforts to survive in its economic life. The "tough-minded" concentrated upon making money and getting ahead. The "soft-minded"
poured their idealism, which had been inherited from Emerson and
Thoreau, into the Populist movement, which in turn was reinforced
by the sentimental iconoclasm of Ingersoll. It is not surprising that
late in life Masters complained that the cultural climate in which
he grew up was destructive to "sensitive natures." Exciting as the
conflict between "tough-minded" pragmatists and "soft-minded" ideal-
ists might have been, the stream of thinking that divided them was
hopelessly shallow, transformed as it was into muddled, muddy, ill-
informed channels of Evangelism. The "soft-minded" were, of course,
doomed to lose each battle. It was not until Masters had reached
forty-five that his insights and intelligence cleared sufficiently for
him to write Spoon River, yet even then in the writing of that book,
inspiration came to him as though he took dictation from a dream.
W. B. Yeats, on one of his visits to New York, quoted what he
called the most memorable line in American poetry, a line from
Spoon River, "All, all are sleeping, sleeping, on the hill," and then
asked who wrote it? Masters who lived in his habitual discontent
many years after the book was published (he died in 1948) did not
outlive its fame.

    In appearance he was the last man who might be taken for a poet;
his profession had left its mark on him: square shouldered, bald
headed, blunt-fingered and with rimless glasses shielding fixed grey
eyes, he looked the part of an able, honest, sturdy Chicago lawyer.
The very writing of Spoon River was in itself a phenomenon. Author
of many unsuccessfully traditional verses, Masters was persuaded by
a friend, William Marion Reedy, editor of a journal, Reedy's Mirror,
to jot down unrhymed epitaphs of the many characters Masters had
once hoped to recreate in a Middle Western novel which was to
have been as massive as Tolstoy's War and Peace. In Masters' eyes
the epitaphs spoken in monologues were never poems, but were

speeches that had taken their form from his reading of prose adaptations from the *Greek Anthology*. Prose versions of Dante's *Purgatorio* contributed further models for him to follow. In spite of Masters' doubts as to whether or not the *Spoon River* monologues were poems, Reedy held him to the task of writing them, and soon the writing of *Spoon River* became Masters' obsession. He found himself writing his monologues during telephone conversations with his clients. His daily life was that of a man who was in a trance; and soon after the last pages of the book had been written he fell ill. Miss Harriet Monroe read the proofs for him, and by the time he had recovered, he was the famous author of *The Spoon River Anthology* but his legal practice had melted away. In Chicago no one would trust a lawyer who was better known for writing poetry than winning cases in a court room.

Nor was he able at any later period in his life to repeat the experience of the strange trance into which he had fallen. Since his practice had left him, he turned to writing unmemorable books of verse, novels and biographies. Of his biographies only one has survived its moment of publication—his life of Vachel Lindsay which was the deeply inspired work of selfless devotion to the memory of a fellow Middle Westerner.

His self-sufficient sturdiness, his crankiness (and in later years he grew to hate Chicago as well as the legend of Abraham Lincoln, for he had turned against the idealistic Populism of his youth) drew respect from Amy Lowell. He was as staunchly his own master as she was mistress of Sevenels.

Yet she was even more at ease with Sandburg, and the Sandburg she knew was a young Socialist whose father had come to Galesburg, Illinois, from Sweden. Sandburg's free verse was far closer to the kind of free verse she wrote than Masters'; to her he seemed a generation younger than the lawyer who had become the author of *Spoon River*. She felt herself at liberty to praise and scold the younger man. Her manner of writing about him was that of an earnest schoolmistress taking a kindly interest in a wrong-headed, yet always promising pupil; he had made her feel that she could guide him and perhaps wean him away from Socialist "propaganda." "So excellently endowed a poet as Mr. Sandburg should beware," she wrote. In her remarks on Sandburg it was clear that the warmth of her maternal affections had been aroused, and at the same time and in his company, she felt free to express *her* opinions on social justice. Of Sandburg's poem in praise of a dynamiter: "a lover of life, a lover of children, a lover of all free, reckless laughter everywhere—lover of red hearts and red blood the world over," she welcomed the chance to say:

That a man loves children, particularly his own, is a good and beautiful thing. But to use that fact as a dazzling screen to obscure the horror of his trade of blowing other men, who possibly also love their children, into atoms, because of a difference in opinions, may be fairly stated as faulty vision on the part of the poet . . . He does not justify his dynamiter, it is true, but he looks at him obliquely, leaving out what he does not wish to see, because of his sympathy with the opinions the man represents. Propaganda is the pitfall of poets . . . propaganda seizes him again in "The Right to Grief." What justification can so honest a poet find for sneering at a father's grief over his dead child and calling it "perfumed sorrow"? Is not grief stark and terrible in all its forms, whether it come to rich or poor? The reformers hurt their cause by showing such a lack of knowledge of human nature . . . Whether the poems are in regular English or in the slang of the streets, they are full of personality. Written, some in *vers libre,* some in a rhythmical prose, some in a cross between the two, they seldom fail to justify their form to the ear.

In these remarks one has a nearly perfect recording of Amy Lowell's voice in conversation—her love of expressing downright opinions, of exerting her intelligence in terms of argumentative talk rather than in those of forceful writing. Certainly in these lines she was earnest enough, speaking in what she called, "regular English," directly to Sandburg, as though she had welcomed him to Sevenels and enjoyed the pleasure of marshaling him into the company of poets she admired. Later, when poets of Left Wing sympathies tried to win her over to their causes, she replied to them in the same language with which she had so vigorously scolded Sandburg. She reserved her sentimental affections for small works of craftsmanship on the subject of dogs, cats or horses. She was far too tough-minded to be swayed in the direction of political causes that were frequently disguised as "humanitarian" and filled with so-called "lofty aspirations." She coolly and sanely rejected appeals for birth control, Socialism and Communism. Although she allowed Louis Untermeyer (who for a brief interval was poetry editor of *The Masses*) to accept her poems for that magazine and to give her friendly pub-

licity within its pages, she refused to sponsor any of the causes that
The Masses advanced. In matters requiring business and political
discrimination, her mind was firm and often just. Nor could she be
bullied into joining causes that her instincts rejected. She had been
too long accustomed to bullying others into accepting *her* opinions.

When she spoke of the character of Sandburg's *vers libre* she was
also describing the kind of verse she was writing, the kind of prose
she wrote. For this reason she could not give Sandburg less than the
highest praise. She loved his lighter verses, particularly "Fog," and
the impressionistic touches in several of his other pieces. "We see
Mr. Sandburg approaching the Imagist technique," she said, and it
was clear that she approved. As in her lectures on "Six French Poets,"
her judgment was colored by a desire to stress the presence of World
War I; she delighted in finding that Sandburg had written "war
poems," which proved that he was unreservedly "contemporary,"
and for her purpose—which was to guide new poets—"up to date"
and "new." His poems convinced her that they—and the poet himself
—were safely arriving in the same covered wagon she had appointed
herself to drive. Sandburg and his "Chicago Poems" helped to give
her the assurance that her leadership was of national scope. She felt
that she could attract even the poets of the Middle West who were
friends of Harriet Monroe and wean them away from *Poetry* and
into her orbit of influence and publicity.

Her attitude toward Vachel Lindsay, the third poet of the Middle
Western triad, was less friendly. There were several reasons for her
lack of feeling for him—and one was his skill in reading his verse
aloud in public. At that time Sandburg had not developed his gift
for entertaining large audiences, and Masters had no talent for reading aloud in lecture halls. It is probable that in so far as public
readings of verse attracted audiences, Amy Lowell felt that Lindsay
was a rival; in this respect he could take care of himself and was
certainly not in need of her maternal protection. Yet there were other
reasons why Lindsay failed to excite her sympathies; and when they
met at the house of a mutual acquaintance in New York, they found
little to say to each other. Vachel Lindsay's poetry did not fall into
the category of *vers libre* which Amy Lowell grew fond of presenting
to startled Chicago lecture goers and bewildered club women. Nor
were Lindsay's personality and his appearance as a fair-haired, awk-

ward farm boy, neatly dressed in "store-clothes" of appeal to her. She
was adept at small talk and quickened turns of literary gossip; he was
not. He was both impractical and earnest; when he travelled to
England and out to Oxford on a reading tour, his mother went with
him—and if wine was served at dinner Mrs. Lindsay not only refused
to drink it, but delivered temperance speeches to the company. Lindsay's taste, or rather lack of taste, in food was no less unsophisticated.
Since he liked both ice cream and thick broiled steaks, he absent-
mindedly ordered the first served on top of the other. His appearance and manner closely resembled those of a journeyman evange-
list, one who travels from one small American town to another to
conduct "revivals." He held his audiences with the same powers of
attraction which were exerted by Dylan Thomas in the 1950's.

The writings and careers of Lindsay and Thomas have other
strong parallels, even to the semi-tragic ending of their lives. Both
poets had read and were attracted to the poetry of the Pre-Raphaelites: Lindsay to Dante Gabriel Rossetti, Thomas to Swinburne. Both
poets were indigenous in the expression of their verse: Lindsay
American and Thomas Welsh. Both poets were of evangelical
temper and were well within the Christian orbit of religious belief.
One of Lindsay's last books, *Every World Is a Circus* can be equated
in its successes and its failures to Thomas's *Under Milk Wood* which
was one of his last books. Both books celebrate the glories of being a
child in a provincial environment, both are an exhibition of childlike
fantasies, and both lend their merits to semi-dramatic performances:
Lindsay's to dance-drama; Thomas's to a BBC performance on the
British wireless. Amy Lowell would probably have kept the same
distance between herself and Thomas as she did between herself
and Lindsay.

Only the more discerning among his readers and his audiences
were aware of the saintliness, the childlike innocence of his gifts,
the thoroughly Utopian nature of his idealism which never ceased
to hope that the town in which he was born, Springfield, Illinois,
would prove itself to be a paradise on earth. He was as divinely
inspired as the eighteenth century British poet Christopher Smart,
and as far removed as Smart from "normal" company in a drawing
room. His cheerfully ecstatic manner, his habit of throwing his head
back and closing his eyes as he chanted his verses, his exaggerated

politeness—a bow from the waist—as he was introduced, made him uneasy, difficult company at tea or dinner. Only in middle age, after his mother's death, and himself newly married to a very young woman, would he relax by smoking a cigarette or taking a small measure of whisky in a tall glass of soda. Writing his poetry, or the recital of it, held the same excitement for him as the drinking of strong spirits had for North American Indians. Nor was Amy Lowell's liking for him increased when she heard gossip of his ecstatic admiration for one of her friends, the poet, Sara Teasdale. She was never unkind to him, yet when they were together in a room neither was at ease, and both fell silent.

The success of her invasion of Chicago became typical of her receptions elsewhere. Editors of magazines and of book-sections on newspapers found themselves overwhelmed by visits from Amy Lowell with demands (and these were usually obeyed) that her books be prominently and favorably reviewed. She herself sought out friends to review her books, and she reported these conquests to her friend and editor, Edward Marsh of the Macmillan Company. In the United States her *Six French Poets* gave additional weight to her appearances on the platform. As a writer she had become as well known in her chosen field as her brother Percival was when he established his reputation as an authority on far eastern culture in Japan and Korea.

9

THE THREE YEARS from 1916 through 1918 were for Amy Lowell her years of rising fame and public accomplishment. Of the many poets whose names were well known during World War I, hers had gained first place. The accelerating events of the war in Europe had brought to America a sense of immediate change in habits of living and thinking: if new modes of warfare were now in sight, it then seemed inevitable that new forms of literature—however experimental, however difficult to understand— should come into being and should continue to change, to bring with them new theories, new subject matter, renewed feelings and excitements, a new language, new means of expression (particularly in poetry) and new personalities. Interest in contemporary poetry— which had been stimulated in the Middle West by the founding of Harriet Monroe's magazine, *Poetry,* and the popular success of Edgar Lee Masters' *Spoon River Anthology* and in the East, by the "discovery" of Edna St. Vincent Millay's first book, *Renascence and*

Other Poems—gave Amy Lowell large audiences for her lectures and readings. Due to the excitement caused by seeing newspaper headlines of "war in Europe and because France had been invaded by Germany, sentimental attachments to France were easily aroused in the United States, and these attachments were among the reasons why Amy Lowell's *Six French Poets* was bought and read outside of colleges and universities.

Moreover, Amy Lowell's books, both in prose and verse, were like informal conversations on timely subjects. Those who read books at all seldom neglected to buy among the novels they read a few books of the "new poetry," and among the new poets least difficult to understand, was Amy Lowell. When in her prefaces to her neatly printed books of poems (the format still designed in the manner of Keats's first book: cloth back and paper sides with firmly pasted labels on which appeared their titles) she explained the virtues of her polyphonic prose, her readers felt they had learned a new phrase with which to describe the newest kind of contemporary poetry. In advancing claims for her own experiments in *vers libre,* her manner was that of one who was happy to teach—even as she protested that "poetry should not try to teach," and that poems like trees should not be asked "to teach us moral lessons." If her experiments in polyphonic prose looked strange enough in print, her arguments in their favor had the appearance of being dictated by well-reasoned expediency.

To her public she conveyed the impression that she led others: "I hope many poets will follow me in opening up the still hardly explored possibilities of *vers libre.*" To them she promised a short-cut to an "avant garde" literature, painlessly applied. She soon found a number of easily converted readers and her enthusiasm seemed harmlessly contagious. In a volume of her narratives, *Can Grande's Castle,* all written in polyphonic prose—their stories taken (as she confessed) from books in her library—passages of description were broken by exclamatory "Tut! Tut!," "Bang! *Bang!* BANG!," "Pup-pup-pup-pup." In one copy, read in 1918, an enchanted reader wrote in its margins "great stuff" and "golly!" and in disappointment at the bottom of one page, "Terrible! It's a shame." The majority of Amy Lowell's readers were caught up in the excitement of watching and hearing description of a German air raid over Italy:

Blackness. One poor devil gone, and the attacking plane is still air-worthy though damaged. It wobbles out of the search-light and dis-appears, rocking. Two Taubes shake themselves free of the tangle, they glide down—down—all round them are ribbons of "flaming onions," they avoid them and pass on down, close over the city, unscathed, so close you can see the black crosses on their wings with a glass. Rifles crack at them from roofs. Pooh! You might as well try to stop them with pea shooters.

Certainly this burst of exclamations has the illusion of being talked rather than written. To read Amy Lowell's polyphonic prose with its irregular passages of phrases that fell into rhyme, was very much like hearing her at the tea table, earnest, but not profoundly serious, intelligent, yet wary in the meaning of what she had to say. More than a few of her younger readers, brought under the spell of Amy Lowell's commands to see and hear, echoed her enthusiasms and were convinced that writing verse resembled marching in a parade. In her narrative, "Sea-Blue and Blood-Red," a series of im-pressions hastily sketched on paper after reading about the career of Lord Nelson and the Napoleonic wars, the following lines appear:

Hip! Hip! Hip! The wheels roll into Vienna. Then what a to-do! Con-certs, Operas, Fireworks too. Dinners where one hundred six-foot grena-diers do the waiting at table. Such grandiloquence! Such splendid, regal magnificence!

Surely the author was enjoying herself with the same exuberance that she showed in dancing at "coming-out" parties in Boston many years ago, when she talked too loud in classrooms at Mrs. Cabot's School, and when she half-bullied, half-charmed her friend Mabel Cabot into the spirit of playing tomboyish games. She made the writing of polyphonic prose seem ridiculously easy—and always a red-cheeked, healthful exercise. There is little doubt that her early readers also enjoyed the literal display of fireworks in her verses: the sight of pin-wheels, fanciful pagodas, Japanese paper lanterns, the blaze of fire from the lips of cannons. All these had the character of brightly painted toys in a rich child's nursery—"And," as she wrote, "everything done to a hullabaloo," as noisy as a group of "spoiled" children at a picnic in New Hampshire or at the keyboard of a piano in a Boston Music-room.

Reread today, Amy Lowell's experiments reflect more of the child who received gifts sent by her brother Percival from Japan than they display any new technique in the writing of poetry. The willful rhymes, the sentences without verbs, the listing of nouns and of adjectives, the many exclamation points, as though the words were to be shouted rather than said aloud, are less shocking than they seemed to be when their author read them from a platform. It was Professor William M. Patterson of Columbia University who first observed that Amy Lowell's personality in print and on the platform was very like President Theodore Roosevelt's—more strenuous than forceful, more vigorous than firm. Roosevelt never questioned his right to fill the President's chair; other men may have questioned theirs or have felt a touch of humility upon entering high office— but not he. And, like Franklin Delano Roosevelt who came after him, he was consciously a member of the Roosevelt "dynasty." As a Lowell, Amy Lowell assumed self-appointed public leadership in modern poetry with the same conviction of her right to do so. John Jay Chapman who had a sane, and later disillusioned, perception of his early leader's character, wrote of Roosevelt in language that could be applied to Amy Lowell by her contemporaries:

He could do the most desperate things in the way of putting a friend down a well and shine on the world like Phoebus the morning afterwards. [Her relationships with Ezra Pound and with Josephine Preston Peabody illustrate this likeness.] I doubt whether he had a true friend, for his friends were dazed by him.

In a number of her friendships with American poets the same notation could be made of Amy Lowell's ability to charm, to dazzle her contemporaries; yet of true friends, Mrs. Russell, her companion, was a singular attachment. Even those who distrusted her ability as poet, were overwhelmed by her radiance as a hostess and dinner table companion; she shone down upon them.

Chapman went on to say that Roosevelt's followers called him "Galahad, Jack, the Giant Killer," and in much the same spirit as that of Roosevelt's young men, a number of younger American poets looked to Amy Lowell as a champion of modern verse. Like Roosevelt she attracted "alternate anathemas and hallelujas," and like him, she "really didn't know there was any principle at the bottom of the matter," but her grasp of "practical" literary politics—as well as the meaning of its gossip—kept her name before the public.

It was during this period of three years that she made the most of her personal likes and dislikes, her mannerisms and her eccentricities. A visitor to her house in Dublin, New Hampshire, reported that he saw her strolling the veranda, smoking a large calabash pipe; others noted that she changed her eyeglasses frequently—a habit which later, as she suffered deeper fatigue, was displayed on lecture platforms. In doing research for her narrative verses in *Can Grande's Castle* she read widely, voraciously, and she attempted to circumvent doctors' orders (which forbade her reading) by carrying in a basket a dozen pairs of pince-nez, each with a differently colored ribbon. This device showed the increasing strength of each pair of lenses, and each was hastily slipped on in ascending order as her fatigue deepened. In her later years, the reading of her notes and papers on the table before her strained her eyes. With considerable effort, since she could no longer stand behind the lectern, she propped herself in a chair behind the table, with her basket at her side. And as she read, the progress of her changing lenses would begin. Her eyeglasses became as much a part of her public accouterment as Theodore Roosevelt's—and these were added to the public's familiarity with her cigar and the image of her in a bathtub at Sevenels.

On entering a city for her lectures, her increasing stoutness made the use of taxicabs imperative. Necessary preparations and ceremonies attended her stays at the Hotel St. Regis in New York: a suite of five rooms was ordered in advance, which included a room for her maid as well as for Mrs. Russell. Instructions were given to cover all objects in the rooms—clocks, mirrors, bric-a-brac—that reflected light with dark cloths; these, and closed curtains to insure Amy Lowell's sleep from six in the morning to half-past-two in the afternoon. All engagements for lunch were cancelled and tea at five became the earliest hour at which a guest of Amy Lowell's could be received. With her companion, her maid, her luggage, an entrance through a hotel lobby became a cavalcade, and more than a mere entrance, a slow march and flourish. Directions and commands were issued in the progress. Wisely enough, for the sake of comfort and of having her own orders followed, she declined—whenever on tour— to accept invitations to stay at private homes. She could well afford the luxury of having a temporary "home" in her suite of rooms at a hotel. This provided a convenient place for interviews with newspaper reporters and private conversations with admirers: it kept her in command.

In the management and display of theatrical decor, Amy Lowell rivaled the rising prominence of Edna St. Vincent Millay. Amy Lowell was the distinguished character actress and Millay was the small, red-haired juvenile lead. Not unlike the public entrances and exits of Hollywood movie stars, the two women from New England in New York gave the "new poetry" a touch of theatrical brilliance that writers of poetry seldom achieved. Byron in early nineteenth-century London was the best known of their predecessors in creating a personal legend, and Edith Sitwell and Dylan Thomas may be called their most recent successors. Of all these, Amy Lowell had the greatest handicaps to master. It demanded intelligence, deft self-management and acquired knowledge of the world for her to surmount her childhood fears that she was ugly to look at and that "God made her a business man." She knew that she had been forced to make herself a poet. These handicaps took physical stamina and psychic courage to overcome.

At Sevenels the "business" of reading and writing verse went forward as though controlled by the general manager of a cotton mill; it was a large-scale industry that kept two secretaries busy typing manuscripts and Mrs. Russell alert to hear Amy Lowell reading aloud—as though in continual rehearsal for public readings—from countless pages of rewritten typescript. Nor was Mr. Marsh, Amy Lowell's editor at the Macmillan Company, allowed to relax, and the annually published series of *Some Imagist Poets* were guided, sales of each volume checked, and royalties paid their contributors, by Amy Lowell's hand at the Houghton Mifflin offices in Boston. Under her commands the mechanical details of Amy Lowell's production ran smoothly enough, and were administered with remarkable poise until midsummer of 1916.

On a country road in New Hampshire near Dublin, riding with Mrs. Russell at her side, Amy Lowell, good driver and lover of horses though she was, steered their way into a right-hand ditch with the carriage in danger of toppling over. Amy Lowell stepped from the carriage and lifted its rear wheel from the rut; the way was straightened again and she drove on. The price of that effort was an internal injury, a strain that later proved to be a rupture, an umbilical hernia.

In April 1917, when in a New York hotel, she attempted to lift a large brass bed into a position that she thought would ensure a few hours' sleep. She never recovered from these disasters. Although their sequel was a series of painful surgical operations, each followed by awkward periods of convalescence, she did not "give in to them." Before she had made up her mind to be a poet, before she had found the means of becoming a celebrity, she was well on the way toward being an imaginary invalid. Now that she was actually faced with continuous ill health, she forcefully resisted her accumulated illnesses. There is no doubt that Mrs. Russell's companionship had its influence upon keeping her alert and active; from Mrs. Russell's example, she re-enforced her own will to be an actress, to take on, as best she could, a routine of public appearances.

In Amy Lowell, the physical courage so often shown by her brothers came uppermost. The very nature of her internal injuries—hernia—was one more frequently visited upon men than women, and she met this discomfort with a show of masculine fortitude. Yet, however gallantly she met this restriction to her activities, renewed signs of thoroughly feminine weakness marked her responses to a sometimes hostile world: she wept more easily—and adverse reviews of her books caused tears to flow as well as violent anger. Even in public a tactless question would find her vulnerable and defensive, with tears beneath the surface of her replies. At a meeting held by an undergraduate poetry group at Harvard, which she attended as the guest of honor and read aloud her poems, John Brooks Wheelwright, one of her more distant Boston relatives (and the most promising poet of his class at college) thoughtlessly asked her: "Miss Lowell, what do you do when you want to write a poem and haven't anything to write about?" The question put her on guard. Was the boy being impertinent? Was he implying that she wrote verses without having anything to say? On this point she became increasingly sensitive, particularly when she met Wheelwright afterwards at dinner parties. After her death, in 1925, Wheelwright wrote a series of ghostly conversations with her, Amy Lowell speaking first:

" 'Yes, my blood pressure is better; and how is your death progressing; —and do you remember asking when we met: 'How do you write, Miss Lowell, when you have nothing to say?' "
His reply was:

"That is unfair. You know I used the 'you' for 'one'; and as for your own
Tact,—

How about calling me, 'Mr. Brooks,' half the time; instead of just plain
'Jack?' "

Her eagerness to answer laughter made her stamp her little feet,—bang,
bang, bang,—down in the dust of the street.

As the dust rose, her neck turned grey, like stale ash of cigars; but
gushes of dead blood mounted her neck.

They flowed through her head; the cheeks turned red; the lips glowed
like scars. But her eyes? Her eyes were frightened.

Our road forked; and she took one tine; and I took the other; and waste-lot
Delta ragweed (fenced by granite posts and hickory rails set diamond-
wise) widened its wedge between.

But I turned for "Good-bye" to Amy Lowell, Biggest Traveling One-Man
Show since Buffalo Bill caught the Midnight Flyer to contact Mark
Twain:

"One would be inclined, at moments, to doubt the entire death!" I
shouted.

Grinning from ear to ear, she shouted back: "Mr. Brooks, you are per-
fectly right;—one would be."

During the remaining eight years of her life, from 1917 to 1925,
high blood pressure was another sign of approaching mortality; her
injuries made her efforts to move her bulk from house to waiting
limousine more cumbersome, more (if she were to avoid pain) difficult. The efforts (even with the assistance of a maid) to dress, to
prepare herself for meeting guests or to leave Sevenels for public
engagements were an increasing demand upon her strength. In her
impatience her blood pressure mounted; her decisions became more
abrupt, more commanding, nor would she relinquish her love of
activity for its own sake. If her tendency to weep increased, she had,
as Wheelwright noted, increased violence in her impulses to laugh
aloud.

The restlessness that her brother Percival displayed in his journeys
to Japan and Korea, took the form in Amy Lowell of writing at least
two books a year, of increasing all ranges of the tasks she set for
herself—the responsibility of urging Houghton Mifflin to continue
annual publication of *Some Imagist Poets*, to write letters to editors
demanding that friends review her books, that her own writings be
promptly published. Only the extremes of New England winter
weather forced her to break public engagements to lecture. Her
lecture engagements west and south of Chicago became journeys of

great trial to her; her complaint was that Middle Western food made
her ill; and it was true that the exertions of train travel brought
with them minor illnesses that seemed to retard the labors of the
mounting schedules of writing she pursued.

Her habit of dictating her correspondence became so firmly established that she seldom addressed her friends in terms other than
those she used in public. The same kind of public informality was
diffused throughout her verses, her prose, and her after dinner conversations. Her letters expressed her enthusiasms, her opinions, her
advice, her imprecise, yet logical defenses of her beliefs. Of the
younger American poets, her greatest affection continued to be
reserved for John Gould Fletcher whom she advised to return to the
United States, even to the city of Little Rock, Arkansas, where he
was born and where he had spent his childhood. Of expatriated
Americans of the younger generation, H. D. held the greatest
measure of her respect. Nor was her admiration for H. D.'s poetry
the only reason why she held her in esteem. Unlike many poets
whom Amy Lowell welcomed as hostess at Sevenels and with whom
she sustained a large correspondence, H. D. was one of the very few
who refused to hint of immediate needs for money. Her letters to
Amy Lowell were those of a gifted friend rather than those sent to a
future patron. Of her own anxieties she wrote nothing; she mentioned only her care in placing her young daughter in Swiss grade
schools, of her preference for London (though the war years brought
privations and Zeppelin raids). Amy Lowell, like other well-to-do
men and women who are friendly to the arts, became increasingly
sensitive to and wary of crude hints to give money to writers less
fortunate than she. The only writer to whom she continued to send
generous gifts of money was D. H. Lawrence whose "bread and
butter" letters tempered candor with feline graces:

But I wish I needn't take the money: it irks me a bit. Why can't I earn
enough, I've done the work. After all, you know, it makes one angry to
have to accept a sort of charity. Not from you, really, because you are an
artist . . . One is denied one's just rights, and then insulted with
charity. Pfui! to them all—But I feel you & I have a sort of odd congenital
understanding.

His books were evidence of what he wrote; they were written and
when published—even his textbook, *Movements in European His-*

tory, written for money and under the pseudonym of "Lawrence H. Davidson"—did not sell. (But twenty years after his death, that book, first published by the Oxford University Press in 1921, did sell and proved a good investment for its publishers.) Nor were his critics and reviewers kind. Of his poems in *Look! We Have Come Through!, The Times Literary Supplement* remarked: "the Muse can only turn away her face in pained distaste," and as he quoted this notice to Amy Lowell he added, "Poor Muse, I feel as if I have affronted a white-haired old spinster with weak eyes." This was a half-humorous complaint that Amy Lowell understood because it seemed to echo her complaints against those who misunderstood her. She saw in Lawrence's image of "a white-haired old spinster with weak eyes," her fancied image of withered, Bostonian "Victorianism," her adverse critics in the Poetry Societies of both New England and New York—all those who gave literal meaning to her lines in "Bath." "Congenital understanding" was also something of which she felt continual need, and in her large appetite for it, replenishment was always necessary. Lawrence's phrase struck deeper than any appeal to her vanity—for her need of being understood was part of her unfulfilled desire, which is so frequently expressed in the actions of a "spoiled" child, the desire to love and to be loved.

In this country she had reached that kind of understanding with Sara Teasdale; and though she had wept over John Gould Fletcher's sympathetic praise of her *Sword Blades and Poppy Seed*, her affections were touched in the same fashion that a nephew's praise touches the heart of a maternal maiden aunt. Her relationship to Sara Teasdale was of far stronger, more enduring fiber. Both women had in common an unyielding devotion to Eleanora Duse; both credited her with being a primary source of their poetic inspiration—she was their "Muse." There were other likenesses that made the bonds of understanding and of friendship secure. Sara Teasdale came from a well-to-do St. Louis family of colonial ancestry; she was the youngest of several children and received, because of ill health, most of her education at home, which was followed by a brief term at a finishing school. Like Amy Lowell's, the important features of her supplementary education came from several years of travel—to the American Southwest and to Europe. Interest in the writing of poetry had rescued her from the extremes of invalidism, and recognition of her gifts—for her book, *Love Songs,* published in 191

distributed praise—gave her further courage to m

pany, to choose friends and to accept the world.

invalidism gave her an excuse to exercise one mild

physician had told her that she seemed to lack a n

a fable she was all too willing to believe, and to

feeling cold, she wore long-armed, high-necked

underwear—which was not concealed by the light

she wore. She was as slender as Amy Lowell

plain-featured woman with attractive grey eye

pince-nez. Her manner was shy, her voice low-pi

her hair the color of dimly lighted gold. When t

for courtesy and distance, she assumed the dignit

angular American school mistress. Aside from th

had in common, Amy Lowell and Sara Teasdal

to and complemented each other: where one s

masculine, the other was yielding and rather m

feminine; where one was all-embracing and worl

reserved, discriminating and finely tempered; t

widely read, their reading followed different cha

tion. One sign of their difference was Sara Teasd

Virginia Woolf and Christina Rossetti.

The points of difference as well as the likeness

ship from growing stale; and there were moment

way—when Sara Teasdale could be as enthusiasti

she felt and thought as Amy Lowell. If Amy L

bring herself to an understanding of Vachel Lind

was always eager to show her liking for him. To

she wrote—and the letter shows how lively, yet

gence was in summing up the charm that Lindsay

He is a real man—full of eccentricities—aggressiv

about middle height, blond, with eager, keen blu

humour; a good talker—almost a monologist if he get

favorite train of thought. His voice is good, but too

time and *very* Middle West. When he reads his ow

rather) in this tiny study of mine, it is like being co

a pipe-organ in an hermetically sealed safe-deposit va

and so do your nerves . . . Yet the fresh humani

beautiful exuberance—fills you with delight. He is a re

tory, written for money and under the pseudonym of "Lawrence H. Davidson"—did not sell. (But twenty years after his death, that book, first published by the Oxford University Press in 1921, did sell and proved a good investment for its publishers.) Nor were his critics and reviewers kind. Of his poems in *Look! We Have Come Through!*, *The Times Literary Supplement* remarked: "the Muse can only turn away her face in pained distaste," and as he quoted this notice to Amy Lowell he added, "Poor Muse, I feel as if I have affronted a white-haired old spinster with weak eyes." This was a half-humorous complaint that Amy Lowell understood because it seemed to echo her complaints against those who misunderstood her. She saw in Lawrence's image of "a white-haired old spinster with weak eyes," her fancied image of withered, Bostonian "Victorianism," her adverse critics in the Poetry Societies of both New England and New York—all those who gave literal meaning to her lines in "Bath." "Congenital understanding" was also something of which she felt continual need, and in her large appetite for it, replenishment was always necessary. Lawrence's phrase struck deeper than any appeal to her vanity—for her need of being understood was part of her unfulfilled desire, which is so frequently expressed in the actions of a "spoiled" child, the desire to love and to be loved.

In this country she had reached that kind of understanding with Sara Teasdale; and though she had wept over John Gould Fletcher's sympathetic praise of her *Sword Blades and Poppy Seed*, her affections were touched in the same fashion that a nephew's praise touches the heart of a maternal maiden aunt. Her relationship to Sara Teasdale was of far stronger, more enduring fiber. Both women had in common an unyielding devotion to Eleanora Duse; both credited her with being a primary source of their poetic inspiration—she was their "Muse." There were other likenesses that made the bonds of understanding and of friendship secure. Sara Teasdale came from a well-to-do St. Louis family of colonial ancestry; she was the youngest of several children and received, because of ill health, most of her education at home, which was followed by a brief term at a finishing school. Like Amy Lowell's, the important features of her supplementary education came from several years of travel—to the American Southwest and to Europe. Interest in the writing of poetry had rescued her from the extremes of invalidism, and recognition of her gifts—for her book, *Love Songs*, published in 1917, received widely distributed praise—gave her further courage to move freely in company, to choose friends and to accept the world. Her many years of invalidism gave her an excuse to exercise one mild eccentricity. Some physician had told her that she seemed to lack a normal layer of skin, a fable she was all too willing to believe, and to keep herself from feeling cold, she wore long-armed, high-necked, long-legged wool underwear—which was not concealed by the light grey chiffon dresses she wore. She was as slender as Amy Lowell was stout—a thin, plain-featured woman with attractive grey eyes glinting behind pince-nez. Her manner was shy, her voice low-pitched and musical, her hair the color of dimly lighted gold. When the occasion called for courtesy and distance, she assumed the dignity of an intelligent, angular American school mistress. Aside from the experiences they had in common, Amy Lowell and Sara Teasdale were in contrast to and complemented each other: where one seemed excessively masculine, the other was yielding and rather more than casually feminine; where one was all-embracing and worldly, the other was reserved, discriminating and finely tempered; though both were widely read, their reading followed different channels of appreciation. One sign of their difference was Sara Teasdale's admiration of Virginia Woolf and Christina Rossetti.

The points of difference as well as the likenesses kept the friendship from growing stale; and there were moments—and in her own way—when Sara Teasdale could be as enthusiastic, as open in what she felt and thought as Amy Lowell. If Amy Lowell could never bring herself to an understanding of Vachel Lindsay, Sara Teasdale was always eager to show her liking for him. To Louis Untermeyer she wrote—and the letter shows how lively, yet precise, her intelligence was in summing up the charm that Lindsay had for her:

He is a real man—full of eccentricities—aggressively himself. He is about middle height, blond, with eager, keen blue-grey eyes full of humour; a good talker—almost a monologist if he gets on a familiar and favorite train of thought. His voice is good, but too loud much of the time and *very* Middle West. When he reads his own poetry (recites it, rather) in this tiny study of mine, it is like being compelled to listen to a pipe-organ in an hermetically sealed safe-deposit vault. Your ears ache, and so do your nerves . . . Yet the fresh humanity of the man—his beautiful exuberance—fills you with delight. He is a real lover of mankind, with a humorous tenderness for its weaknesses. You forgive the celluloid collar and the long craning neck that seems to grow unspeakably when he lifts his voice in recitation . . . He has, quite literally, clean hands and a pure heart.

The first lines of her description of Lindsay also show something of the charm that Amy Lowell had for her: "full of eccentricities—aggressively himself . . . eager, keen blue-grey eyes full of humour; a good talker—almost a monologist . . . ," the kind of personality that sustained pointed contrasts to her own retiring, diffident, sensitized temperament. As for Lindsay, she encouraged a legend that she was vaguely in love with him, and he in return, with his attachment to his mother still unbroken, held Sara Teasdale as the "pure," unattainable ideal of the woman and poet he wished to marry. Her actual choice in marriage was a heavily built, kindly, well-to-do proprietor of a shoe store in St. Louis, who remained in awe of her wit and her poetic gifts—while she remained as outwardly virginal as a nineteenth-century nymph carved out of marble. Her later poems had the same external purity of line and diction. Her marriage lasted twelve years, then quietly she secured a divorce in Reno. Meanwhile, as her verse improved and she grew more critical of its values, her public reputation waned. The enthusiasm with which reviewers had greeted her *Love Songs* had been transferred to a younger, more fashionable, more flagrantly outspoken poet than she—Edna St. Vincent Millay. Readers of her poetry were numerous enough, but reviewers forgot to mention her name and during the turn of the late 1920's into the 1930's, she had drifted into semi-obscurity. She rented a small apartment in New York and attempted to write a biography of Christina Rossetti, but the invalidism which had clouded the early years of her life returned—and she failed to adjust herself to the changes in literary personalities and fashions. In January, 1933, eight years after Amy Lowell's death, she died from an overdose of sleeping tablets.

The rapport that she had established with Amy Lowell was a friendship that brought out the best qualities, the most generous impulses, in both women. Sara Teasdale knew and understood the least public side of Amy Lowell's character, and of the people Amy Lowell met and entertained at her New York hotel, Sara Teasdale was the most welcome, most intimate of her friends. In her poems

Amy Lowell often showed her feminine liking for fragile, scarcely animate things and finely if curiously made objects of art; to a few, very few women this contrasting side of her kindliness was shown. It was both protective and maternal and was known to H. D., Sara Teasdale and Bryher, the modest young Englishwoman who had written an appreciative pamphlet on Amy Lowell's writings and is known today as the distinguished author of memorable historical novels. In these three incidents of friendship Amy Lowell concealed her vanity and shrewdness. She felt instinctively that her three friends understood *her* in a way that the rest of the world did not. In these decisions she was not wrong. Proof of H. D.'s disinterestedness came in her letters asking her to help—not herself—but D. H. Lawrence; and the other two women had the same selflessness in their attitudes toward the world. In this kind of discrimination, Amy Lowell was nearly faultless; she could be fooled while in a mild frenzy of book collecting into buying sham first editions, but she was almost never deceived in her sharp, and final estimations of human character. This was a side of her abilities, her gifts that entered into the encounters of her social life—and all too seldom into the writing of her verses. In her management of people she was on firm ground, and no public relations counselor could have given her better advice than she was able, instinctively, to give herself.

As hostess at Sevenels she had ample opportunity to observe the world, to discriminate among her guests, to judge their usefulness to her, their genuineness of spirit, their weaknesses and their strength. She made a point of entertaining her guests with a show of lavishness.

At Sevenels where she invited reviewers, editors and poets in to dinner, she had the advantage of observing her guests within a setting designed by her own showmanship. Her service and food were excellent: her dining room glowed with a somewhat heavy late nineteenth-century luster; her seven long-haired English sheepdogs sat at attention in a wide semi-circle beyond the chairs in which guests were seated. After dinner her guests were ushered into the now familiar routine of being seated in deep, comfortable chairs and each given a large clean bathtowel to spread across the knees so as to protect their clothes from the affectionate pawing and mouthing of the dogs. All this was done with a half-humorous air of informality, yet something less than true ease was achieved. However kindly the hostess was, however intelligently Mrs. Russell guided the conversations, the presence and feeding of the dogs among the guests gave the entire scene a Circe-like atmosphere. It was one in which Amy Lowell—as Circe—was in command of a small kingdom where the distinction between literary guests and the friendly sheep dogs had nearly disappeared. Within this circle it seemed inevitable that most of the talk was literary gossip.

One victim of fright caused by the dogs, so legends ran, was Maxwell Bodenheim, the Bohemian Chicago-New York poet. Bodenheim, born in Mississippi and self-educated, had wandered, after a brief career in the U.S. Army, north to Chicago and into the offices of Margaret Anderson's *The Little Review*. He was poor and ingenuous. In Chicago which was then in the first stages of a "poetic renaissance," Bodenheim, who knew little or nothing of either and—so far as his legend carried him—combined the fantastic characteristics of Petrus Borel, *le Lycanthrope*, and the young Rimbaud on their arrivals in Paris. In manner he was as frightening as Borel in his guise as Werewolf; and in his careless dress, his aggressive speech—"he walked as though he wore hobnailed boots," wrote Margaret Anderson—he was as spectacular but by no means as violently offensive or as gifted as Rimbaud. If Bohemian Chicago had not had a Bodenheim at hand and readymade, it is nearly certain that it would have had to invent him. To Chicago newspapermen, Bodenheim was a figure that suited their wildest dreams of what a poet should be: destitute, cadging his wares—which were poems in manuscript produced from torn pockets—loud in his abuse of the world, and quick with insults to those who refused to print his poems. To anyone who would listen he would fix their attention by a stare from pale blue eyes and with a pronounced stutter proceed to a loud reading of what he had written five minutes before. In his own way he could bully an editor as effectively as Amy Lowell, yet with this great difference, he awakened feelings of pity and of marked repulsion. That he was unlearned, that his sometimes strange use of words was of his own and often meaningless invention, that he was strident in his demands—all worked in his favor. Since verse was acknowledged to be "free," all bars were down, and the extremes to which he carried his unrhymed verses created the illusion of being "new" and extraordinary. For the moment he held the admiration of all who feared to say what they felt and thought; he was far outside the pale of conventional society—and some of his listeners half-envied his complete lack of respectability, his outward show of courage.

From Chicago streets he came to New York and transferred his attention to the larger, more fluid Bohemia that then existed in Greenwich Village—where a recited poem could be used as currency for a meal in a cheap restaurant or offered as pay for a drink in a saloon or "speak-easy." Brookline and Boston were close enough to allow the sale of a poem to a magazine to furnish a round-trip ticket (and with a kindly invitation from Amy Lowell in his pocket—for she was curious about all who wrote unrhymed verse) he came to Sevenels.

In his eagerness to meet the wealthy sister of Harvard's President, and in his absent-minded fashion, Bodenheim mistimed his eight o'clock dinner invitation. He came two hours early; and on the broad front lawn of Sevenels, walled from the road, Amy Lowell's seven English sheepdogs were innocently taking their late afternoon exercise. As he walked up the drive Bodenheim saw the dogs and was fearful of their size, their shagginess, and their awkward leaping in the air. He became terrified; he began to run and the dogs ran after him. They were more than eager to have him join in a game he had no desire to play. He hid behind trees, but the dogs were too many for him; the seven surrounded him, leaping, barking, playfully tearing at his ragged coat. Under a large stone statue of Flora above a columned entrance he saw the small figure of a housemaid and toward her he escaped, up the stone steps through the darkened doorway.

When he sat down at dinner Bodenheim found a check for ten dollars under his plate. He protested: was ten dollars enough to buy a new overcoat, a new suit, a new jacket and trousers? His hostess quietly replied that all his clothes—ties, shirt, suit, overcoat—even before his encounter with her dogs, were worth no more than ten dollars for the lot; surely the amount of her check covered the damage that had been done to him; he was unhurt. Fantasy seized Bodenheim: he insisted that his nerves had suffered irreparable damage and that he would never recover from the shock. He demanded a hundred dollars. To calm his nerves he would have to go back to Chicago and visit his first love's grave in a cemetery there.

Bodenheim, since he had little to lose except his temper, and felt he had been meagerly patronized by a rich woman, could well afford to be violent in his demands. Amy Lowell was unimpressed: in situations of this kind, she was neither to be bullied nor to be moved by pity. To her mind Bodenheim was as Bohemian as Gaudier-Brzeska —and more so than Ezra Pound. Her curiosity about him had been satisfied. If many years later her brother Lawrence was in error in passing judgment on Sacco and Vanzetti, he was governed by the same repulsions Amy Lowell felt for Bohemians, for the overtly ugly, for the helplessly poor, for the crippled. Because of her own mis-shapen body—her care in not seeing it reflected in hotel mirrors—there was a deep, if flickering shadow of self-hate in her horror of visible human deformities. She had learned to use and to spend her body—not to pamper it beyond indulgence in elaborate dinners at Sevenels and well-chosen mild Havana tobacco. Louis Untermeyer reported that her attitude toward Randolph Bourne, the dwarfed and hunchbacked liberal essayist of *The New Republic* (who on visiting her had also been frightened by her dogs) was the same as that with which she regarded Bodenheim. In telling this story Untermeyer quoted James Oppenheim, who was an editor of *The Seven Arts*, a magazine that had published Amy Lowell's long poem "Guns as Keys" with unrestrained enthusiasm. To Oppenheim she insisted that Bourne's writing (which was not true) had "tortured style and twisted mentality." "Everything he writes," she said, "shows he is a cripple." Oppenheim in reply said, "Aren't we all cripples?"—at which Amy Lowell suddenly, childishly contrite and frightened, said, "Yes. Look at me. I'm nothing but a disease."

There were many rumours that grew out of the presence of Amy Lowell's seven English sheep dogs. It was said that a specially com-missioned servant guided guests to the door past hostile, growling creatures, who became friendly only when and if their mistress appeared. At an interview granted to a reporter from *The Sunday Herald* (Boston), June 24, 1917, Amy Lowell disclosed their names: the seven were Jack, John, Tommy, Rosine, Mary, Lydia and Colum-bine. It was said that women visitors to Sevenels, overcome by the dogs' attention, suffered torn gloves and skirts, that when Amy Lowell traveled to Dublin, New Hampshire, with her dogs, a local physician, called in because two or three of the dogs had fallen ill, grew angry when he learned that for their comfort he had been roused from bed at night. Since the dogs cost their mistress sixty dollars a week in butcher bills—and since she never paid a bill oftener than once in three years—they were the cause of additional quarrels with Brookline meat dealers whenever they presented their bills. With the exception of their mistress's affection, the dogs were not loved by the household at Sevenels; that much is clear. With the dogs in mind, one of Amy Lowell's secretaries called the house, "Seven Hells," yet the same secretary had the illusion that nineteen dogs surrounded her—fifteen very large, and four smaller.

In 1918, rules of war rationing prohibited the dogs' usual diet of top round beef, and ptomaine poisoning from badly preserved horse meat was the result; five were ill; the sixth fell dead. Amy Lowell ordered the five to be "put to sleep" painlessly—and the seventh lingered on in ill health for ten months longer. On this occasion Amy Lowell probably remembered that her beloved horses had died in a fire, that their stables had been the site of Hylowe Kennels where the sheep dogs were bedded when the six dogs died. "Winky," a black tomcat, was their substitute, and to Amy Lowell's guests he was a more amiable pet.

The celebrity Amy Lowell had acquired outside of Boston and Brookline gave heightened color to and intensified her reputation at home. Among her guests at Sevenels was William Stanley Braithwaite, an editor of *The Boston Evening Transcript,* which was once the most conservative of American newspapers, and which in an early, witty, youthfully irreverent poem, T. S. Eliot immortalized by writing "Cousin Harriet, here is the *Boston Evening Transcript.*" Braithwaite was a Negro, born and educated in Boston; he was a small-boned, delicately featured little man whose writings were informative, decorous, selfless in their devotion to poetic literature. He never allowed racial discrimination or political propaganda to modify his responses to poetry. Of all journalists who praised the writings of Edwin Arlington Robinson his comments were the most perceptive, and of Robinson's critics he was among the first to recognize the touch of elegance in Robinson's wit. It was said that Amy Lowell, with Mrs. Russell as chaperone, held private interviews with Braith-

waite, that on his invitations to dinner at Sevenels the three dined
alone. It was true enough that Braithwaite avoided literary gatherings; the poets he admired he dined with tête-à-tête; and on his visits
to New York, he would spend entire nights listening to Robinson
talk while the poet emptied many tumblers of speakeasy gin. In Boston his recognition of Amy Lowell and her Imagist anthologies were
read as signatures of respectable approval. Through his acceptance
of her verse a balance was struck between flagrant notoriety and
mildly conservative literary opinion. Her conquest of Braithwaite
represented a decisive local victory.

Although dinners at Sevenels and Amy Lowell on lecture platforms had reached their apotheosis in newspaper celebrity, the
shadows of Amy Lowell's illnesses darkened. After the carriage incident of August 1916, her illnesses grew more frequent and of longer
duration. Her physicians prescribed doses of morphine which caused
visions of fireworks flashing in the corners of her top-floor nursery
bedroom. During one of the first of these visitations (in November
1916) her brother Percival died of a cerebral hemorrhage at Flagstaff,
California, where he had founded the Lowell Observatory. She was so
ill that she was not informed of his death. Her cycles of illness, her
three surgical operations and the periods of influenza which followed
them, made her labors in writing both sporadic and increasingly
heroic in size and energy. The cheerfulness with which she invited
controversy on lecture platforms began to waver. The First World
War ended on Armistice Day, November 11th, 1918; and after that
date the hearing of Amy Lowell's war poems lost their patriotic
relevance, nor were the diversions of listening to Imagist verse as
fresh, as shockingly "new" as during the years preceding 1919. The
temper of Amy Lowell's audiences was changing; conservative members of the audience were less easily caught off guard, and were
more severely critical. Among younger groups a self-consciously post-
war generation was being formed—one that was less innocently
"experimental" than the poets Amy Lowell dreamed of leading, and
who as the 1920's reached their meridian, welcomed the growing
reputation of T. S. Eliot.

Signs of a break in Amy Lowell's cheerfulness came at her lecture
on "Walt Whitman and the New Poetry" at the Contemporary Club
in Philadelphia on November 12th, 1919. A member of the audience

loudly refuted her definitions and defenses of "free verse." She burst
into tears; she claimed that she objected to all controversies, and that
the club in debating against "free verse," had broken faith with her.
She protested that she had agreed to lecture and not to being forced
into a debate. According to newspaper reports two days later, she
denied her tears—and exhibited only anger against those who had
refuted her. In actuality her conduct showed the results of her continued illnesses. She was aware that her earlier defenses of Imagism
for its own sake were wearing thin. Though her name now carried
its own weight (even her bulk could be sustained by her reputation),
she still lacked authority for a number of her opinions. The rest of
her life was to be spent in an effort at scholarship in biography—her
John Keats and in furthering her claims that she understood Oriental
poetry.

Chinese Gardens and John Keats

10

IN THE YEARS immediately following World War I, from 1919 to 1921, Amy Lowell's energies were devoted to the further production of *belles lettres*. The distractions of her patriotic duties, of contributing funds to Government war efforts, of giving lectures and reading poems to further them, had decreased in number. Four of her books of poems had gone into several editions, and so had her two books of prose, *Six French Poets* and *Tendencies in American Poetry*. As a literary figure she was becoming less of a curiosity than a national institution. Harvard and Princeton undergraduates took pleasure in receiving her at their literary clubs for readings and lectures. E. E. Cummings, who a few years earlier was at Harvard—and as an undergraduate—remembers how Amy Lowell's great bulk was steered, a boy on each side supporting left and right arms, between the aisles of a small lecture hall to a chair behind a table. Her good nature was uppermost, high enough at least to surmount her awkwardness in size, her obvious and painful infirmities.

To walk at all had become an effort that was Samuel Johnsonian, yet she created the impression of being brisk and gay—a visible sign of courage that in the eyes of her youthful audience stirred an impulse to cheer. To them and in her own right she was less their President's sister than Amy Lowell, the unpredictable commentator on everything "new" in literature.

Before the War had come to an end, still another legend had been added to the cluster of stories that were remembered whenever and wherever she appeared in public. At a New York dinner she had overheard a young British officer who was on leave in the United States tell of how he had misdirected a fat, perspiring poorly dressed woman, burdened with heavy bags, in a railway station. The woman —because of his uniform—had mistaken him for a porter—and he, to teach an American a lesson, had abruptly and with authority misinformed her. He was pleased with his joke, but Amy Lowell was not: she called him a cad and threatened to telephone a complaint against him to the British embassy in Washington. It took all the ingenuity of Mrs. Russell's tact to prevent Amy Lowell from placing a long distance call to Washington at once. The young officer, frightened at Amy Lowell's anger, pleaded he was not completely certain he misdirected the unfortunate woman—he apologized to Amy Lowell, which did not improve his defense. She had lost her temper; the young man had lost his poise. An hour later she had taken a train back to Boston and Brookline, but through the early hours of the following morning her New York friends were kept awake by long distance telephone calls from Sevenels, Amy Lowell alternately weeping and storming. She did not carry out her threat of complaint against the young Englishman, yet her effort at self-control was costly; she lost sleep; her illnesses had increased their discomforts.

Her own identification with the woman in the railway station had awakened her defense of women in general; her humane temper, seldom touched, had been aroused by the inhuman conduct of the young officer. Nothing in her character was more constant than the contrasts she displayed in her views on women. She had rejected all movements in favor of birth control. Verses she had written which showed the pitiful fate of unmarried mothers and of which "The Forsaken" in Sword Blades and Poppy Seed which had become notorious, misled a few of her friends into thinking she would join crusades which advanced political feminism. Nothing was further from Amy Lowell's sympathies and intentions. She approved of neither Margaret Sanger nor the Lucy Stone League. When Louis Untermeyer tried to get her support to defend a young man who distributed birth control leaflets in the streets of Boston, she vehemently refused to act, and Heywood Broun, who was then a special feature writer on the staff of *The New York World* reported:

Amy Lowell leaned back in a big easy chair, puffing one of her Manila cigars. 'I have (puff, puff) no patience with the new-fashioned woman (puff, puff) and her so-called rights. I believe (and here she drew deep on the cigar) in the old-fashioned woman and all her limitations.'

Today it seems strange that her politically minded friends did not realize how deeply rooted Amy Lowell was in the conventions of the Lowell family; except for her opinions of the new poetry and her own rights to indulge in personal eccentricities, she was at one with the conservative opinions of her mother, father and elder brothers. With this particular brand of Lowell conservatism she fused the working of her own clear-headed mind. She was never to be swayed, either by sentiment, or pleas in favor of humanitarian causes, and became even more decided in her attitude against Left political opinions. In the face of such opinions she was "tough-minded," intelligently aware that her name might be used to advance causes in which she did not believe, and was quick to avoid any trap that had been prepared for her.

All these were signs of her growing maturity. Her conservatism was also furthered by drifting away from "little magazines" to the pages of *The North American Review*, the very publication of which in the latter 1870's James Russell Lowell had been an editor. *Poetry* magazine of Chicago was the only *avant-garde* publication in which Amy Lowell sustained an interest. She had withdrawn—because by that time Ezra Pound had joined its staff—all connections with Margaret Anderson's *The Little Review*.

In American literary circles, Amy Lowell was now definitely within a New York-Boston orbit; she shared its fashions, its gossip, its literary opinions and disagreements. Among the fashionable topics—which became the subject of talk at cocktail parties during the early 1920's —was sexual emancipation. "Free love," Left politics, Freud, and a revival of interest in the Shelley legend were prominent subjects of

dispute—and as for Shelley, there were many efforts to emulate the
more commonly known and lurid features of his beliefs and conduct.
In the late 'teens and early 'twenties of the present century, the image
of the Shelley legend had taken on large proportions in the United
States and, fused as it was with ideas of sexual freedom, with atheism,
with Godwin and with Mary Wollstonecraft (that handsome "blue-
stocking" whose name had been associated with "rights for women,"
who had been the wife of Godwin and the mother of Shelley's second
wife), the legend acquired romantic attractions. These were all the
more glittering and brilliant because Shelley had been a rich young
man—and in the United States, the prestige of unearned wealth has
never been despised. To have casual love affairs, an urge to travel
on the European Continent and to write poetry, to be careless in
respect to everyday responsibilities, to participate in cults of walking
naked and of vegetarianism, to be wilfully scornful of conventions—
all these were then traits and attainments to be admired and
achieved. The most peculiar fusion of the Shelley legend took place in
the imaginations of two women poets, Edna St. Vincent Millay and
Elinor Wylie, and in their writings it was recreated as a cult of
youth. One of Mrs. Wylie's novels, *Orphan Angel*, was a fictional
life of Shelley, thinly disguised and boldly reconstructed with the
superimposition of her own image, her sunset-tinted hair and graceful figure, over that of a young man who had been a notorious poet
a hundred years before her book was published. Mrs. Wylie collected
Shelley manuscripts with the same joy and devotion that Amy Lowell
collected Keats. Not unlike Amy Lowell's, Mrs. Wylie's career as a
poet began late. Though at the age of twenty-seven—in 1912—she
had privately issued a small book of poems, it was not until 1921, with
the publication year of her second book, *Nets to Catch the Wind*,
that her name became known. Born Elinor Hoyt (her grandfather
had been Governor of Pennsylvania, her father Solicitor General of
the United States in Theodore Roosevelt's administration), she
moved brilliantly in Washington society. She married Philip Hich-
born, the son of an admiral, and broke her relationship with him to
elope and live for several years in England with Horace Wylie. In
her conduct, she was more like the heroine of an unwritten novel by
Edith Wharton than the idealization of herself as a reborn Shelley;
she was cooler headed, had greater worldliness and no passion what-

soever for economic and social reform—and, of course, was far better looking, far more aggressively poised than he. The only outward resemblance she had to the poet was a voice that was harsh, nervous and shrill. It was enough for her that certain features of the legend around him held fascination: truly, he had deserted his first wife, the childlike Harriet, with the same careless air of indifference that she had left her first husband for her second. Yet even with these points of resemblance, her devotion to the Shelley legend and her affinity with its hero were more fantastic than deeply felt or realized. Both she and Edna St. Vincent Millay took from the Shelley legend the idea that "poets are the trumpets which sing to battle . . . poets are the unacknowledged legislators of the world," an eloquent statement once made by Shelley which was used as an epigraph on the title pages of the Everyman's Library series of English poets. The epigraph gave them a precedent to do as they pleased, to give advice to their admirers who were many and of both sexes which was:

> Avoid the reeking herd,
> Shun the polluted flock . . .

—and to say, not without self-knowledge and a touch of wit:

> My candle burns at both ends;
>   It will not last the night;
> But ah, my foes, and oh, my friends—
>   It gives a lovely light!

These lines were not, of course, of a kind that Shelley might have written, but behind them floated ideas of "equal rights for women," rights to be unfaithful to their lovers, children, or heavy-minded, devoted husbands—and it was logical enough that this attitude lacked humility, and that it bolstered without effort personal vanity and ego. It expressed in the fewest number of words the temper of a post-war generation, the right to say whatever it felt, to say it loudly, barbarously, and without regard for the feelings of other human beings. There were moments (as in the case of Mrs. Wylie) when the attitude seemed affected, brittle, strained—it was nearly vulgar in its blatant snobbery, in its claims to be possessed by "the chosen few." Surely the desire to be sexually unfaithful has always—and in all ages—been the wish of many young men and women, and the desire to be "superior," to be a legislator, acknowledged or not, is a

common ambition. Both Millay and Wylie took pride and a sense
of glamour from their own good looks: Millay, short in stature,
girlish, fluttering, sometimes petulant, sometimes gay, red-haired,
green-eyed, and utterly charming to undergraduates from Princeton, Harvard and Yale who saw her perform behind the footlights on
the stage of the Provincetown Theatre in Greenwich Village. Wylie
was taller and more restrained in her movements than Millay. Her
stage was the cocktail lounge of a fashionable hotel or the floor of a
drawing-room where she walked as though aware of her reflection in
tall, silver-tinted, gold-rimmed mirrors. The image of Mrs. Wylie was
reflected accurately in her lines on "Beauty":

> O, she is neither good nor bad,
> But innocent and wild!
> Enshrine her and she dies, who had
> The hard heart of a child.

A not too far-fetched analogy can be made between Britain's newly
rich "age of elegance," with its rapidly acquired snobberies, its
Byronic love-affairs, its own cults of youth and post-Napoleonic-war
disillusionments and the early nineteen-twenties in the United States.
In fashionable literary circles speech was as candid, conduct was as
naughty as it had been in London a hundred years before. At no time
in New York had the literary heroines of the hour been so prominently, outrageously pretty and so glitteringly dressed as Millay and
Wylie. This was, of course, one of the secrets of their sudden popularity—and the reason why their convictions of being "superior" were
sustained by so many admirers. They were the obvious rivals to the
position held by Amy Lowell; and they were also the followers (at a
very great distance) of Shelley. Many years ago Amy Lowell's father
had forbidden Shelley's poems a place on the shelves of his library
at Sevenels. His daughter did not share the force of his prejudice
against the poet who wrote a memorable elegy on Keats—she went
so far as to find a title for her own book of poems in a line from
"Adonais," "Life, like a dome of many-colored glass." Yet Keats, not
Shelley (the Lowell curse against him was modified, but not erased),
became in Amy Lowell's imagination a long-sustained center of
attraction. During the nineteen-twenties, the two "revivals" of Keats
and Shelley had much in common. In time the two poets were farther
away than the Victorians were, and had acquired the charms of

distance and embellished legend that the Victorians lacked—but among their admirers something of a split, a difference in temperament, was indicated by showing prejudice in favor of either Keats or Shelley. This division depended less upon an actual reading of poems written by either than the mysteries and legends of their lives. Beneath the surfaces of these discriminations rivalries, if never openly displayed, were felt. Broadly, it was clearly understood that Keats was the more respectable figure, but being less wealthy, was less socially acceptable than Shelley. He had also been more deeply injured by adverse reviewers of his day than Shelley, yet his posthumous fame had increased, and this aspect of Keats's legend gave hope to those who felt their own writings had received less than justice at the hands of critics. To Amy Lowell the legend of Keats's life combined several attractive elements: first of all, there was no question as to his stature as a poet, and as a collector of books and manuscripts, it was clear that her buying of first editions and manuscripts of his poems had been a safe investment. She never forgot her early reading of Leigh Hunt's writings—and Hunt was among the earliest as well as the most enthusiastic of Keats's admirers, an editor who was both a champion and friend. The figure of Keats never lost its appeal to Amy Lowell's protective instincts; even at the distance of a hundred years, she felt the need of some righting of justice, some compensation, however posthumous, to make up for the unhappier moments of his short life. For all these reasons Amy Lowell, as opposed to Elinor Wylie's championship of Shelley, was on Keats's side of a division in the ranks of those who took as standards for the conduct of their own lives the lives of two well-known romantic poets.

Amy Lowell's relationship with Elinor Wylie, though never warm, was watchful without dispensing excessive praise, and not openly unfriendly. Amy Lowell felt herself socially superior to Mrs. Wylie; as with all the Lowells, Amy Lowell's domestic life was irreproachable, and it was obvious that Mrs. Wylie's family, the Hoyts, were less wealthy, less prominent, even though recognized in Philadelphia and Washington, than the Lowells. A grandfather who had been Governor of Pennsylvania was scarcely a match for a well-to-do and living Lowell who was President of Harvard.

In 1955 Miss Amy Loveman, who for many years was an editor

of *The Saturday Review of Literature,* remembered being witness to
a meeting between Amy Lowell and Elinor Wylie. The time was the
winter of 1923, the place was William Rose· Benét's apartment in
New York, the occasion was a small evening party to celebrate Mrs.
Wylie's third marriage, this time to William Rose Benét. Long
before he met her, as early as his undergraduate years at Yale, Benét
had heard of Elinor Hoyt, and at Yale he numbered among his few
intimate friends (another was Sinclair Lewis) her brother, Henry
Martyn Hoyt. Hoyt was a promising painter, and shortly after the two
young men received their degrees at Yale, they moved on to New
York and shared a studio-apartment. An easy and somewhat romantic
friendship was sustained between the young poet and the young
painter; both young men possessed great social charm. Benét had
inherited through his family's tradition (his father had been an
officer in the Ordinance Department in the United States Army) a
military erectness and poise. At social gatherings his wit concealed
his emotions. Hoyt was more volatile, and was subject to stormy fits
of elation and depression. His small income helped pay the rent of
the studio. Benét, since he had been an editor of undergraduate Yale
publications, sought out editorial appointments in New York. His
first efforts failed, and temporarily he was forced to leave the city, to
venture west to California, where he found jobs on newspapers. His
friendship with Hoyt led to his sending his friend's sister, Elinor, rare
books of seventeenth-century verse with instructions in their margins
as to how to appreciate the poems. His stay in the west resulted in
his marriage to a sister of Kathleen Norris. His marriage and the
distance between Washington and California interrupted his correspondence with Mrs. Wylie, and some twelve years elapsed (and this
after his young wife's death and his return to New York) before it
was resumed. As an editor of *Century Magazine,* and later, as an
editor of *The Saturday Review of Literature,* Benét encouraged Mrs.
Wylie in the writing of verse. As with his younger brother, Stephen
Vincent Benét, William Rose had been her most instructive and inspiring teacher; as her editor, he became her protector and champion,
and through his efforts, her verse became well-known.

His marriage with Elinor Wylie seemed to be a logical conse-
quence of their interest in poetry. In outward appearance they were
at ease in literary society, and many welcomed their gay and fash-

ionable good looks. Elinor Wylie's poise scarcely veiled a violent, self-consuming temper, turned inward with the force that destroyed Narcissus; Benét's poise was a mask for his romantic aspirations, his diffidence, his distrust of his own gifts, and the shyness of one who failed to be the military hero of his father's hopes. Both skimmed the surfaces of New York's literary Bohemia in Greenwich Village, and found their true level several layers above it: Benét in literary journalism on *The Saturday Review of Literature*, Wylie in the editorial offices of Condé Nast's *Vanity Fair*, a place where smartly dressed young women from Vassar, Smith or Bryn Mawr and young men from Princeton or Yale (and recently returned from the battlefields of France as well as the Café du Dome in Paris) played at knowing the latest fashions in dress, painting and literature. Chief among these were Edmund Wilson and John Peale Bishop; and Edith Wharton-like, the circle moved into and around the peripheries of New York Society. As the 1920's advanced, some of its members moved fashionably Left. Max Eastman, the handsome young professor of philosophy at Columbia, had pointed the way by becoming the editor of the then Socialist *Masses* and its successor, *The Liberator*, which in turn became the Communist *New Masses*. Meanwhile the marriage of Elinor Wylie to Benét had the outward show of being a match of social and literary genius, with Mrs. Wylie as a latter-day Shelley, to use their own analogies, and Carl Van Doren, a specialist in eighteenth-century history at Columbia and an editor of *Century* magazine, became the circle's Thomas Love Peacock.

To Amy Lowell, Benét had been an hospitable, kindly, humourously tempered editor, welcoming her to the half-liberal, half-conservative pages of *The Saturday Review*. It did not take much to seem to overwhelm him; he listened to writers with a courteous, absent, slightly relaxed, faintly ironic military air. In spite of and perhaps because of his degree from the Sheffield Scientific School at Yale, he applied himself (after leaving the University) to the acquisition of far-reaching literary knowledge. His father had been an active reader of the same kind, and this with a particular appreciation of English lyric poetry. Benét's love of reading had made him as learned as his London contemporary, Desmond MacCarthy; nearly every book in his large library had signs of his marginalia written in his fine, clear hand. Amy Lowell's practical eye surveyed him sharply, and it is likely that she saw through and behind the mask of his courtesy a diffident man recently married to a woman whose ambitions were ruthless and self-absorbed. As Amy Loveman recalled the incidents of that winter evening in 1923, Mrs. Russell preceded Amy Lowell's entry into the apartment by several minutes, carrying on her arm her companion's fur coat. The apartment was a walk-up of two flights; the weather had turned unexpectedly warm, and the climb upstairs, though carpeted, and the flights short, meant heated exertion for Amy Lowell. She took her time, for she did not wish to show herself too obviously out-of-breath or ill at ease. She entered the door to take command of the scene and was as brisk as ever. She turned to Mrs. Wylie and congratulated her on her fortunate marriage. "But if you marry again," she said, "I shall cut you dead—and I warn you all Society will do the same. You will be nobody." There was a moment of silence; then smoothly, cheerfully Amy Lowell started a quick round of literary gossip; the breach was swiftly closed. Further drinks were served and two hours later, Mrs. Russell went down the stairs to summon a taxi, and the pair left the house for their suite at the St. Regis.

Amy Lowell's duties in furthering her career as a woman of letters kept her confined in the rooms above her library at Sevenels. Each succeeding illness that had followed three operations for hernia meant that each succeeding journey away from Brookline became a greater tax upon her strength. The successes (in the United States) of her two critical studies, Six French Poets and Tendencies in Modern American Poetry, encouraged her to try her hand at translations from the Chinese, her book of verses which later carried the title of Fir-Flower Tablets. Two immediate reasons for undertaking this venture presented themselves. Though she admired—even praised—Ezra Pound's adaptations from Chinese, which had been steered and directed by Ernest Fenollosa's notes and translations of Li Po's ideograms, and though helplessly ignorant herself of the Chinese written characters and tongue, she felt that she could do better translations than Pound, and with a firmer hand than his. Among her childhood friends was Florence Wheelock, afterwards Mrs. Ayscough, who in 1916 on her return from China, brought with her a collection of Chinese paintings to be placed on exhibition in

Boston. It was then that Mrs. Ayscough and Amy Lowell conceived
the idea of transforming "written Chinese pictures" into verse. Some
few adaptations were made, but by 1920 when Amy Lowell heard
that Witter Bynner was at work on a book of translations from the
Chinese, she decided that with Florence Ayscough's help she could
publish a book of Chinese verses at greater speed than he. As she
wrote to Mrs. Ayscough, she was out "to kill him." The violence of
Amy Lowell's desire to "kill" Bynner recalled an earlier quarrel with
him that dated back to 1918.

Harold Witter Bynner had gone to high school in Brookline
and to Harvard from which he graduated in 1902. Bynner's taste
in the writing as well as the appreciation of poetry was finely tempered and conservative. His own gifts were distinctly lyrical which
were shown at their best in his *Grenstone Poems,* published in 1917.
Bynner had wit, a tall, gentlemanly presence, and a compelling, gay,
easy sense of humor. The combination of his lightness and his humor
made him the perfect guest at any tea table or cocktail party, but it
also prevented him from taking himself or the world of literary
politics with the smallest degree of seriousness. Nor could he accept
the presence of Amy Lowell with the serious concern that she demanded. In 1916 and in collaboration with Arthur Davison Ficke, he
composed a book of parodies, *Spectra,* taking off the various extremes
of the new, unrhymed imagist verse. "Emanuel Morgan" was his
pseudonym while Ficke took the name of "Anne Knish." A few
"little magazines" treated the verse as though it was the work of
newly discovered free verse poets, and Bynner's joke became the talk
of a literary season. The quality of the verse in *Spectra,* however,
annoyed Amy Lowell; she felt that the book was an attack on her
and the kind of verse she wrote, nor did she welcome the possible
association of her name with those of "Anne Knish" and "Emanuel
Morgan." On June 5th 1918 she wrote to Bynner:

Dear Emanuel:
You certainly did well with 'Spectra!' And how glad I am that I always
said it was charlatanism! I verily believe that you began to respect me
from the very moment that you asked me what I thought of it, and I
told you that I thought the authors were insincere. Of course, I had no
idea it was a genial hoax. I simply thought that Miss Knish and Mr.
Morgan were trying to gain notoriety out of a singularity in which they

themselves did not in the least believe, and perhaps you will remember that I never acknowledged the presentation copy which you so kindly sent me.

She then quoted Bynner's signed reference to the "Spectrists," "Knish" and "Morgan" which had appeared in *The New Republic*:

If I have over-estimated the importance of "Spectra," it is because of my constant hope that out of these various succeeding "schools" something better may develop than an aesthetic dalliance of eyeglass and blue-stocking—

The last phrase (because of her wearing pince-nez) could be taken to be a reference to her, and the company of "Knish" and "Morgan" was more than she could bear.

Because he had defended her poem, "Guns as Keys," at a meeting of the New York Poetry Society, she was willing to announce a truce, but an atmosphere of ill-will persisted between them. Nor did the quarrel have an easy death. Years later (in 1946), seventeen years after his own book of Chinese poems, *The Jade Mountain*, had appeared, Bynner reviewed a book of Ayscough-Lowell correspondence for *The Saturday Review of Literature*. From that book he learned all that Amy Lowell had said of him in 1920. This was an unhappy moment for Bynner, nor did John Gould Fletcher's letter, written to him because of his review, ease his discomfort. "I have meant to tell you," Fletcher wrote,

for years that you need not fear any reprisal on my part, for anything you may choose to say about Amy. I learned her bad side, long before she died; and it is awfully manifest in these letters. Indeed, I recall her telling me (in 1920 or maybe 1923) that she considered you her enemy; a statement which I took at that time with a considerable grain of salt, knowing that Amy simply could not help exploiting everything and any-body with whom she came into contact, and if that person happened to show any independence; or if some other person happened to interfere with any pet project of hers, she simply tried ruthless extermination. It really is a fact that the same knock-you-down and drag-you-out manner was, in her case, tried out with everybody: even with Florence Ayscough. She was as innocent, and as cruel, as a spoiled child, with all her literary projects. . . .

Jessie Rittenhouse also sent Bynner a letter:

In the summer of 1921, I think it was, I was in Boston and phoned Amy. She said to come right out to Sevenels and spend the afternoon with her. When I got there she had me shown up to her room on the third floor (she always kept her childhood rooms, as being above the noise). She was just over one of her many operations for hernia and said the doctor had forbidden her to get out of bed for three weeks more, but she was up, wearing a voluminous white robe which made her look like a swami, and immediately launched forth into the matter of Fir Flower Tablets.

Mrs Ayscough was there with her and they were feverishly working to get ahead of your Jade Mountain. Amy said if she did not get hers out first that it would fall flat and people would say she had imitated you; that she had heard yours was about ready and at all hazards she must get hers out first, therefore she was not listening to the doctor.

She began to read me some of the poems, insisting upon standing up, and as you know she read with much gusto and fine effect. . . .

If not in appearance, in spirit at least, Amy Lowell herself was not without resemblance to the kind of "Beauty" Elinor Wylie spoke of when she defined it as having "The hard heart of a child."

To this degree Amy Lowell shared some few of the flaws of the younger generation of the early nineteen-twenties; driven by the forces of literary ambition, she, too, might well have felt, if not written, "My candle burns at both ends . . ."

As in the days when she went to school with Amy Lowell, Florence Ayscough, now in her forties, was quickly swept into the tempest that surrounded her friend's activities. It was useless for her to protest that she knew little Chinese, that she had no pretensions to scholarship in that or any other language, that she would be forced to hire tutors to help *her*—and it was true enough, as one of her friends remarked, that Mrs. Ayscough spoke no Chinese, but rather "Shanghai pidgin to her servants." The misadventure into Chinese scholarship, the strain of supplying Amy Lowell with rough drafts of Chinese poems in English had little pleasure for Mrs. Asycough, and much difficult, vaguely mastered labor. The procedure was as elaborate as a Chinese puzzle to her, yet Amy Lowell, as director of the scheme, contrived tables of linguistic cross-references between verbal sounds and written characters. The performance was fantastically laborious and had a touch of madness in it, yet in English the poems were both flat and tame. One tablet read as follows:

PASSIONATE GRIEF
BY LI T'AI-PO

Beautiful is this woman who rolls up the pe
She sits in an inner chamber,
And her eyebrows, delicate as a moth's anter
Are drawn with grief.
One sees only the wet lines of tears.
For whom does she suffer this misery?
We do not know.

Amy Lowell wrote "We do not know" with
One is reminded of Percival Lowell's contentio
were an "upside down" people and that they fe
contrary to those who lived in and walked the str
was a Lowell conviction and with family loyalt
Lowell held to it—no external authority was to
against it. Nearly all the verses could have b
drawn shades in Brookline without the labors of
which both Amy Lowell and Mrs. Ayscough
drawn. To keep Mrs. Ayscough working at a
hers, Amy Lowell insisted that the work should b
be overwhelming enough to impress Harriet
Ayscough should be presented to Miss Monr
authority on Chinese poetry. Modest Mrs. Aysc
a power far greater than she could control.

In addition to the method that had been cor
lation of Chinese into English, the constructi
tables, the reading of the verses aloud by Amy L
of final versions with first drafts, the book conta
166 notes. For those unused to scholarly resear
as Amy Lowell and Mrs. Ayscough were, this ta
short of "colossal." The notes were done in a st
nineteenth-century encyclopedists who made
answer questions of bright children. The notes
created the atmosphere of an earlier day in Bost
the voice of an instructive governess speaking t
ery, now converted into a classroom:

"The Sorceress Gorge is often referred to in a fi
in this poem. The allusion is to the story of
dreamed that a fairy, calling herself the Lady of th

In the summer of 1921, I think it was, I was in Boston and phoned Amy. She said to come right out to Sevenels and spend the afternoon with her. When I got there she had me shown up to her room on the third floor (she always kept her childhood rooms, as being above the noise). She was just over one of her many operations for hernia and said the doctor had forbidden her to get out of bed for three weeks more, but she was up, wearing a voluminous white robe which made her look like a swami, and immediately launched forth into the matter of Fir Flower Tablets.

Mrs Ayscough was there with her and they were feverishly working to get ahead of your Jade Mountain. Amy said if she did not get hers out first that it would fall flat and people would say she had imitated you; that she had heard yours was about ready and at all hazards she must get hers out first, therefore she was not listening to the doctor.

She began to read me some of the poems, insisting upon standing up, and as you know she read with much gusto and fine effect. . . .

If not in appearance, in spirit at least, Amy Lowell herself was not without resemblance to the kind of "Beauty" Elinor Wylie spoke of when she defined it as having "The hard heart of a child."

To this degree Amy Lowell shared some few of the flaws of the younger generation of the early nineteen-twenties; driven by the forces of literary ambition, she, too, might well have felt, if not written, "My candle burns at both ends . . ."

As in the days when she went to school with Amy Lowell, Florence Ayscough, now in her forties, was quickly swept into the tempest that surrounded her friend's activities. It was useless for her to protest that she knew little Chinese, that she had no pretensions to scholarship in that or any other language, that she would be forced to hire tutors to help *her*—and it was true enough, as one of her friends remarked, that Mrs. Ayscough spoke no Chinese, but rather "Shanghai pidgin to her servants." The misadventure into Chinese scholarship, the strain of supplying Amy Lowell with rough drafts of Chinese poems in English had little pleasure for Mrs. Asycough, and much difficult, vaguely mastered labor. The procedure was as elaborate as a Chinese puzzle to her, yet Amy Lowell, as director of the scheme, contrived tables of linguistic cross-references between verbal sounds and written characters. The performance was fantastically laborious and had a touch of madness in it, yet in English the poems were both flat and tame. One tablet read as follows:

PASSIONATE GRIEF
BY LI T'AI-PO

Beautiful is this woman who rolls up the pearl-reed blind.
She sits in an inner chamber,
And her eyebrows, delicate as a moth's antennae,
Are drawn with grief.
One sees only the wet lines of tears.
For whom does she suffer this misery?
We do not know.

Amy Lowell wrote "We do not know" with complete sincerity. One is reminded of Percival Lowell's contention that the Orientals were an "upside down" people and that they felt and acted exactly contrary to those who lived in and walked the streets of Boston. This was a Lowell conviction and with family loyalty and tenacity Amy Lowell held to it—no external authority was to refute an argument against it. Nearly all the verses could have been written behind drawn shades in Brookline without the labors of nervous activity into which both Amy Lowell and Mrs. Ayscough were so unhappily drawn. To keep Mrs. Ayscough working at a speed comparable to hers, Amy Lowell insisted that the work should be voluminous, should be overwhelming enough to impress Harriet Monroe, that Mrs. Ayscough should be presented to Miss Monroe as an established authority on Chinese poetry. Modest Mrs. Ayscough was swayed by a power far greater than she could control.

In addition to the method that had been contrived for the translation of Chinese into English, the construction of cross-reference tables, the reading of the verses aloud by Amy Lowell, the rechecking of final versions with first drafts, the book contained an appendix of 166 notes. For those unused to scholarly researches and disciplines as Amy Lowell and Mrs. Ayscough were, this task alone was nothing short of "colossal." The notes were done in a style made popular by nineteenth-century encyclopedists who made up "fact books" to answer questions of bright children. The notes had charm; they re-created the atmosphere of an earlier day in Boston. One almost hears the voice of an instructive governess speaking to children in a nursery, now converted into a classroom:

"The Sorceress Gorge is often referred to in a figurative sense, as it is in this poem. The allusion is to the story of a certain prince who dreamed that a fairy, calling herself the Lady of the Sorceress Mountain, came and passed the night with him. On leaving in the morning, she told him that it was she who ruled over the clouds and rain, which would ever after be symbols of their love."

This was the kind of notation at which Amy Lowell excelled, but it was not of a nature that was likely to impress such authorities in Oriental literature as Arthur Waley. Her ambitions had been to outdo Pound's *Cathay* if not in beauty, then in scholarly interpretation— and after this, to dim the prospects of Bynner's collection of Chinese verse. The book obviously fell short of both objectives: Arthur Waley wrote of its errors in *The Literary Review* of the *New York Evening Post*, and Bynner, unruffled by Amy Lowell's rivalry, completed his book and published it four years after her death, in 1929. An attack on her book in *The Chinese Students' Monthly* gave Amy Lowell a wild headache, so she wrote, and a sleepless night; "scholars are the enemies of literature"—and then with a touch of her matchless Lowellese, she concluded—"They have nearly killed the Greek for us, and up to date they have killed the Chinese." Was it possible that in her fear of admitting she had made a mistake in doing the book at all, she had forgotten Waley's own exquisite version of 170 *Chinese Poems* which had been in print since 1919? Perhaps she had. The reception of *Fir-Flower Tablets* placed her on the defensive. In her writings, at least, the time had come for her to change the scene, to veer swiftly back from imagined Chinese landscapes to familiar Boston, to "Cousin James's" *A Fable for Critics* as well as to the literary gossip of her own day. Among her admirations were Louis Untermeyer's parodies in verse of his contemporaries, which as early as 1916 had established him as a writer of thoroughly engaging, witty and candid light verse; and no one in America has excelled him in that particular skill. With something of the same elaborate structure she had devised in her labors of writing new versions of Chinese verse, she planned the publication of an anonymous pamphlet, *A Critical Fable*.

As a precedent for her anonymously published *Fable,* she had James Russell Lowell's *A Fable for Critics* which delighted the members of his generation and time has justified their approval of his wit. The young man of twenty-nine had proved himself by a single, neatly sustained *tour de force* in verse to be the equal of England's early Victorian masters of light verse; his outrageous puns were superior to Thomas Hood's, and he converted whatever he had learned from reading Byron's *Don Juan* into engaging breakneck rhymes and metrics of his own. In its particular genre Lowell's *Fable* has not been equaled since the day of its publication—and seldom in the history of American criticism has there been a more brilliant display of youthful learning and shrewd summing up of transient literary opinions. Amy Lowell's *Fable* was a direct imitation of his: whatever she had taken from it in the way of inspiration was, of course, family property, and within the Lowell tradition; her energy and shrewdness took the place of James Russell's wit; her ear and learning had been less well trained than his, yet her boldness in writing her *Fable* was far more fortunate and appropriate than it had been in its attempt to make English versions of Chinese verse. After the labors of *Fir-Flower Tablets* the writing of her *Fable* came as a holiday; to write it was relief from the boredom of illness and of convalescence. She enjoyed voicing her opinions recklessly, and the *Fable* gave her a better excuse to do so than speaking them aloud in lecture halls. Nor was the portrait of herself in the *Fable* without self-knowledge:

> When I push at a wheel it must go or I'll break it.
> Once embarked on a mission I never forsake it.

Her list of poets mentioned in her *Fable* was: Robert Frost, Edwin Arlington Robinson, Carl Sandburg, Edgar Lee Masters, Vachel Lindsay, Emily Dickinson, herself (a transparent choice which was made to bolster transparent claims to anonymity), "H.D.," Conrad Aiken, John Gould Fletcher, Sara Teasdale, Hilda Conkling (the "child poet" of the day), Alfred Kreymborg, the two Untermeyers— Jean Starr and Louis—T. S. Eliot, Ezra Pound (both of whom she disliked, misreading Eliot as a pedant, and Pound as one "who knows nothing at all"—in these comments Amy Lowell showed how clearly she had become the Boston club woman of her generation), William Rose Benét, Wallace Stevens, Edna Millay and Maxwell Bodenheim. These names were from her world of literary gossip and speculation, and some were of the company in which she moved whenever she visited New York. The T. S. Eliot of whom she had heard so much was then the author of a slight book of poems which included "The Love Song of J. Alfred Prufrock" and nearly as slender a book of essays, *The Sacred Wood*. The well-known controversy over "The Waste Land" was yet to come. For her, Bodenheim was the "exotic" poet, and though her opinion and placing of him seem strange today, he was "the La Fontaine," so she thought, of her generation, which was precisely a misjudgment that James Russell Lowell (with his knowledge of comparative literature) would not have made. This also was the kind of misstep that showed how thin her readings in French had been.

She went to some trouble to spread rumours that Leonard Bacon, the author of much bookish light verse and a contributor to Henry Seidel Canby's *Literary Review* of the *New York Evening Post* was the true author of her *Fable*, but her efforts to deceive such readers as Conrad Aiken failed and he knew the gossip of the moment as well or better than she. At a Boston party he was quick to accuse her of the authorship which she denied. His argument with her had gone far enough for him to say: "Well, since you persist that you didn't write it, I can say what I really think of it. I think it's damn rotten." The *Fable* was not as clever as she had believed it to be. If anything, her *Fable* proved the superiority of James Russell Lowell's original, his greater skill in sustaining mastery of the form he chose, as well as its underlying wit and the shrewdness of the criticism he advanced. Amy Lowell's habits of hasty writing reduced many of her later experiments in conventional forms to the level of doggerel; her lines had none of the necessary brilliance of a tour de force—they limped, thumped, rattled on to their conclusions. Nor was Conrad Aiken the only one who remained undeceived as to the authorship of her *Fable*; there were many, far too many, who suspected that its true author was Amy Lowell. As a last hope for the *Fable*'s popularity, Amy Lowell as chairman of *The Bookman Magazine*'s poetry committee tried to get the pamphlet adopted as required reading for American women's clubs, but even that attempt was not successful. Today the pamphlet has something of the half-pleading, half-pathetic value of an historical document that once had had pretensions to literary fame.

But *Fir-Flower Tablets* and *A Critical Fable* were scarcely more than by-products of Amy Lowell's literary activities. To distract herself from the terrifying presence of her illnesses, she was at last surrounded by and immersed in her gigantic, two-volume life of John Keats. From the age of eighteen onward, all things she cared to

call her "inner life," held at its center the image and legend of
Keats, and these were more appropriate possessions than Elinor
Wylie's identity with the image of Shelley. The first steps toward
the writing of the biography were taken, as Amy Lowell confessed,
as part of her book-collecting activities. Her collection of Keats manuscripts and first editions increased in value, and in 1920 their prices
on the book-collecting market were not likely to decline. So far her
romantic, instinctive love of possessing Keatsiana had practical
rewards, almost as practical in their way, as her investment in D. H.
Lawrence. Lawrence's letters to her were growing evidence that she
had not been wrong in sending him money; even as his reputation
grew he had made thrifty use of it. These two investments were safe
enough and chances of disillusionment concerning them were few.

Amy Lowell's *John Keats* was to be her masterpiece; and the
writing of its more than twelve hundred pages also included efforts at
scholarship which had made *Fir-Flower Tablets* more of a nightmare
than a happy control of the disciplines of research.* In writing a life
of Keats, and as she confessed, "Keats is killing me," she was, as
contrasted to the efforts at understanding Chinese poetry, on firmer
ground. Her sources were written in English, and she had formed a
friendship with John Livingston Lowes, a talented and discursive
professor of English at Harvard. In 1918, Professor Lowes had delivered a series of lectures, "Convention and Revolt in Poetry," at the
Lowell Institute in Boston. He was an inspiring speaker, who had
admirable control over broadly scattered readings in English poetry;
his mind was well-disciplined and alert; he spoke with vigor and his
manner was non-pedantic. Since 1919 he had been at work on a
brilliantly conceived essay on Coleridge's poetry, *The Road to
Xanadu*, and in 1927 when at last the book was published, it became
and still remains today an authoritative study of Coleridge's mind.
Of all extended researches into the poetic imagination, Professor
Lowes's book is among the few of its kind, which, as twenty years
later E. M. Forster noted, kept itself free of critical jargon, and yet
sustained its standards of accuracy. The very writing in the essay was
on a parity with the clearest merits of Coleridge's prose. At its best
Amy Lowell's intelligence had much of the quickness and verve that

* According to Mrs. August Belmont, Mrs. Russell greatly assisted Amy
Lowell in her Keatsian researches.

were among the attractions of Lowes's personality; and both she and Lowes shared a nineteenth-century prejudice against eighteenth-century poetic diction. Both loved (and were tolerant of the flaws of) romantic poetry. Their likes and dislikes were on common ground.

If he considered himself an authority on romantic verse in English (which he was), Professor Lowes paid Amy Lowell the compliment of accepting her as an authority on the subject of contemporary verse. He was the very man to give her confidence in the progress of writing her life of Keats; he had already quoted her remarks concerning *vers libre* as well as lines from her verses in his *Convention and Revolt*. Lowes was a friend to whom she could entrust more than a few of her speculations about Keats—nor (since he was deep in his researches of the books that Coleridge had read before writing "The Ancient Mariner") did she fear him as a rival authority on the subject of John Keats. There was no likelihood of his writing a biography of any poet—and he was both courteous and generous in giving her the literary sources of some of Keats's poems. With equal courtesy she expressed her gratitude to John Livingston Lowes; and in guiding her toward the disciplines of literary research, he was by far the most valuable of her friends.

In 1921 she had been invited by Professor William Lyon Phelps to deliver the commemorative address on the one hundredth anniversary of Keats's death. Phelps shared the same nineteenth-century heritage of teaching English literature that Lowes possessed in his *Convention and Revolt in Poetry*. "Billy" Phelps, with the tall build of a football captain, had made the appreciation of Shakespeare an exercise in athletic enthusiasm at Yale and he applied the same cheerfulness to the reading of contemporary fiction. Under Phelps's spell, even the most indifferent of Yale undergraduates became converts to the pleasure of reading a book; and so great was his power to charm his listeners that he drew unlikely visitors to his lectures. One of his more notable conquests was the heavyweight champion of the world, Gene Tunney. Tunney, after defeating Jack Dempsey in an historic bout, earned a fortune, and since he felt the need of knowing arts other than those of boxing, turned to Professor Phelps and learned to enjoy a reading of Shakespeare. Literature, under Phelps's genial direction, became one of the liveliest of the "seven lively arts." Both Lowes and Phelps belonged to a generation of lecturers who accepted the broad learning of George Saintsbury as a standard of scholarship—and Phelps transformed the British critic's far-ranging and relaxed studies of literature into platform adventures which were as exciting as Theodore Roosevelt's accounts of his hunting trips into Africa. Like Lowes, he admired Amy Lowell's abilities to confront an audience, and from his encouragement she renewed her determination to begin her long journey through writing the story of Keats's life.

Amy Lowell's *John Keats* is an overwhelming document in American literature. The huge, two-volume work carried within it (and thinly disguised) her own aspirations, her "spiritual autobiography," as well as a nearly day-to-day narration of Keats's life. In her *John Keats* Amy Lowell was both Keats's belated patroness and Keats in her own image. She endowed him with her love of moonlight, much of her energy, her enjoyment of genial company, her moments of loneliness, her thoroughly sublimated sexual frustrations—all of which she could relate with freedom as long as the name she chose was that of John Keats and not that of Amy Lowell. Her many years of collecting Keatsiana made such an identification possible. Her great enjoyment in collecting first editions of Keats and Keats's manuscripts were experiences that had become fused with facts she had unearthed about his life. These involved her intimate feelings and responses.

Many of the impulses and traits that Amy Lowell gave to Keats were not entirely false. Truly enough, though ill, he possessed great energy. The large volume of his letters, his long poems are proof of that. There was also a genial side to his character, and with Amy Lowell he shared a love of sweets. It is also famously true that his love for Fanny Brawne resulted in the sublimation of emotions stirred by sexual impulses. These were literal facts, easily arrived at and not to be contraverted. It was Amy Lowell's intention to be supremely accurate in the factual detail of Keats's life—so far, she was relatively safe. Her errors were those of interpretation, founded upon self-identification with her hero, and supported by prejudiced convictions.

In the same fashion that she had drawn Keats into the orbit of her own temper and feelings, she drew Keats's mother to her side and transformed her into a vivid self-portrait. She described her as "a woman of strong passions and appetites, with no particular desire to curb either, but with something redeeming and attractive about her just the same." If the comment fitted Amy Lowell supremely well, it also prepared the reader, since it appeared early in the first chapter of her *John Keats,* for her role of Keats's maternal patroness. With these opening remarks, she defended his mother who was the daughter of a prosperous stable keeper, and later, wife of his successor, against irresponsible gossip about her behavior. Even the strictest measures of latter-day research into the origins of Keats's family, and the lives of his parents, have failed to modify the facts of Amy Lowell's observations of who and what they were. In matters such as these she outstripped, outpaced all previous biographers of Keats, and like an able lawyer preparing a brief to defend his client, she laid the foundations of her case. In this respect her book on Keats proved her contention that she could, if forced, outdo the claims of academic research. She also proved that her years spent in collecting Keats's manuscripts and letters were not entirely wasted; this, in itself, was an initial victory. As Keats's biographer, she herself was "a woman of strong passions and appetites," and openly partisan in her defense of her chosen hero.

Lawyerlike she proceeded with the briefing of her case, and her comment on Keats at fourteen when he heard of his mother's death and hid himself under a desk was: "Poor little shaver, so pitiably unable to cope with his first sorrow!" No Boston lawyer making his appeal to a jury could have made a better gesture. As Amy Lowell stepped into the company of men and women related to Keats, the family of Fanny Brawne (and she defended the character of Fanny Brawne with the same vigor that she defended her young lover), Keats's publisher, Keats's editors and friends, the same lawyerlike shrewdness prevailed, and with it a Boston lawyer's comments on sexual morality. She observed that:

. . . Keats pleased to live a decidedly clean and strenuous life [not too much unlike her own] . . . He had a good healthy liking for the broad speaking of sixteenth and seventeenth-century writers, and was quite capable of relishing a lively, animal pleasantry, but the painful and cynical making of mudpies which is the principal preoccupation of our modern novelists [Amy Lowell had once written of D. H. Lawrence that she thought he "had a sort of erotic mania"] was as far from his attitude as it was from that of Congreve.

Nor was Amy Lowell less shrewd in her comment on the dangers Keats faced as he dedicated his *Poems,* 1817, to Leigh Hunt. "Keats must have known," she wrote, "that Hunt was the perpetual butt of Tory criticism," and that he was open to attack from Lockhart; she continued her clear-headed explanation of Keats's difficulty:

Poetry is one thing, the politics of poetry is quite another, and poor Keats, through his association with Hunt, was immediately and heavily thrown into the very centre of the political arena.

And no less sensible were her remarks on Keats's publisher Taylor and his editorial advisor, Richard Woodhouse. Taylor was the kind of business-man-publisher that she had met at the Macmillan Company and at Houghton Mifflin. And Richard Woodhouse, Keats's kindly editor, was not unlike editors she had known; her portraits of the two men were done with the ease of a writer who knew her models well. Yet her sketch of Keats in the act of writing a poem was more than all else a mirrored reflection of herself, or rather as she felt herself to be, ill and distracted, trying to write verses among the labors of her book on Keats. To say the least, the sketch was histrionic:

I do not suppose that any one not a poet can realize the agony of creating a poem. Every nerve, even every muscle, seems strained to the breaking point. The poem will not be denied, to refuse to write it would be a greater torture. It tears its way out of the brain, splintering and breaking its passage, and leaves that organ in the state of a jellyfish when the task is done.

There is nothing in Keats's letters that has the slightest resemblance, either in language or imagery, to this passage of pure Amy Lowellese. Whenever she turned to Keats's poems, what she saw in them was often what she read in her own verses. Her comment on these lines:

> Lo! I must tell a tale of chivalry;
> For while I muse, the lance points slantingly
> Athwart the morning air

ran into the following digression:

This is as vivid and reticent as a Japanese print. We have the exact atmosphere: the faint blue of the sky; the fresh, rather damp air; the silver, not the golden sun.

However one may interpret her interpretation of Keats's lines, her view of them is closer to a description of a walk through her gardens at Sevenels on a late spring morning, than any thought of "a tale of chivalry" and "the lance points slantingly/ Athwart the morning air."

Whenever Amy Lowell attempted to paraphrase Keats's poems, a large measure of her realistic common sense deserted her. On these occasions she was the Amy Lowell having her way with Keats's poems in the same fashion that she talked aloud in a classroom and bullied her classmates at Mrs. Cabot's School. Yet she was not entirely unconscious of the kind of liberty she took in rereading Keats's poems for her biography; in her comments on "Endymion," she wrote, "Poetry is avowedly what one makes of it. A poem should mean different things to different people"— and with these two truisms she was ready to advance whatever she felt Keats's poetry meant to *her*.

With more relevance to what Keats had written in prose she identified her love of food with his, and quoted two extracts from letters to his sister Fanny:

I got to the stage half an hour before it set out and counted the buns and tarts in a Pastry-cook's window and was just beginning with the Jellies.

"There the sentence ends," she wrote, "and leaves us with our mouths watering." Then she continued with a passage from another letter to Fanny:

I should like now to promenade round your Gardens—apple-tasting— pear-tasting—plum-judging—apricot-nibbling—peach-scrunching—nectar-ine-sucking and Melon-carving.

Amy Lowell's love of food had always been candid enough. As though she were a Victorian herself, she objected to D. H. Lawrence's mention of sex in his novels—and like Dickens, and more pointedly Thackeray, she substituted food for the pleasures of sex. Nor did the literary company she kept in New York show less delight in the enjoyment of food than she; her friend Louis Untermeyer chose as a title for one of his books of verses, *Food and Drink*.

As an excursion into literary criticism, Amy Lowell's life of Keats was almost as erratic and willful as her lectures on *Six French Poets*; and successful only when (guided by suggestions from John Livingston Lowes) she found sources of Keats's poems in Keats's readings.

The values of her immense labors in writing the book were of another kind. In collecting Keats's manuscripts and first editions of his poems, she contributed many facts of bibliographical importance and established with reasonable accuracy a chronology of his writings in this respect her book was a large step forward in Keatsian scholarship. Through her defense of Fanny Brawne she destroyed sentimental prejudice against her and in doing so, clearly recreated a portrait of a young woman of nineteenth-century London's middle class, who within the conventions of her time and place, loved Keats, yet kept her closely guarded self-respect. Young as Fanny Brawne was, she was intelligent enough to know that marriage with a poet, dying of consumption, held dangers of her own destruction rather than hopes of saving her lover's life. With the same clarity Amy Lowell described Keats's friendships with Hunt, and the painter Haydon, as well as the last friendship in his brief life, with Joseph Severn, the mediocre draughtsman and painter who tended him at his deathbed in Rome, and who afterwards made a career by sharing the glories of Keats's posthumous fame. If she failed to perceive the finer qualities of Keats's imagination, she succeeded admirably in recreating the circle of men who knew Keats, from Charles Armitage Brown to Joseph Severn, from Leigh Hunt to Benjamin Haydon.

Her understanding of the Keats circle—which has been supported by Hyder Edward Rollins' two-volume publication of letters written by those who moved within it in 1948—also explains why her book on Keats was among the more popular of books on Keats in the United States. As she wrote of the men in the Keats circle her pragmatic sanity, her intelligence in portraying London's businessmen and editors came forward in vigorous, skilfully guided "Lowellese." Her understanding of Keats's situation among Londoners who were not poets was a merit that American readers welcomed and respected. In America her interpretation of Keats balanced romantic legend with a "practical" view of Keats's place in middleclass society. The very bulk of her work was impressive, and its monumental size and weight gave proof that the author had nearly killed herself as she said in the writing of it.

The British reception of Amy Lowell's Keats was distinctly cool; the book had the appearance of a two-volume invasion of Keatsian scholarship, and its latter-day Bostonian and autobiographical asides were sufficient evidence that she had heeded neither the warnings of Arthur Waley's review of *Fir-Flower Tablets* nor Lytton Strachey's wit when he wrote of how she saw French poets "through Boston eyes." Yet the invasion of her *John Keats* into the British Isles was not without serious accomplishment. Her work stimulated rather than retarded scholarly appreciation of Keats. After the publication of her monumental *John Keats,* ignorance of a Keats chronology, whether in the literal facts of his career or in the progress of his writings, was no longer permissible. H. W. Garrod's definitive edition of *The Poetical Works of John Keats* (1939) paid just tribute to her researches in Keatsian bibliography.

In the writing of her *John Keats* the conservative elements in Amy Lowell's character had found a renewed facet of expression. Her devotion to Keats, however wilfully she misread the meanings of his poems, reasserted her devotion to traditional verse. Her biography of Keats showed how superficial her championship of the "new poetry" had been. If her first crusade had been a campaign in favor of her right to appear as champion of the "new poetry" with Amy Lowell leading its formations, her last crusade was to further the cause of rereading Keats. Outwardly at least, her last efforts were less strenuously planned to promote the career of Amy Lowell, Poet than her earlier ventures into critical literature. In her *John Keats* she became the belated protector of Keats' reputation.

In her life of Keats there are also countless signs that the greater number of its pages were dictated to secretaries rather than written by a weary hand. The two volume work had little or no regard for economy in the use of words; its pages of print seem to overflow their margins; at no time during the composition of the book did she restrict the Mississippi-like flow of her opinions. In speaking of Lockhart's attack on Keats she said:

O Lockhart! Lockhart! Aged twenty-three! With what a proud and strutting air you deployed your erudition!

She defended Keats's experiments in the writing of verse with the following exclamations:

How hard, how desperately hard, is the way of the experimenter in art! How cruelly do those persons, whose blunt-edged senses cannot keep pace with his alert ones, treat such a man! Keats was, all his life, an

experimenter. He knew his English public, but he changed his way not
a jot to placate them.

This was, of course, prose that is declaimed, not written. The echo
of her voice sounds at the end of each exclamation mark; and no one,
even today, can deny that the accents of her speech had "personality."
It was as though she had accepted D. H. Lawrence's instruction to
put herself, the expansive Amy Lowell, between the covers of two
large books.

Another sign that the book had been talked into existence was
the note of thanks she gave to her secretaries in its preface:

. . . whose unwearying labors have so materially lightened mine. By
their devotion, complete indifference to the passage of time, and enthusiastic eagerness, a long and difficult task has been made almost easy and
brought to a conclusion in a surprisingly short time.

She could not have been unaware that her "labors," however
"lightened" by her secretaries, were beyond her strength. She had
signed the contract with Houghton Mifflin to write her book on
Keats on January 16, 1924; it was her intention to complete the book
that summer. She kept her local lecture appointments, and even
traveled as far away from Brookline as Washington, Bryn Mawr
and New York where she spoke at a Lucy Stone League dinner,
saying briefly that she had no sympathy for married women who
retained their maiden names—and once more her opinions on that
subject were firmly said. She went back to Sevenels and with a renewed effort of will worked on her manuscript of *John Keats* until
she suffered injury to her eyes: blood vessels had broken in both
retinas. This warning that she had overtaxed her strength was followed by news that Eleanora Duse on a last tour of the United
States had fallen ill and was near death. Her death in April brought
to a close a source of inspiration that Amy Lowell cherished. This
also came as a warning of another kind; she had begun to feel that
life was short, and as her strength declined, her impatience to complete the book mounted above all warnings. She worked as best
she could throughout the summer, but it was not until November,
and with the help of Mrs. Russell, that the last pages of the second
volume were typed and set up in galleys while the page proofs of
Volume One were read. The year brought with it recognition from
Poetry magazine of Chicago; Amy Lowell received its highest poetry

award, the Helen Haire Levinson Prize. This was gratifying enough, but the sustained anxiety of writing and anticipating the publication of her *John Keats* took fatal toll of her energy.

On February 5, 1925, she received advance copies of *John Keats*, and as she turned to unwrap the packages she was given the news that her sister, Katherine Bowlker, had been killed by a fall from a window of the Hotel Vendome in Boston.

To celebrate the publication of her book she made plans to sail to England on April 15, to answer her English critics by an appearance on British soil, but by the first of that month renewed signs of her illnesses became so clear that her doctors forbade any further plans for travel; a fifth operation for hernia was prepared. She had lost the desire to eat; she had lost weight; she was afflicted with nausea. For two years she had overridden all her doctors' orders to rest. She would insist upon rising from her bed if only to walk downstairs to sit in a chair for a short time and then slowly make her way back to her bedroom. By the tenth of May she whispered to Mrs. Hill by phone, "Alison, I feel like hell." Her weight was reduced to 159 pounds—and Mrs. Russell noted that she seemed weaker than at the times she suffered attacks of influenza after her four operations for hernia.

Two days later she woke to say to Mrs. Russell, using the nickname she had given her, "Peter, I'm done. Why can't they let me alone. The operations never have been any good."

She rose from bed and seated herself before her dressing mirror. Mrs. Russell tried to assist her in adjusting the bandages that corseted the wounds of her operations, but Amy Lowell with a return of her usual independence attempted to pin the bandage herself, only to discover that her hand was numb. "I can't use it," she said. Then in the mirror she saw the right side of her face drop and whispered, "Pete, a stroke." A nurse and a maid moved her chair to a sofa, and while Mrs. Russell telephoned a doctor, they lifted her to the sofa. When Mrs. Russell returned Amy Lowell said "Get Eastman" —this was the doctor she wished to see—and fell unconscious. An hour and a half later, at five-thirty in the afternoon, Mrs. Russell and the doctor announced her death.

The career of Amy Lowell came to its end with a peacefulness that was seldom achieved during her active life. The wide notoriety she had received was echoed in newspapers after her death. Perhaps the best of these tributes was written by John Hunter Sedgwick in the pages of *The Boston Evening Transcript*; Sedgwick's view of her accomplishments was in terms of her being a good New Englander, "a very good citizen, than which there can be no more honorable title in a democracy whose lap is full of the dark gifts of fate." His very language had a curious resemblance to hers, the vernacular of Boston, in which he continued,

>   . . . in her head was the noble tradition of those things called in-tellectual, and neither tradition nor duty was lulled to sleep by the possession of that wealth which has so often cheated the country of help and training . . .

He saw in Amy Lowell an example of industry that was among the civic virtues of a Puritan capital, and, almost in words she might have said, he spoke of her *John Keats* as a work that had the follow-ing merit: "She would have her hero, but no nonsense about him or the book."

She was then as she is now a peculiarly American figure, around whom affectionate legends could be woven, and none was better known than one recited by her good friend and editor, Ferris Greenslet:

>   She liked to tell of an occasion when the mulberry motor had ceased suddenly to function and the proprietor of the village garage hesitated about charging the cost of repairs.
>   "I'm Amy Lowell," she told him, "the sister of the President of Harvard. Call him up and he'll tell you I'm good for the bill."
>   The proprietor called Kirkland 7600, and did so, stating the case in some detail.
>   "What's she doing now?" asked Lawrence.
>   "She's sitting across the road on a stone wall smoking a cigar!"
>   "All right, that's my sister."

The story was also the best of a series that have now become part of the fabulae of Cambridge and of Harvard. Seen in perspective, the three Lowell children of Augustus, Percival, Lawrence and Amy, complement one another. Time has moved them closer; and their contrasting characters seem no more than a usual variety of features in a family portrait, a "conversation piece" of the three Lowells. After Amy's death four books of her verses were published, and in 1928,

What's O'Clock, the first of these posthumous volumes, received a
Pulitzer Prize, which was a wreath in memory of her stout commanding presence. In 1928, her friend, John Livingston Lowes, still conscious of a "revolt," a revolt, even then growing less brilliant than
it had seemed in poetry, edited a selection of her poems. All these
were in the nature of last words. Even the posthumous publications
of her writings could not bring to life again the most flagrantly
romantic figure of Lowell heritage. Her commanding presence was
gone.

From a stanza in one of her best poems, "On Looking at a Copy of
Alice Meynell's Poems Given to Me Years Ago by a Friend," a
fragment of self-knowledge comes to light:

> How strange that tumult, looking back,
> The ink is pale, the letters fade,
> The verses seem to be well made,
> But I have lived the almanac.

Perhaps her lines consciously echoed the stanzas of Tennyson's
In Memoriam; if not, instinctively they echoed an elegiac mood
that she felt forced to put aside:

> Between us I must shut the door
> The living have so much to do.

It was in doing things, not writing of them, that she excelled. Her
John Keats was almost a superhuman effort in a display of ceaseless,
almost sleepless industry. She had forced the act of writing into a
medium that came very close to the quickly performed, then as
quickly forgotten, engagements with both enemies and friends.
Writing became the means by which she participated in literary
adventures. It was very nearly the by-product of her personality. It is
the reason why her poem "Patterns" with its closing phrase, "Christ!
What are patterns for?" is the most frequently quoted of all the many
lines she wrote. Action in voice, in gesture, was the medium that
gave her greatest pleasure, and is her monument.

Preface
as Epilogue

N WRITING a portrait of Amy Lowell I have made no attempt to give the reader a conventional biography. All who wish to read of Amy Lowell as she lived within a Brookline-Boston environment, closely witnessed by New England eyes, are referred to S. Foster Damon's official biography. The present book carries a conscious debt to Damon's presentation of Amy Lowell, and his book, the official biography, is likely to remain a source of Amy Lowell anecdotes for many years to come. His book on Amy Lowell may be compared to John Forster's *Walter Savage Landor*, a well-sustained and weighty Victorian labor of love.

My portrait of Amy Lowell is of a different nature. It is lighter in weight than Damon's book and is an interpretive historical essay that attempts to place Amy Lowell among other poets of her day. No one can deny that in the United States during the First World War she was the most spectacular of all those who advanced the cause of the "new poetry." In her recent book of memoirs, Mrs.

August Belmont affectionately speaks of her as a circus "barker" in that cause—and so she was. But to be a "barker" for poetry old or new is a curious distinction, and one should not conclude that the "barker" because of his activity is a poet. Poetry in itself is not a cause; a good poem has a hardiness that lives beyond the poet. It also lives beyond other causes, political or social, of its time. There is, however, a continuing interest in figures that speak in the name of poetry, figures like Leigh Hunt (appropriate here because Amy Lowell was introduced to a reading of poetry through one of his anthologies called *Imagination and Fancy* found in her father's library. Any picture of the literary scene in Boston, London, New York, and Chicago between 1914 and 1925 would remain strangely incomplete without her. As for Hunt, and with small loss, few remember his poems today. Old-fashioned anthologies of verse retain such favorites as "Jenny Kiss'd Me" and "Abou Ben Adhem." Biographers of Keats, Shelley, and Byron never fail to mention him, for his personality and name hold their places in studies of the romantic school, the "Cockney" school in London. Students of Dickens recognize Hunt as the lay figure for Harold Skimpole in *Bleak House.* Amy Lowell's long sustained admiration of Hunt was innocent girlish affection for one who never wavered in his admiration for Keats's poetry. In his own mild way, Hunt, too, was a "barker," active in liberal politics and in literary journalism, happy to share the fame (and to promote it) of Keats, Shelley (though later he was to quarrel with him), Byron. In his youth he proved his courage by attacking the Prince Regent in print and gaily serving time at Newgate for libel. Though Amy Lowell consciously imitated James Russell Lowell's *Fable For Critics* in *A Critical Fable,* Hunt as early as 1811 anticipated both Lowells by writing a satire on contemporary poets called *The Feast of the Poets* in metres and rhymes that the latter two poems seem to echo and recall. Hunt's satire is happily forgotten. At the very least Amy Lowell was as vivid a figure in the United States as Hunt was in London in 1815.

Amy Lowell was not, of course, another Leigh Hunt. Hunt was an English phenomenon of his day. Amy Lowell was an American phenomenon of a period that welcomed a "renaissance" in American poetry. The more important figures of her day were Ezra Pound, H.D., Edwin Arlington Robinson, Robert Frost, Vachel Lindsay,

Edgar Lee Masters, Carl Sandburg—all Americans of various accomplishments and gifts. In actuality, she trailed at some distance behind them; she was never clear in her knowledge of what the "new poetry" was or hoped to be; her true affinities were of a nineteenth-century origin, gathered from her readings in her father's library at Sevenels and among the book shelves of Boston's Athenaeum. Her love of the Keats legend was consistent with whatever she knew of poetic literature. She read herself into it. She created the illusion that she possessed it with the same magnetic force that it attracted her. Among the members of her family, she was an archetypical "romantic" Lowell, born to promote whatever interest occupied her mind, and then with equal vigor, command the scene around her.

Any European reading writings by Amy Lowell or about her would be moved to say, and this, perhaps, with an air of patronage, "How very American Amy Lowell is!" The European would be right. Even to the bright, staccato, "practical" way she jotted down her observations about things that caught her eyes she was "very American," and quick in movement:

> I came from the country
> With flowers,
> Larkspur and roses,
> Fretted lilies
> In their leaves,
> And long, cool lavender.

Or in these few opening lines from "Dog-Days":

> A ladder sticking up at the open window,
> The top of an old ladder;
> And all of Summer is there.

The view is seen in passing. It has no emotional associations, nostalgic or otherwise. It is real enough, even to the imprecise colloquialism of "a ladder sticking up at the open window"—and all distinctly American in accent and phrasing. It is the "hands-off-don't-touch-me" speech of the busy American clubwoman in a hurry. This is one of the reasons why so many of Amy Lowell's writings, either in polyphonic prose or verse, fail to touch the emotions of the reader, nor do they convey more than a transient glimpse of the writer. The lines I have just quoted have no nonsense about them, but it is also true that they do not spring from a center of poetic imagination. Their surfaces present all they have to say.

If Amy Lowell was an archetypical "romantic" Lowell, she was also an archetypical American clubwoman of her day: well-to-do, clear-minded in the management of practical civic affairs, valiantly interested in education (until her interest in "Amy Lowell: Poet" overshadowed it), outspoken, vigorous. In these characteristics she transcended Brookline, Boston and New England. She also transcended specific causes in favor of "Rights for Women." She herself became the embodiment of those rights, the right to speak opinions frankly, to smoke in public, to express her feelings in anger, or tears, or smiles. If she had not had the support of Lowell wealth and prestige behind her, her courage might well have been forced to take on other forms. As it was she could literally "buy" her way into public notice, a practice that she enjoyed rather than rejected. Like any well-to-do American of her generation, she took great pleasure in "running things," making deals with her publishers, and as she paid contributors to her Imagist anthologies, she delighted in her abilities in accounting and bookkeeping. These pleasures were signs of Lowell genius, the same genius that had enabled her father to increase the fortune he had inherited. All these abilities were transcendent forms of the activities performed by the American clubwoman who skilfully takes charge of household accounts, drives a station wagon, serves on boards of parent-teacher associations, and by efficient management of the day's routine, finds time to attend, even contribute to, weekly discussion groups that had been formed to review current events in politics or the arts.

It is wrong, I think, to overstress the so-called "neurotic" aspects of Amy Lowell's character. During the latter years of her literary activity, she was gravely ill, and she believed that she was "killing" herself with too much industry, with overwork. Perhaps she was, yet her self-imposed discipline of producing rapidly written, monumental quantities of prose and verse, distracted her mind from recurrent cycles of pain. The habit of writing had its reward as self-imposed therapy, but it could not remove the cause of illness. If Amy Lowell was not ideally well-balanced, she was eminently sane. Her eccentricities were never as pronounced, or as unconventional as she made them appear to be. It is not too much to say that she adroitly dramatized her love of tobacco; and this she did in much the same fashion that she retained and slept in her childhood bedroom at Sevenels.

Earlier in her career she had cured her headaches, her fits of depression by the same therapy—the *activity* of writing, which for her became a substitute for imaginative and aesthetic creation. And to this she added the histrionics of the lecture platform. By these means she kept herself "in balance" and could face the world with smiles. She had found a way of keeping herself in business—with something to sell, her personality, her writings placed on view before the world. All this was consistent with a philosophy that was essentially pragmatic and realistic. She could and did make things "work"; she had the money (with which she so often made the original investment on her publications by paying for the printing of her books), she had the prestige of the Lowell name—and the very name had transatlantic glories. Before coming to America D. H. Lawrence wrote of Amy Lowell to his agent in the following terms: "Her brother is the principal of Harvard and she can touch the pulse of *The Yale Review* and things like that." This description may seem blasphemous to a Bostonion, but it does show how far the aura of the Lowell name had shed its light. Amy Lowell was never shy in making the most of her resources.

Even at her unhappiest in her loss of temper, her short-lived rages, and her moments of depression, her sense of sadness and of despair did not strike much deeper than the feelings expressed by a "spoiled child." Her moments of self-hatred were all too obviously caused by the consciousness of her ungainly figure, and from this came her conviction that she was unloved. She could be charming, and she knew it. Her charms as a benign if commanding hostess mitigated the ungainliness of her appearance. To play the part of a deranged and tragic heroine was not a rôle that destiny prepared for her.

For all these reasons a portrait of a "neurotic" Amy Lowell falsifies her character. She was sane; she was no fool. She knew that in America money "talked"; and in London, among certain younger poets, if it could not earn respect, it could demand attention. In the United States, she used all the tricks of showmanship (which was a kind of salesmanship) her instincts and intelligence told her to provide. This knowledge was no midnight reverie. The years of "The

Poetic Renaissance," a period from 1911 to the end of World War I, gave her salesmanship of "polyphonic prose," vers libre, and all the kinds of verse she chose to write, a backdrop for her presence on a platform. The founding of Harriet Monroe's magazine, *Poetry*, the manifestos issued by Miss Monroe's foreign editor, Ezra Pound, gave her all she needed to promote, to sell a kind of verse to which Pound gave the title of "Amyism." She could well afford to name other poets, some older and better known than she, as well as a group of younger unknown poets in her recitals, to read their verse, to "sell" them to an audience whose curiosity had been aroused by talk of a "new poetry." This she did willingly—provided that her own opinions had their voice, and that she herself would always take the center of the stage.

In America in our day as well as hers, there is a general pragmatic, even democratic, conviction that a product, however good, bad, or indifferent, can and *must* be sold. The quality of the thing sold is of small importance, provided that it is "new." The hope is that it is better than the thing like it that had been sold some twenty years before. Amy Lowell was archetypically American in this conviction. And in respect to the selling of verse her technic was not unlike that of the successful commercial anthologist of verse, one who shifts his standards to the taste of the moment and is shrewd enough never to be in advance of the times. It was to Amy Lowell's advantage that aside from the fact that most "free verse" did not rhyme, she did not understand what the "new poetry" was. She could simplify its theories at will. She was nearly as ill-informed as those who heard her read, and therefore her explanations of the poem she read aloud to them were presented in terms of every-day, commonsensical remarks. To know that most of the "new poetry" was newly written was enough to insure its merit to her and her listeners. She sold the "new poetry" in the same spirit that a new brand of breakfast food or headache pill is sold. All difficult questions of aesthetic distinction were smoothed away. She could never understand the meaning of Ezra Pound's remark and warning: "There is no democracy in the arts." In her eyes critical discrimination meant a free-for-all pitched battle in an arena of literary politics. That was why she felt herself at war with Ezra Pound, or at war against his polar opposite, the Poetry Society of New York.

As soon as she felt that a general curiosity concerning the "new poetry" had declined (and she saw warnings of this as the sales of her Imagist anthologies of verse dropped off and received less notice in the reviewing columns of newspapers), she turned her energies to the promotion of John Keats's reputation. To her this venture became a completion of her life-work. In a bibliographical sense she was on familiar ground; her readings in Keats had begun so long ago! Her book on Keats also closed the cycle of her ideas about poetry, her enthusiasm for her readings that had been awakened in her father's library. From these she could recover from the disasters of attempting to translate Chinese verse. She had earned notoriety and now had the fame of Keats to support it. Her public would listen to what she had to say; she had readers waiting, ready to buy a two-volume biography of a famous poet.

Within a dozen years, the years from 1912 to 1925, the year of her death, Amy Lowell had achieved a great personal victory. She had made herself far more than the mere sister of a president of Harvard. She was a legend in New York as well as in Boston and newspapermen of her day were not wrong in regarding her as an American phenomenon. She gave added variety, if not pathos, to a literary generation that had first welcomed Sara Teasdale, and was enchanted by the public appearances of Edna St. Vincent Millay and Elinor Wylie. She never failed to be "controversial" in a thoroughly respectable way that Americans enjoyed. It is not without significance that Edmund Wilson, a year after her death and writing as a journalist, included her name in his "all-star literary vaudeville."

During the thirty years following her death, Amy Lowell's reputation has acquired a legendary glamour, which was rekindled in 1935 by the publication of S. Foster Damon's *Amy Lowell* and in 1946 by Ferris Greenslet's *The Lowells and Their Seven Worlds*. Both books were of first hand and Bostonian reminiscence, Damon's from the view of one who had been an undergraduate at Harvard during the years of Amy Lowell's fame, Greenslet's from the less awed perspective of being Amy Lowell's first and last editor at Houghton Mifflin in Boston. Today whatever light surrounds her name is

largely the reflected light of other literary figures of her time. Her
histrionic presence gave an air of excitement to readers who for the
first time had read the Symphonies of John Gould Fletcher, the early
poems of H.D., the pastorals of Robert Frost, who had heard the
lilt of Vachel Lindsay's Simon Legree, the unrhymed cadences of
Sandburg and Edgar Lee Masters. All these were poets of greater
promise and accomplishment than hers. Her distinction had no relevance to the writing of poetry; it was clearly and cheerfully the pub-
lice expression of a personality, a literary celebrity of its day.

Proof of how fragile, though voluminous, her verses were, may be
found in *The Complete Poetical Works of Amy Lowell,* a six-hun-
dred-page book, published in 1955. Nor is there much of Amy Lowell
in it. The verse is the expression of extraverted activity and observation, most of it as clear as daily reports upon the weather, and as
perishable as last year's almanac. Amy Lowell's nearest approach to
a revelation of whatever she felt or thought is in her prose, her
Tendencies in Modern American Poetry, her life of *John Keats.*
D. H. Lawrence's remarks on one of her best books of verse, *Men,
Women and Ghosts,* which opened with her well-known "Patterns,"
are as true today as when he wrote his letter to her in 1916:

> You see it [the book] is uttering pure sensation *without concepts,*
> which is what this futuristic art tries to do. One step further and it
> passes into *mere noises,* as the Italian futurismo poems have done, or
> mere jags and zig-zags, as the futuristic paintings. There it ceases to be
> art, and is pure accident, mindless . . . You might have called your book
> 'Rockets and Sighs.' It would have been better than Men, Women &
> Ghosts.

This was and still is as true as his warning to her, "Do write from
your *real* self, Amy, don't make up things from the outside, it is so
saddening."

For this very reason *The Collected Poetical Works of Amy Lowell,*
and this in spite of its glimpses of gardens, flowers and rockets, is a
sad book, a lifeless monument to ten years of industry in jotting
observations down on paper.

Sevenels, inherited by Mrs. Russell, and sold by her, is now no
longer in Lowell hands. The Amy Lowell Estate sustains a fund of
yearly grants to poets as well as funds to buy rare books and manuscripts for the Houghton Library at Harvard. Her name recovers

some of its orignal and transient brilliance in the letters written to her by D. H. Lawrence, and it is in these that she is assured of an immortality.

If at Sevenels a spirit still haunts the magnificent gardens, it is one of Amy Lowell, her weight held upright by her walking stick. She, however, is not a sad ghost, nor a meditative one. At one moment she may be all smiles, and at the next show a phosphorescent glow of anger—then calmed, resume her slow pace at evening through garden paths.